THE MILLION-DOLLAR FINANCIAL SERVICES PRACTICE

THE
MILLION-DOLLAR
FINANCIAL
SERVICES
PRACTICE

THE MILLION-DOLLAR FINANCIAL SERVICES PRACTICE

A Proven System for Becoming a Top Producer

2nd Edition

David J. Mullen Jr.

HarperCollins
LEADERSHIP

AN IMPRINT OF HARPERCOLLINS

Published by HarperCollins Leadership, an imprint of HarperCollins Focus LLC.

Any internet addresses, phone numbers, or company or product information printed in this book are offered as a resource and are not intended in any way to be or to imply an endorsement by HarperCollins Leadership, nor does HarperCollins Leadership vouch for the existence, content, or services of these sites, phone numbers, companies, or products beyond the life of this book.

Bulk discounts available. For details visit:
www.harpercollinsleadership.com/bulkquotes
Email: customercare@harpercollins.com

ISBN 978-1-4002-3880-4 (TP)

To my loving family, which has always provided
unconditional love and support.
Thank you Cynthia, Nathan, David, John, and Katie.
Also to my parents, the late Dave Sr. and Rosemary Mullen.
Not only were they wonderful parents,
but they both were teachers who inspired in me
the sharing of knowledge with others.

Contents

PART 3

Acknowledgments

TO THE FINANCIAL ADVISORS I HAVE WORKED WITH over the past thirty-two years: You have been my teachers and students. Without you, this book would not have been possible.

To my many mentors: Al Thornton, Morris Copeland, Bill Crawford, Jim Billington, Larry Biederman, Rob Knapp, Bob Sherman, Dave Middleton, Mike Thompson, Bob Mulholland, and John Dozier. You have been the role models I have learned from and who have shaped my career as a manager.

To Jan Jones, who helped me in countless ways.

To Joe Yanofsky, for being my partner in developing many of the concepts presented in this book.

To Pam Liflander for her fine editing work.

To Jim Dullanty, my business partner and friend, for his help throughout this 2nd edition. His insight and understanding of our industry was invaluable and his contributions were considerable.

To Wendy Keller, my agent, for her support and confidence in me.

To Bob Nirkind, my publisher, for encouraging me to write this 2nd edition; without his gentle persuasion this updated edition would not have been written. And lastly, to AMACOM, for believing in me with my first book, successfully publishing my second, and allowing me to bring you the most up-to-date information on successfully achieving a million-dollar financial services practice.

THE MILLION-DOLLAR FINANCIAL SERVICES PRACTICE

THE
MILLION-DOLLAR
FINANCIAL
SERVICES
PRACTICE

THE FOUNDATION

Introduction

Building a million-dollar financial services practice is not complicated, but I'm not going to pretend that it is easy. If it were, there would be a lot more financial advisors making millions. In the thirty-two years I have been in the business, I have seen hundreds of people fail to make it past the first two years and few who have reached the million-dollar level. Yet those who reach or exceed $1 million in business have one of the best jobs imaginable. The autonomy and income of, and the excitement experienced by, million-dollar and multimillion-dollar producers are unparalleled.

There are many books and training programs that claim to help you build your financial services practice. This book is different, however, because it gives you step-by-step instructions for carrying out a proven, comprehensive, tactical process that will make your practice more successful.

The Million-Dollar Financial Services Practice covers every aspect of a financial advisor's job, from prospecting to client service. No matter where you are in your career, it will give you all the tools you need to build your financial services practice to a million dollars and beyond—including templates, scripts, contact plans, lists, tasks, marketing plans, letters, and resources, each of which is integrated into the overall process, and it will show you when to use them, how to use them, and how often to use them. The process I present here has for thirty–two years guided financial advisors, whether working at large firms or on their own, and it will do the same for you.

The book also addresses each of the three distinct stages of an advisor's career. Stage one is building the foundation. This is done during the first two years. During this stage, the advisor should spend 70 percent of his time on marketing, with the objective of getting a minimum of eight appointments with new prospects a week and building a "practice" of fifty client relationships and a prospect pipeline of one hundred.

Stage two runs from the advisor's third year through the fifth year of service. Now she must balance client service with marketing. The number of client relationships should be increased to one hundred, and the client relationships and the one hundred prospects should be upgraded at a higher level of affluence compared to your existing average client. The advisor needs to spend at least 50 percent of her time on marketing—on client-leveraging activities, on niche marketing techniques, and on attempting to identify and acquire all her existing clients' assets. At this stage, the advisor should have at least four appointments per week with new prospects.

Stage three is beyond five years. The advisor should continue to cull through his client list, retaining only the top one hundred client relationships and focusing on attracting increasingly affluent clients. A minimum of fifty prospects should be in the active pipeline. At this stage, the advisor should spend a minimum of 25 percent of his time marketing, and he needs to see at least one new prospect per week.

The road to a million-dollar practice is a series of steps that build on one another. The new advisor needs to understand that building the right foundation greatly increases the chances of creating a million-dollar practice and greatly reduces the time required to get there. An advisor can commit to the million-dollar road at any stage of her career, but the fastest and easiest way is to take the proper steps at the beginning. As the practice grows, the fundamentals remain the same, but the allocation of time changes.

HOW THIS BOOK IS STRUCTURED

This book is divided into three parts and an Appendix.

Part 1, "The Foundation," comprises Chapters 1 through 8. Of particular interest to new advisors, it outlines the first things you need to do on the pathway to building a million-dollar practice; it shows you how to build the foundation you need for a million-dollar business. But I encourage any advisor, no matter how much experience she has, to review the information in this section. The importance of motivation (Chapter 3) and the marketing process (Chapters 3 through 7) outlined in this part of the book applies to experienced advisors as well as to new ones.

Part 2, "Taking It to the Next Level," includes Chapters 9 through 19. If you are a more experienced advisor, it will be particularly useful. You will find everything you need to do once you have built the proper foundation. If you are a new advisor, these chapters will be helpful because they provide a vision for how to reach a million-dollar practice once you have built the foundation of your business.

Part 3, "Market Action Plans," contains Chapters 20 through 34. It includes more than fifty approaches to fifteen different markets. Each market action plan gives you all the tools you need to succeed in that market: when the action plan is appropriate, how to implement the plan, sample phone scripts and letters, and case studies.

At the end of the book, the Appendix provides you with resources for finding names and directories for each market.

WHAT IS NEW IN THE SECOND EDITION

Lots of things have changed since I wrote this book in 2007. Back then, most of us in the industry had no idea of the financial turmoil that would occur a year later. Since the book was published in 2008, the job of a financial services professional has been challenging as the financial markets have struggled. This doesn't mean that you can't create a million-dollar practice, it just means that you need to be on top of the changes in our industry and learn how to adjust your business to keep up with them.

In this new edition, I've thoroughly updated the business model to meet these changing times. I've interviewed dozens of million-dollar practitioners and learned from both their successes and failures, especially in terms of how they have weathered the storm. In general, I've found that the million-dollar practices established before the recession have continued to thrive, which gives me great optimism for the future of this industry.

I've also taken a close look at every chapter and adjusted the content accordingly, including snippets of my interviews and their firsthand responses to my questions. In addition, I've culled my list of distinct markets and updated my targets for potential clients to include different types of professionals and referral networks, Realtors, and alumni marketing.

New ideas on how to set and reach new targets are included as well in this edition. The most important of these is the implementation of an effective social media marketing plan. I've found that social media—especially LinkedIn—are important for every financial advisor to master. While the

Internet has become an indispensable tool for all of us, the ability to navigate and increase the reach of your marketing efforts will have a positive impact on the growth of your practice.

Finally, I've taken a much deeper look into the wealth-management process, which I believe must be the cornerstone to any million-dollar financial services practice. Chapter 10 has become a must-read for every practitioner, whether you have been in business for five months or fifteen years. What's more, the earlier you can adopt it, the more successful you can become.

I hope you find this industry as compelling as I do. The most successful financial advisors have made a 100 percent commitment to this business. To them, it's more than a job, it's their career. With that attitude and the lessons in this book, you're off to the best start imaginable. Together, we can set the stage for you to create a long-term, million-dollar practice that will be both challenging and enjoyable for years to come. Let's get started.

CHAPTER 1

The Concept Behind the Process

THE FIRST STEP TO BUILDING A MILLION-DOLLAR PRACTICE is to understand the basics of success. As I was writing this book, I interviewed dozens of top-tier financial advisors. What became easily apparent was that they all shared many of the same characteristics in terms of how they approached their business. At the same time, my years in the industry as both an advisor and a professional coach have led me to identify five targeted ways that financial services practices can grow. It is important that you understand both the five characteristics of million-dollar producers and the "five fundamentals" of growth, which together are the foundation on which the million-dollar practice is built. These two subjects will be the focus of this chapter.

THE FIVE CHARACTERISTICS OF MILLION-DOLLAR PRODUCERS

My observations of successes and failures in this business have led me to the conclusion that million-dollar producers do not possess any extraordinary skills. But they do possess five characteristics that distinguish them from advisors who do not reach the million-dollar level:

1. They set business and activity goals and track their progress.
2. They are motivated.
3. They market relentlessly.
4. They manage their time effectively.
5. They make establishing relationships with affluent individuals their first priority.

These characteristics apply to any advisor who wants to build a million-dollar practice, no matter where he is in his career.

Million-Dollar Producers Set Business and Activity Goals and Track Their Progress

Studies done on the differences between more successful and less successful people indicate that the most successful people set goals. To reach a million dollars in business, you must set goals and measure your progress.

The first step is to understand that your business corresponds to the number of affluent households (those with more than $250,000 in investable assets) you have and the total amount of assets you manage. The average million-dollar producer I have worked with manages at least $120 million in assets for about one hundred affluent households. To determine how many assets you need in order to attain a $1 million practice, take your current ROA (return on assets, the percentage of sales on assets under management) and divide a million into that number. For example, if your ROA is 80 basis points (0.8 of 1 percent) divide a million into that number and you will see that you need $120 million in assets to reach your million-dollar business goal.

Then take the number of affluent households (100) and the amount of assets ($120 million) or your calculated number of assets based on your ROA and subtract from that the amount of assets and the number of households you have currently, if any. The result is the amount of assets and number of households you need to add to reach $1 million. If you divide that number by the number of years within which you want to reach $1 million, you will see the number of households and the amount of assets you need to add to your practice each year to reach your goal by that time.

I tell new advisors that building a million-dollar practice in ten years is a challenging but realistic time frame. Certainly, this can be done in less time, but I have seen very few do so—most advisors who reach $1 million take between ten and twenty years. But if a new advisor is trained to follow the guidelines presented in this book on how to build a million-dollar practice from the beginning, and understands and executes the program, she can realistically expect to reach $1 million in ten years.

Those advisors who want to reach $1 million and who have been in the business for a while can expect that the training in this book, if followed, can add at least $100,000 in business each year. As an example, if you are currently producing $500,000 per year, following and executing the guidelines presented throughout this book should result in your reaching $1 million within five years.

Once you have set your overall production goal, you should set goals in the following two areas:

1. You have set your goals for the number of affluent households and the amount of managed assets required to reach a million-dollar practice; now you should break down these goals into daily, weekly, monthly, and annual goals, and you should monitor your progress at least every week; track the difference between your goals and where you currently are.

2. You should set activity goals every week for the number of client contacts to make, the number of prospect contacts to make, and the number of appointments with new prospects to have.

Million-Dollar Producers Are Motivated

Once you have established your goals and your time frame for reaching them, you must make sure you have a truly high level of motivation to fuel the process. Merely understanding the five fundamentals of building a million-dollar practice is not enough. To execute them every day, you must have a high level of sustainable motivation.

Executing the fundamentals is no easier for the million-dollar producer than for those who never reach that level, but the successful advisor can make himself execute the fundamentals while the less successful advisor cannot. Million-dollar producers make themselves do the more difficult tasks that this business sometimes requires, in spite of the rejection they receive. Less successful advisors avoid them. Remember what I said at the beginning: Building a million-dollar practice is not complicated, but it is difficult. Having a high and sustained level of motivation is essential if you are to do the difficult things required to succeed in this business.

Million-Dollar Producers Market Relentlessly

After you have made your commitments (motivation) and set your goals (and the time frame for reaching them), you must understand that the most important characteristic is sustained marketing. The most successful million-, multimillion-, and decamillion-dollar advisors I have worked with never quit marketing. Their individual marketing processes may be different, but they always do them. The only way to reach a million-dollar practice is to understand that you must always be carrying out effective marketing.

This book provides a proven marketing process, as well as fifteen different marketing plans, that any advisor at any point in her career can implement. This is certainly not the only marketing process that works, but it has been used by hundreds of advisors, and it has been proven to work very well.

Million-Dollar Producers Manage Their Time Effectively

It is essential that you have sound time-management techniques, especially in order to perform—every day—the five fundamentals discussed in the next section. Your day should be divided between proactive and reactive activities. Proactive activities include what I call the "Big Three":

+ Setting investment policy and strategy and implementation
+ Proactive client contact and appointments
+ Marketing activities

The most successful advisors spend at least 50 percent of their time doing these activities.

Reactive activities are everything else, including administrative and operational work, e-mail correspondence, research, return calls, internal meetings, and presentation preparation. Use your client associate to protect your time throughout the day and to help increase your service to your existing clients.

You should have a process-based practice: Establish a process for most everything you do, and then spend the day executing the processes you have established. Preparing and setting up these processes in advance is required to maximize your execution time.

You should also become a master at executing the three basics of time management: prioritization, delegation, and time blocking.

Million-Dollar Producers Make Establishing Relationships with Affluent Individuals Their First Priority

This is primarily a relationship business, and million-dollar producers focus more on their relationships with affluent individuals than do less successful advisors. Without strong relationships and all the elements that strong relationships are based on, it is very difficult to reach the million-dollar level. Taylor Glover, the most successful advisor I have ever worked with, summed up this characteristic best: "The most important attribute that has contributed to my successes is the relationships that I built with my clients and prospective clients."

THE FIVE FUNDAMENTALS OF GROWTH

The five fundamentals of growth (LEARN) are:

1. Leverage: Leverage current clients to get new ones.
2. Expand: Expand the products and services each client uses.
3. Assets: Get all of your clients' assets.
4. Retain: Retain your clients by providing extraordinary service, setting the stage for leveraging those clients to grow your practice.
5. Niche: Develop your niche markets and build a marketing process around them.

Developing a niche market means acquiring a level of expertise and experience in working with a specific occupation, profession, or type of investor and focusing your marketing efforts on that particular niche. Potential niches might include business owners, executives, retirement plans, medical or legal professionals, sales professionals, retirees, or individuals preparing for retirement.

The process for niche marketing should:

♦ Include one to five marketing plans for different niches.
♦ Make getting a face-to-face appointment a first priority.
♦ Have a follow-up process that is tailored to each prospect's needs.

In order to open the number of new accounts that will lead to a million-dollar practice, you should be servicing between fifty and one hundred prospects. Most prospects are underserviced by their existing advisor, and if you service them better, you will convert them to clients. This means providing them with consistent follow-up tailored to their personal and financial needs.

Once you have at least fifty affluent client relationships of at least $100,000 each, you can now tackle the other four fundamentals of growth. Knowing what these five fundamentals are and developing a plan to incorporate these fundamentals every day is how a million-dollar practice is built in the shortest time possible.

WHAT IT ALL ADDS UP TO

The formula for building a million- and multimillion-dollar practice is not a complicated one. It involves building the right foundation first, then taking it to the next level by doing ongoing marketing, developing strong relationships with clients, and providing outstanding service. This formula is much easier to understand than to execute. It takes a high level of commitment and motivation to do the activities necessary to build such a practice. It takes strong organization and time-management skills to fit these activities into every day, to build an effective team, and to build processes that support the practice. It takes making relationship building the highest priority.

This can all be condensed into the following equation: *The right foundation + marketing + strong client relationships + outstanding service = $1 million practice.*

There are so few million-dollar advisors and even fewer multimillion-dollar advisors not because the formula for success is complicated, but because it is so hard to carry out the right activities daily. If you are committed, develop the characteristics of million-dollar producers, and follow the fundamentals I have outlined in this book, then a million-dollar practice can be yours.

CHAPTER 2

Motivation

THE FIVE FUNDAMENTALS I MENTIONED at the end of the last chapter form the foundation of a million-dollar-plus practice. These five fundamentals are the foundation, and motivation is their cornerstone.

Everyone who enters the financial services business wants to succeed. To truly succeed, however, an advisor must have more than simply the desire to succeed. There must be a far deeper level of motivation. An advisor's motivation will be tested over and over throughout her career, and her motivation reservoir must always be deep enough to replenish her. It is possible to write down all the correct processes and techniques for succeeding in this business, but without deep motivation, none of them work.

There are two components to motivation:

1. Building and keeping motivation
2. Time allocation

BUILDING AND KEEPING MOTIVATION

In order to achieve a million-dollar practice in financial services, you must market, and if you market, you must be ready to face rejection. This is especially true at the early stages of your career. Marketing is difficult, and over the course of your career, you may not feel that your motivation level is high enough to do it. You are not lost, though, because you can renew or increase your motivation any time. In order to build and keep your motivation, you need to do two things:

1. You must understand the low-percentage/high-payoff dynamic of the business.

2. You must clearly understand your own personal reasons for wanting to have a million-dollar-plus practice.

The Low-Percentage/High-Payoff Dynamic

A fundamental aspect of the financial services business is that it is a low-percentage/high-payoff business: A high number of rejections (low percentage) is *required* to reach the reward (high payoff). Notice that I used the word required: It is required that you have a high number of rejections in order to reach the high payoff. The payoff is so high because the number of rejections is so high. They go hand in hand.

Every affluent investor has a current provider; it is difficult to disrupt an existing relationship, and it takes time. You face an uphill battle to capture affluent investors, which means that you must market as effectively as you possibly can in order to succeed. The most effective marketing practice I have seen is the "Rolodex technique" (calling the list of personal contacts you have built over the years), which generates a 50 percent call-to-appointment ratio (50 percent of calls lead to appointments); the worst is a mailing, which generates about 1 percent. Cold calling generates about 5 percent. These numbers reflect a low-percentage success rate, which means that doing these tasks every day requires a very high level of motivation. The payoff, however, is high: To have a million-dollar practice, an advisor needs to have approximately thirty $1 million-plus households. While it is hard to get a new million-dollar household (low percentage), it takes only three per year to put you on track to build a million-dollar practice (high payoff).

If you understand this dynamic, it is easier to accept rejection. You are prepared for it because you know that only a few successes have a significant impact on the growth of your business, and that in order to get those few successes, you must go through a lot of rejection. Please take note: It is easier to be rejected than to fail. In other words, you pay a greater psychological price if you fail than if you are rejected.

Your Reasons for Wanting a Million-Dollar Practice

Think through and even write down why reaching a million-dollar-plus practice is important to you. Your reasons might be:

♦ Professional accomplishment and status
♦ The extra things the income could provide, such as a new dream car, a

European vacation, a second home, a bigger home, remodeling your
home, a country club membership, or a boat or plane

- Financial independence at a younger age
- Charitable giving
- A top college education for your children

Your reasons should be very definite and very clear. You need to fill a deep
motivation reservoir with a clear idea of what reaching this goal will mean.
In too many cases, advisors set a goal and have not spent much time
thinking through why they want to reach it. Setting general goals without
thinking through the details and without generating real desire leads to
superficial motivation that is not enough to make a behavioral difference.

Once your goals are set and your desire is high, you have the ammuni-
tion you need to make the right time-management choices. As you work
through the day, when the time comes for you to choose to risk rejection or
not, you must be able to draw on your reservoir of motivation to make the
right choice: You must vividly recall why it is important to you to grow your
business, you must call up strong images that fuel your desire to grow, and
you must remember that doing the difficult tasks is worth more than failing
or not growing.

Each day, you will face the decision whether or not to do those tasks that
expose you to rejection, and each time, your deep motivation will push you
toward the choices that fuel growth. The tasks that expose you to rejection
and that build your business are marketing tasks, because when you are
marketing, you are putting yourself in the position of asking for new money
from a client or a prospect. Marketing activities are the ones that require
deep motivation.

You should decide in advance at what times during the day you will
market. Interestingly, once you start on marketing tasks, they actually get
easier and require less motivation. Once you make marketing a daily
practice and do it for at least a month, starting the marketing activities
requires less motivation. One of the reasons for this is that you get better
and more relaxed by doing them. As with anything else, "practice makes
perfect."

You must have high motivation to engage in activities that have a high
risk of rejection. You must have high motivation to engage in marketing
activities. At the same time, if you don't perform these marketing activities,
you will not build a million-dollar practice.

TIME ALLOCATION

Many people in financial services have a superficial level of motivation. Superficial motivation is the simple desire to do well and to work hard. This alone will not lead you to a million-dollar-plus practice. You need a deeper level of motivation: motivation not only to work hard, but to spend a high percentage of your time every day risking being rejected.

Deeply motivated advisors spend their time doing the tasks that build their business most effectively, and they spend little time doing tasks that do not. How you spend your time, then, will be a good indicator of how motivated you are. Another way of looking at this is that when you choose how you will spend your time, you are really choosing how successful you are going to allow yourself to be—how you spend your time is the most important choice in building a million-dollar practice.

There are no shortcuts to building a million-dollar practice. In the end, it is simple math. To have a million-dollar practice, you should have:

+ Between $100 million and $150 million in investable assets
+ At least one hundred relationships that have more than $250,000 in investable assets
+ At least thirty of those one hundred relationships with assets over $1 million

To build a million-dollar practice, you should bring in:

+ At least $12 million net new assets per year (net means assets in minus assets lost)
+ Nine $250,000 to $1 million-plus relationships per year
+ Three $1 million-plus relationships per year

This seems like a simple formula, and it is, but it is also very hard to reach these numbers every year. The only way to bring in $1 million in new assets and one new $250,000-plus household every month is to spend time marketing. It is a cause-and-effect relationship: Do those tasks that are effective in bringing in this new money, and the effect will be that you will build a million-dollar practice.

The most effective marketing is to get in front of affluent prospects, follow up with affluent prospects, and get more assets from existing clients. For most advisors, the time spent marketing is "hard time" because they are putting themselves in the position of being rejected.

If your level of motivation is high, you will do these tasks. If it is not, you will not, and you will not succeed in building a million-dollar practice. The choice you make will be obvious each day when you choose how you will spend your time.

You have to spend a much greater percentage of your time marketing when you are building a new practice. But no matter where you are in your career, if you want your practice to grow at an above-average rate, you must market. As a guideline, in the first two years, you should spend 70 percent of a ten-hour day, or seven hours, directly on marketing activities. In years three through five, you should spend 50 percent of a ten-hour day (five hours daily); and in years six and after, you should spend 25 percent of an eight-hour day (two hours per day). As your experience and expertise increase, you will be able to leverage your clients more, which means that it will take less time to get each new affluent household. Upgrading a household to a $250,000 household counts as one of the twelve households you need; this is much easier for an experienced advisor to do than for a new advisor.

Motivation becomes the cornerstone of success when, each day, you make choices about how to spend your time. Some tasks put you at risk of being rejected. These are hard tasks and require high motivation. These are also the marketing tasks that will advance your practice most effectively. The hard tasks put you at risk of being rejected, but they also lead to a high pay-off: building a million-dollar practice. As I stated earlier, high rejection and high payoff go hand in hand.

MOTIVATION FOR EXPERIENCED ADVISORS

Many experienced advisors had high levels of motivation earlier in their careers and, as a result, built the foundation for a million-dollar practice. Yet as they achieved early success they reached a comfort level and slowed down. It is easy, and even understandable, to reach a comfort level once a certain level of income is achieved and the motivation to do the difficult tasks required for sustained growth is diminished. This comfort level, combined with the fear of rejection, is what keeps most experienced advisors from building a million-dollar practice. So if the experienced advisor wants to reach a million-dollar and ultimately a multimillion-dollar practice, he must sustain the high level of motivation he had at the beginning of his career.

The first step in regaining the required motivation is having a strong enough desire to reach the goal of a million-dollar plus practice. For many experienced advisors that can come from the pride of being among the most successful in the industry. For others it can be a monetary goal that will provide them a certain lifestyle, and for others it can be the sense of fulfillment of reaching their potential. But whatever the goal, it must be intense and real, and you must have faith that you can achieve the goal.

The good news is that as a financial advisor, a million-dollar income is completely achievable. There is enough wealth, wealth transfer, and opportunity for any advisor in any market to reach the million-dollar level if she has the right amount of motivation to fuel the required activities. Just as important as the decision to spend time on the right activities is the decision not to spend time on the wrong activities. The wrong activities during the day can include spending time with other advisors, paperwork, administrative tasks, preparation, and reading. It's not that these tasks aren't necessary, but they should not be done if they can be delegated or done during non–prime marketing times (later in the afternoon, evening, weekends). The right activities include proactive contact and appointments with clients, proactive contact and appointments with prospects, and prospect pipeline contacts.

Financial advisors can learn from Olympic athletes who spend time not only training for their sport but also visualizing success to increase their motivation. Psychologists train Olympic athletes to prepare mentally for success, and part of that is to visualize winning and how they will feel when they win. Experienced advisors should do the same mental preparation that elite athletes do and visualize how they will feel when they reach their million-dollar goal. Visualize the office you will be in, the income you will earn, and the pride you will feel in being among the elite financial advisors. This visualization will trigger your subconscious to keep you focused on those things that will result in achievement of your goals.

The most successful advisors are "pulled" by their goals rather than "pushed" by their goals. When you are "pulled" toward your goals you are motivated and excited about doing those activities that will enable you to achieve your goals rather than feeling "pushed" to do things you don't want to do. The result of being pulled toward a goal you want to achieve is that you lose your fear because the excitement of achieving a goal that is important to you offsets the fear of doing that activity.

It takes courage to be successful as a financial advisor. You have to be willing to face rejection, you have to be willing to spend money, you have to be willing to accept failure if you don't reach your goals, and you have to be willing to try new things. But those advisors who have the courage and the motivation to set challenging goals and do the activities that will lead to the achievement of their goals have all the necessary ingredients that are required to reach the goal of building a million-dollar financial services practice.

The high level of turnover in financial services has more to do with a lack of deep motivation than with a lack of talent. Most people are not willing to face, over the long term, the low-percentage/high-payoff dynamics of this business—they cannot stand the pain of rejection long enough to reap the big rewards. The advisor must want, at the deepest level, this kind of success and be very clear about why that success is so important; that desire is the essence of the motivation you must have to face rejection and to ensure success.

There is such an information overload in financial services that it is easy to get distracted and not focus on the right activities and the right numbers. No matter where you are in building a million-dollar practice, it is critical that you understand the numeric measures that lead to it. This understanding will allow you to focus on the right activities and to set the right goals. In Chapter 3, I will explain these numeric measures and goals.

SUMMARY

- ♦ To succeed in financial services, you must market, and to market, you must have deep motivation.
- ♦ How you spend your time shows how motivated you are.
- ♦ The activities required to build a million-dollar practice put you in the position of being rejected, which is hard.
- ♦ Financial services is a low-percentage/high-payoff business.
- ♦ You must spend time on direct marketing activities every day in order to build a million-dollar practice and beyond.
- ♦ The price you pay for being rejected must be less than your fear of failure.
- ♦ The key to deep motivation is being clear on how important success is to you and what tangible results you will receive.
- ♦ You make a hard choice every day of how to spend your time. Your motivation must be high for you to make the right choice.

- The more time you spend on marketing, the easier it gets.
- It is not easier for successful advisors to face rejection, but they can make themselves do it.
- Experienced advisors must re-establish the high level of motivation they had earlier in their careers to move past their comfort zone to reach the goal of a million-dollar practice.
- Visualizing the goal of achievement is an essential ingredient in developing the motivation required to perform the necessary activities.
- It takes courage to set challenging goals and engage in the activities required to achieve the goal of a million-dollar practice.

CHAPTER 3

The Numbers You Need to Succeed

ANY ADVISOR IN FINANCIAL SERVICES can build a million-dollar practice. Reaching the million-dollar level generates an income that few other occupations provide. Only about 20 percent of financial advisors, however, survive their first two years and of those who survive, only 5 percent ever reach the goal of a $1 million or greater practice. This means that only 1 percent of financial advisors hired ever achieve the coveted goal of a $1 million practice.

If most advisors aspire to the million-dollar goal, why do so few reach it? There are two reasons:

1. A lack of deep motivation—not being willing to pay the price of facing rejection to achieve a million-dollar practice
2. Not knowing how to build a million-dollar practice, or building a practice that limits growth

What I am about to outline is how to build a million-dollar practice within ten years of starting in the business, or, for advisors who are not just starting out, how to add $12 million in assets and $100,000 in business each year. Building a million-dollar business starts with understanding the six numeric elements you should have in order to reach that level.

THE SIX NUMERIC ELEMENTS OF A MILLION-DOLLAR PRACTICE

Element 1. You should have at least $120 million in assets under management.

Element 2.   You should have one hundred relationships with affluent investors ($250,000-plus).

Element 3.   You should set relationship minimums and continue to raise those minimums as your business grows, limiting your total client relationships to 100.

Element 4.   You should have at least one $1 million-plus client for every three clients in the $250,000 asset class.

Element 5.   You should develop and maintain a prospect pipeline of between fifty and one hundred qualified prospects (one hundred prospects for advisors with three years or less of experience and fifty prospects for advisors with more than three years of experience).

Element 6.   You should work toward having 100 percent wallet share with your core affluent clients, those fifty to one hundred clients who make up 80 to 90 percent of your business and assets.

If you have all six elements, then you will have built the right business practice to reach $1 million in business; you should be generating about 80 basis points on all assets under management under most circumstances and market conditions. An advisor can manage a conservative practice and still generate 80 basis points in most financial cycles.

Here is how these six elements work.

Element 1: You Should Have at Least $120 Million in Assets Under Management

It takes approximately $120 million in assets to generate $1 million in business (with a ROA (return on assets) of 80 basis points; ROA equals fees divided by assets).

Element 2: You Should Have One Hundred Relationships with Affluent Investors

It is nearly impossible to manage more than a total of one hundred relationships effectively: If you contact each client once a month, and if three of these contacts include a quarterly review and one includes an annual review with a planning session, and if you spend time with your clients at one or two events a year, then you will be spending at least ten hours per year on each client relationship. Given one hundred relationships, this is 1,000 hours per year.

If you have between fifty and one hundred prospects and treat your prospects like they are your affluent clients, you will be spending ten hours a year with each prospect. This is 500 to 1,000 hours per year. This adds up to approximately 1,500 hours that you need to spend on your current clients and prospects. The average advisor works approximately 2,300 hours per year, which leaves only 800 hours for all administrative work, client service, and other marketing activities.

There are not enough hours in the day to service more than one hundred client relationships and fifty to one hundred prospect relationships properly. The same principle applies to the advisor's client associates. To keep these one hundred clients, you should provide "raving fans" service, which limits the number of total relationships you and your client associates can have.

Element 3: You Should Set Relationship Minimums

As a guideline, every relationship should have at least $250,000 in investable assets, or the potential for that amount. If you are an advisor with a length of service of five years or less, it's reasonable to have accounts with less than $250,000 as you build up to a total of one hundred relationships, as long as those relationships are over $100,000. Every relationship should generate at least $1,000 in fees per year. Million-dollar-plus relationships should average at least $10,000 per year and be doing at least $5,000 per year in business. These numbers should be relatively easy to achieve if you contact each relationship twelve times per year and you expose each one to a broad mix of products and services. If a client does not generate the minimum level of business during the course of a year, consider replacing him with a client who will.

Constantly raise the minimums for assets and business. Your number of client relationships should always be constant—one hundred—but you should keep raising the minimum level of assets and business.

Element 4: You Should Have at Least One $1 Million-Plus Client for Every Three in the $250,000 Asset Class

You need to have approximately seventy relationships with at least $250,000 but less than $1 million in investable assets, with an average of $500,000 to $700,000 in assets. You need to have at least thirty relationships that have at least $1 million in investable assets, with an average of $2.5 million in assets.

Element 5: You Should Develop and Maintain a Prospect Pipeline of Between Fifty and One Hundred Qualified Prospects (one hundred prospects for advisors with three years or less of experience and fifty prospects for advisors with more than three years of experience)

To grow your assets by $12 million each year, keep a pipeline of one hundred active prospects at all times (fifty for advisors with a length of service of three years or more). You should spend time daily contacting the prospects in this pipeline and setting appointments with new ones. These prospects will ultimately replace the lower end of your existing one hundred client relationships as you increase the minimums each year. Your goal should be to have fifty to one hundred prospects that are all more qualified than your

> **FUNDAMENTAL TRUTH:**
> You grow your business by raising the level of minimum assets, not by increasing the number of relationships

smallest and least productive client relationships. Ideally, your prospects will all have more assets than your average size client. To grow your business at the rate that will lead to a million-dollar practice, you need to upgrade both your client list and your prospect list every year.

Element 6: You Should Work Toward Having 100 Percent Wallet Share with Your Core Affluent Clients

The goal is to have 100 percent wallet share with your top one hundred clients. You may never achieve that goal but you should never stop trying to reach it. The key to 100 percent wallet share is continuously exposing appropriate financial products and services to your top one hundred clients. In many cases, if you double the products and services a client uses, you can triple the business the client generates. If a relationship has more than $250,000 and uses six or more services and products, client retention is typically more than 98 percent.

Note: These six elements are interrelated. Having relationships of this size automatically limits the total number of relationships you can have; clients at this level of affluence want and need a greater variety of products and services and require more contact and a higher level of service.

HOW NEW ADVISORS NEED TO START OUT

If you are a new advisor and you want to build a million-dollar practice in the shortest time possible, you need to understand from the outset how the numbers work. This increases the probability of building a million-dollar practice and decreases the time it will take.

As a new advisor, you have two goals above all others:

Goal 1.   Build a pipeline of one hundred qualified prospects quickly.

Goal 2.   Bring in $1 million in net new assets per month.

Goal 1: Build a Pipeline of One Hundred Qualified Prospects Quickly

First and most important, you need to build a pipeline of one hundred qualified prospects as soon as possible. The definition of a qualified (or "legitimate") prospect is a person who:

♦   Has met you.
♦   Meets your minimum level of investable assets.
♦   Agrees to a second appointment and/or will be receptive to your follow-up efforts

It should take six to twelve months to build this pipeline. Remember that once you **build** this pipeline of one hundred prospects, you will continue to upgrade it throughout your entire career. The number of one hundred prospects should not change until your length of service is six years or more, and then your goal should be at least fifty qualified prospects.

After six months, you, as a new advisor, should set a goal of acquiring one new $250,000 client a month, and within a year, one of those should be at least a $1 million client. This means that by the end of your first twelve months of production, you should have:

♦   One hundred qualified prospects
♦   Five $250,000-plus client relationships
♦   One $1 million-plus client relationship
♦   Six $100,000-plus client relationships that have potential for $250,000-plus

Goal 2: Bring In $1 Million in Net New Assets Per Month

The other important goal is assets under management. Your goal should be to bring in $1 million net in new assets per month (with net meaning assets gained minus any assets lost) after the first six months. Any affluent clients or large assets you capture in less than six months is unpredictable, because in most cases, it takes six months to cultivate a prospect's trust to the point that she will let you manage her money. Therefore, you should have at least $6 million in assets after your first twelve months in order to be on track to reach a goal of a million-dollar practice within ten years.

After the first twelve months, a new advisor's numbers stay essentially the same. You need to add an average of one new affluent relationship ($250,000-plus) per month, of which three, after twelve months, should be $1 million-plus. Additionally, you need to bring in $12 million net in new assets per year. Note that existing clients who turn over new money to you count toward new assets and new affluent households if they cross the $250,000 or $1 million mark; this gives the more experienced advisor an advantage because at least 50 percent of these goals can be achieved by upgrading current clients, which is much easier that bringing in new ones.

WHAT IT ALL MEANS

Any advisor who is motivated to reach $1 million needs to set a goal of adding approximately one new $250,000-plus household per month net (of which three per year need to be $1 million-plus) and $1 million in new assets per month. This will lead to a million-dollar practice.

Reminder: Upgrades of clients and additional client assets count toward these goals.

Now that you understand the numbers, move on to the next step, which is to have a good overall marketing process for reaching those numbers. Without a good process, all you have are goals and motivation. Chapter 4 covers the first step of that marketing process, called niche marketing.

SUMMARY

- It takes a deep level of motivation to build a million- or multimillion-dollar business.
- With the right focus and motivation, a new advisor can expect to reach a goal of a million-dollar practice within ten years from starting.
- With the right focus and motivation, an advisor can expect to increase her business $100,000 per year.

- To support a million-dollar practice, you need to bring in $12 million net new assets per year and add at least ten net new $250,000 households per year, of which two or three are $1 million-plus.
- Limit your total number of client relationships to one hundred. If you are working within a team, look to achieve no more than one hundred client relationships per team member and, ideally, fifty total per team member.
- Work toward each client relationship having at least $250,000 in assets.
- Deep penetration of each relationship is important; make it a goal to have five to six different products and services per relationship.
- To grow beyond $1 million, you should limit the number of affluent client relationships to one hundred, but always increase the minimums.
- In most market conditions a well-managed financial practice that follows all six elements should generate 80 basis points on assets managed.
- Set a minimum amount of business for a relationship to qualify as one of your one hundred. As a guideline, set a $1,000 revenue minimum for relationships with $250,000 to $1 million in assets, and $5,000 for relationships with more than $1 million.
- Depending on your experience level, keep fifty to one hundred active prospects in your pipeline at all times.
- Set a minimum for a prospect of at least $100,000 and a target of at least $250,000+ in assets if you have a length of service of zero to three years, and $250,000 in assets if you have a length of service of three years or more until you reach $1 million. Never have more than one hundred prospects at once, but increase the qualifying minimums constantly.
- Upgrading an existing relationship to above $250,000 or $1,000,000 is just as valuable as bringing in a new one. It all counts the same in building a million-dollar practice.

CHAPTER 4

Niche Marketing

IF YOU WANT TO BUILD YOUR BUSINESS TO $1 MILLION-PLUS, you must develop an effective marketing process. The first step in doing this is to identify the markets you want to focus on. Once you have identified your markets, the second step is to develop a well-thought-out market action plan. These two steps create what is called a niche marketing plan because the plan is focused on a small number of specific markets.

Part 3 of this book gives market action plans that advisors can choose from, complete with sample scripts and sources of names.

WHY NICHE MARKETING WORKS BEST

Niche marketing works because each market requires a high level of expertise and experience to capture it effectively. The more you understand the dynamics of a particular market, the easier it is to get appointments with prospects and referrals in that market. You will capture your market most effectively if you select only a few markets (narrow) and understand and work them deeply—niche marketing is narrow and deep. As your familiarity and expertise with a market increase, so will your confidence and ability to build trust with potential investors. As individual investors' affluence increases, so does their belief that their circumstances are unique, and they want to work with a financial advisor who has both expertise and experience working with people like them. Your competition will also be reduced because most financial advisors don't focus on a niche market and don't develop a deep level of experience and expertise working with a particular type of investor or occupation. Examples of potential niche markets include business owners, corporate executives, retirement plans, individuals preparing for retirement, stock option plans, attorneys, medical professionals, and retirees.

The goal is to build depth within the markets you choose. How?

- Join their professional associations.
- Subscribe to their trade journals.
- Develop professional and personal relationships with centers of influence within your targeted market.

These activities will enable you to "talk the talk" and "walk the walk" of your target markets. They will give you credibility and visibility so you can build trust with potential investors in those markets. Typically, each market has individuals who are leaders and centers of influence within that market. The only way you can identify and connect with these centers of influence is to have a level of expertise in their market and to know who the "movers and shakers" are. It is hard to do this for more than four to five markets.

ELEMENTS OF AN EFFECTIVE MARKET ACTION PLAN

An effective niche market action plan should have four parts.

Part 1: Approach

The approach is a description or set of ideas regarding how best to approach the target market. Develop this description by:

- Interviewing the most successful advisors for that market about what they do to succeed
- Reading books on the target market
- Collecting information from local management, wholesalers, home-office training, and other sources

Your objective is to get appointments with affluent investors within your niche markets. Whenever possible, these should be "warm calls," not cold calls. To make the initial contact warmer, try:

1. A referral from someone that person knows
2. A connection, something you have in common
3. Knowing something about your contact's area of expertise

One way of developing this information is to enter the name of the person you will contact into a Google search before contacting her. Or if you follow the guidelines in Chapter 22 and have some level of connection with the prospect, you can see her credentials on the website LinkedIn. This can provide some interesting background that can make the contact "warmer." Warm calls go much further than cold ones; making warm contacts is what niche marketing is all about.

Part 2: Expertise

You must develop some level of expertise before you approach your target market. You should identify people and resources that your firm has to offer that can support your targeted market. In addition, reading books and other materials can provide you with expertise in your target market. Investing time developing your expertise will pay off in dividends as you approach your target markets and are able to immediately distinguish yourself as someone who understands the unique needs of your target market. As you focus your efforts on a particular target market you will learn from your experiences and gain insights and expertise.

Part 3: Scripts

The third part of the market action plan is the scripts. These scripts link the theory of the market action plan to reality by getting appointments. You develop these scripts from the market intelligence you gathered in Part 1. Sample scripts are provided in Part 3 of this book for each of the market action plans featured.

Part 4: List of Names

The fourth part of the market action plan is a list of names of potential prospects who are in the target market. The source for these names can be the library, the Internet, or leads lists you purchase (see Appendix/resources). The objective is to have between 3,000 and 4,000 names representing all of your selected niche markets. Try to screen each person on this list to be sure he or she fits your qualifications before the first contact is made (see how in Chapter 5). The more time spent developing and prescreening these names, the more productive each contact will be. There are few things more valuable than a prescreened list of qualified names within a target market.

The market action plan is complete and ready to execute once it has all four parts. All that's left is to execute by contacting the qualified names. To do that, you must have a deep level of motivation that pushes you through the inevitable rejection you will get.

AN EXAMPLE OF DEVELOPING A MARKET ACTION PLAN

Let us say you choose to target attorneys. In Parts 1 and 2 of your market action plan, you might discover that attorneys are generally too busy to spend much time on investing because they are paid for billable hours. You might also find out that most attorneys are responsible for their own retirement plans and that by becoming an expert in retirement plans, you become more valuable to this market. Becoming familiar with the resources your firm provides to support retirement plans will help develop your expertise. To complete Part 4 of the action plan, you could start a list of all attorneys in your market with the telephone directory business pages (which is only one example of the many sources for finding names of attorneys), and you could use a Google search and visit the attorneys' web-sites to narrow that list to the most experienced and successful attorneys in town. You might also identify and read local publications or trade maga-zines that your local attorneys read and attend the meetings of the bar associations they belong to; as you do, you will quickly find out who the centers of influence within that market are. Let's say that you then make a connection with one of these centers of influence—she can provide you with insights about attorneys in your market and then potentially refer you to other qualified attorneys. Now, armed with the information you have gathered, you can write out several scripts (Part 3) you will use when con-tacting the attorneys on your list (Part 4) to set up initial appointments.

THE MARKETING PROCESS FOR NEW ADVISORS

I recommend that new advisors initially target four to five markets and develop market action plans for each. I believe that new advisors need to focus on more markets than experienced advisors because at the early stages of your career, you may not be certain which markets you will be most effec-tive with. You need to experiment to see what works best; then, over the course of your first two years, you can narrow your five initial market action plans to one or two, based on your success. I further recommend that new advisors consider the following two market action plans among their first five:

1. **Past experience market action plan** (see Chapter 24). As a new advisor, one of your first market action plans should be based on your past experience. For example, if you were previously in the software business, then one of your market action plans should focus on people in the software industry. You know who the most qualified prospects are in that industry; use your insider knowledge and contacts to make a connection with those prospects.

2. **Personal contacts market action plan** (see Chapter 24). Your second market action plan should be based on personal contacts, which is essentially a list of all potentially qualified personal contacts. This approach is also called "Rolodex marketing," and it has the highest ratio of contacts to appointments: 50 percent of contacts lead to appointments. The chapter later in this book on social media marketing (Chapter 22) can provide some additional ideas on how to most effectively market through your physical or electronic Rolodex.

Choose your other two to three market action plans based on the types of markets you are interested in or you think you would do well with. Part 3 of this book contains fifteen market action plans and more than fifty approaches. Find ones that appeal to you and develop them fully, complete with sources of names, before you receive a production number. You should have at least three thousand names among all your market action plans. If possible, do all this work in advance so that when you receive your securities licenses you'll be ready to go.

The Notebook

Maintain a notebook or a spreadsheet that contains each of your targeted market plans, with a tab separating each market plan. In each section of your notebook list the affluent individuals you plan to contact, along with all their contact information and any information you have researched about them, as well as the script you plan on using. There should be a total of between 3,000 and 4,000 representing all of your different market plans in the notebook. Researching your prospects, practicing your scripts, and organizing your target market notebook will increase the odds of success once you start implementing your plans and contacting your prospects. The goal is to start each day with your niche market notebook prepared so that all you have to do is to execute your plans throughout the day.

THE MARKETING PROCESS FOR EXPERIENCED ADVISORS

Experienced advisors can choose from among the seven market action plans I outline here. (You don't need all seven to be successful, and you can choose others that may suit you better—see the fifteen market action plans in Part 3 of this book.) These seven are based on leveraging your current client relationships and on your outside interests. Parts 2 and 3 of this book have more detail on each of the seven market action plans, but I will outline each of them here.

1. **Referrals** (see Chapter 12). Every senior advisor must have an active referral program in place. A proactive referral plan is essential because the majority of new relationships are opened as a result of referrals. Furthermore, the majority of clients would refer if they were asked to do so by their advisor. Most clients indicate, however, that they are never asked.

2. **Professional referral network** (see Chapter 23). All experienced advisors should have a network of CPAs and attorneys who refer prospects to the advisor. The number one way millionaires get a financial advisor is by referral from their CPA or attorney. The best way to build this network is through the CPAs and attorneys your current clients use—take advantage of this natural leverage point of the mutual acquaintance. Many advisors who are successful in building this kind of network find that they need a total of five CPAs and attorneys (combined) to generate a good number of referrals. Support and strengthen this network by offering these people continuing edu-cation sessions and fun events, by being an information resource, by educating them about investments and wealth management, especially as they relate to taxes, and by showcasing the strengths of your practice.

3. **Seminars** (see Chapter 20). Most of your clients belong to outside organizations, such as chambers of commerce, church groups, garden clubs, and business service clubs, such as Rotary and Kiwanis clubs. Offer to speak to these ready-made audiences about investing, and follow up with a response card after the seminar. This way, you can reach hundreds of new potential prospects per year (example—twelve organizations with twenty participants in each organization).

4. **Prospect events** (see Chapter 21). The experienced advisor should host client events focused on his clients' interests, and invite his clients to bring friends. These events can be educational, activity-based, or both.

People like to be with other people with whom they share common interests; this is a nonthreatening way for clients to introduce you to potential referrals.

5. **Natural-market board of directors and niche markets** (see Chapter 14). If you look at your clients' demographics, you will see that many of your clients are clustered in the same occupation or the same stage of life; these groupings are your "natural market." Form a marketing board of directors, with the directors coming from this natural market, then ask these clients how to market to people like them. They will give you good ideas, and it's an ideal time to ask them for a referral to someone they know or work with.

You can take your natural market further by using the same narrow and deep approach within this niche market: Read publications, join local organizations, network within your natural market, become the financial services expert whom everyone in that market knows about, and contact qualified prospects in it.

6. **Nonprofits** (see Chapter 34). In this market action plan, you take a leadership role in an organization that you have a passion for. This can be a philanthropic, civic, or social organization. The key to making this work is to be in a leadership role and to be committed to the organization. Qualified investors who have a similar passion will be in this organization, and they will be drawn to you.

7. **Right Place–Right People**. Putting yourself in a position to meet affluent people through your involvement in the community, organizations, country clubs, children's schools, and other social or philanthropic activities you are interested in is one of the most effective and productive way to develop relationships with affluent individuals. Once the relationships are developed, having transition strategies to convert these individuals into personal relationships is required. Join the organizations that have the kind of members you want to have as clients, and build relationships with these individuals. This can take twelve months or more. In this way you can transition them from personal to business relationships.

MARKETING EFFECTIVENESS

The following table gives approximate ratios of how many contacts each technique requires in order to produce one appointment:

Marketing Method	Contact-to-Appointment
Mailing	100:1
Cold call	20:1
Influencer networking*	10:1
Seminar follow-up	5:1
Referrals	2:1
Personal contacts (Rolodex)	2:1
Networking**	2:1

* Number of influencer meetings needed to get one referral.
** Referral from a network member.

The key to building a million-dollar practice is to increase your business by twelve new affluent investors ($250,000 in investable assets or more) per year and $12 million in new assets. The first step to achieving that goal is to identify specific market niches and to develop market action plans for these niches. Each action plan should contain a well-thought-out approach, expertise, scripts, and qualified names. Niche marketing is effective at all stages of your career.

Once you have your action plans, your next step is to contact the names in each plan. As you do this, be very clear about why you are making the contact and that your objective is a face-to-face meeting; otherwise, you will squander all your hard work and you will not be effective. In Chapter 5, I outline how you go from your list of names to actually getting an appointment with each person you contact.

SUMMARY

♦ The first step in growing your practice is to identify three to five niche markets and develop a market action plan for each one.

♦ Each market action plan should include a detailed plan for how to approach the niche market, a plan to develop expertise, scripts to get appointments with people in that market, and sources of names.

♦ Economies of scale work in favor of going deep and narrow in each niche market. Knowing local centers of influence in each one provides great leverage for penetrating that market effectively.

+ You must be deeply motivated to execute the market action plan each day.

+ The key focus of each market action plan is getting appointments with new prospects in that market.

+ All experienced advisors should choose among seven market action plans and consider using one or several of the other market action plans in Part 3. These seven plans are referrals, a CPA/attorney network, seminars for clients' organizations, client/prospect events, developing prospects within your natural market, taking a leadership role in non-profit organizations, and putting yourself in position to meet affluent individuals through your outside interests and developing transition strategies to move them from personal to business relationships.

+ Network within new or existing social groups and develop them as distinct target markets.

CHAPTER 5

Getting the Appointment

IN BUILDING THE FOUNDATION FOR A MILLION-DOLLAR BUSINESS, a new advisor's highest priority should be to get as many appointments with affluent prospects as possible. In fact, getting new appointments with affluent prospects should be one of your highest priorities throughout your entire career.

YOU MUST MEET YOUR PROSPECTS FACE TO FACE

The ability to build a million-dollar practice has more to do with psychology than with financials. This is a people business, and your success is determined by building relationships with people, affluent investors in this case, and opening accounts with them in a reasonable time frame (six to twelve months).

Next to physical health, fiscal health is the highest priority for most people. An affluent investor has so many choices of advisors that he would never enter into a relationship without trusting and liking the advisor he will be working with. This is especially true if he is cur-

> **FUNDAMENTAL TRUTH:**
> You cannot build a relationship without meeting a prospect face to face.

rently working with another advisor, which most affluent investors are.

It is essential to understand that nothing good will happen without your first meeting a qualified investor face to face. The first important skill for achieving marketing success and building a million-dollar practice is to be able to get an initial face-to-face appointment with a qualified prospect. Any activity that postpones the face-to-face appointment delays building the relationship that leads to doing business with the prospect. Appointments with affluent prospects should be priority 1.

Most advisors will do anything to get a "feel-good" response from a prospect and will delay rejection for as long as they can. This tendency to get a feel-good response is like a one-yard play in football—the ball is moving down the field, but after four one-yard plays, you lose the ball. Examples of one-yard plays include mailing a prospect something or calling her back before you have met her. Getting a first appointment is harder to do, but in the end, it is much more productive. It is like getting a first down—you are moving the ball and you keep the ball.

If you focus on getting the appointment, then you are absolutely clear about what you want when you first contact the prospect. The mistake most advisors make when they are marketing is that they do not really know what they want to get out of the initial contact. They want to get a positive response, but they are unclear about where they want the contact to go. If you know with absolute clarity where you want the first contact to go, your probability of success is much higher. When you contact the prospect, he has no idea where the contact is going; if you make a strong case initially about the value of an appointment, the prospect is much less likely to object.

You might assume that giving the highest priority to getting an appointment applies only to cold calling. That is absolutely not the case. Whatever your market action plans are, your first priority must be to get a face-to-face appointment. Remember the Fundamental Truth just given; it applies to networking, seminars, prospect events, CPA referrals, Rolodex marketing, or any other market action plan. Consider cold calling as a last resort when you can't get an appointment any other way.

PREQUALIFYING YOUR PROSPECTS

It is important that you prequalify the prospect before contacting her to get an appointment. It is a complete waste of time to set appointments with unqualified prospects. When developing your market action plan and building the lists to support the plan, spend as much time as you can qualifying the prospects on the list. You can do this in a variety of ways:

♦   Determine what job title the prospect holds. An executive who holds the title of vice president or higher is most likely qualified.

♦   If the prospect owns a business, find out if it is generating $1 million or more in revenue or if it is consistently profitable and has been in existence for five years or longer.

- Find out where the prospect lives; for example, many qualified investors live in older neighborhoods that have larger homes.
- If the prospect is a professional (attorney or physician), find out if he owns the practice or is a partner. Determine how long he has been in practice.
- Check out websites of businesses and professionals. These websites often contain all the information you need to know about the revenues, experience, and longevity of a business or practice.
- Use LinkedIn or other social networking. If you are connected to the individual or if she is connected to one of your connections you can see her past experience and current position, which is an excellent source of information to qualify a potential prospect. Please see more on this in Chapter 22, on social media marketing.
- A Google search is a good way to help qualify a potential prospect. Through a Google search you can often determine the person's involvement in different organizations and levels of charitable contributions, and you can find other information about the success, interest, and activities of your target prospect.
- If the prospect is an executive of a public company, check public records for information on his holdings and compensation, specifically the proxy section of the annual report.
- It is also possible to purchase or lease lists of people who have been prescreened for different selectors (income, job title, value of home, and so on).

QUALIFYING REFERRALS

Try to prequalify prospects who have been referred to you by others as tactfully as possible. To do this, you can ask questions of the person making the referral, such as:

- "Do you believe the net worth of the prospect you are referring is similar to yours?"
- "Do you believe the referred prospect has at least [minimum qualification] in investable assets?"
- "I find I am most valuable to prospects who have investable assets of [minimum qualification]. Do you believe the referred prospect has at least that amount?"

QUALIFYING ON THE FIRST CONTACT

If you have not prequalified your list or if you want to confirm that the prospect is qualified before making the appointment, you can do it during the initial contact. Here are some examples of how to do that:

+ "I am looking forward to meeting you, and I have found that I provide the most value to investors who have [minimum qualification] or more. Would that apply to you?"

+ "Before our meeting, it would be helpful for me to have some preliminary information; would you estimate that you have over or under [minimum qualification] in investable assets?"

+ "In preparing for our appointment, it would be helpful for me to have an estimate of your investable assets. Would you be comfortable providing me with an estimate?"

+ "In preparing for our appointment, it would be helpful to know some preliminary information about your situation. Currently, do you invest in mutual funds or use separate account managers? Do you invest in municipal bonds? Do you have any concentrated stock positions?"

+ "My practice because of my high commitment to service is tailored to individuals who have investable assets of at least (state minimum). Would that apply to you?"

I recommend that you do as much prequalification as you can because having to qualify the prospect during the first contact can be awkward and might offend him or her. You should, however, qualify the prospect before the appointment, and if the only way to do it is during the initial contact, do it then to avoid wasting time with an unqualified prospect.

The bottom line is that the more time you spend prequalifying your list before you contact a prospect, the more hours you will save by avoiding meeting with unqualified prospects. Your ability to prequalify is limited only by the time you are willing to spend researching the qualification level.

HOW TO DETERMINE THE MINIMUM QUALIFICATION

Determine the minimum qualification level based on the size of your current clients. A rule of thumb is that a prospect should have at least as many investable assets as your least affluent client and your target prospect should have more assets than your average client. A new advisor has very few, if any, client relationships, so the minimum qualification should be at least $100,000 in investable assets with the potential to have more. Another guideline is based on your length of service (LOS):

(LOS in Years)	Minimum Investable Assets Guidelines
0–2*	$100,000
3–5	$250,000
6+†	$250,000

* Potential for $250,000.
† "If over $1 million in production, prospect minimum should increase.

IF THE PROSPECT IS NOT QUALIFIED, "UNSELL" THE APPOINTMENT

If you have to "unsell" an appointment because the prospect does not meet the minimum qualification, it is okay to do so. The following script gives some idea of how to do this:

Mr./Ms. Prospect, based on what you told me about your investments, I am not sure an appointment makes sense right now. I would like to send you some information on what we have available, and you can call me if you are interested.

MAKING THE CONTACT AND GETTING THE APPOINTMENT

The objective of your contact is to get the prospect to commit to a meeting so that you can make a face-to-face connection with her to discuss her investments—only a face-to-face investment discussion counts here. You should understand this and remember it at all times.

Most affluent investors are bombarded with offers to invest their money—solicitations in the mail, in newspapers and magazines, on television, from telemarketers, and so on. Other obstacles are that the affluent investor most likely already has an advisor, and affluent investors tend to be very busy people.

On the other hand, take confidence from the fact that the majority of investors are underserviced and will change advisors at some point. Also, despite the obstacles, getting an appointment is not complicated, although it is difficult. When contacting a prospect to ask for an appointment, you will greatly increase the probability of getting one if you:

♦ Remember that your first priority is to get a face-to-face meeting.

♦ State your experience and expertise in the prospect's particular niche market.

♦ Quickly describe why it is in the prospect's best interest to take some time to meet you ("value-added").

♦ Provide a sincere compliment—whenever possible.

♦ Request an appointment.

Remember that the objective of the appointment will be to make a personal connection, which will set the stage for building a strong relationship with the prospect; that, in turn, will become the catalyst for the prospect to transfer at least a portion of his assets to you. In order to make this connection during the appointment, add value by focusing on the prospect's needs. This is why niche marketing, the research behind it, and your expertise are all so important. The value you will give to the prospect when he meets with you is based on your understanding of that prospect's needs.

The more you know about the prospect in advance, the stronger the case you can make for why the prospect should meet with you. If you have any common connection with the prospect, that will further increase the value of the appointment. The following are some examples of how you can add a sense of value when you contact a prospect to set up your appointment.

Examples of Scripts for Getting an Appointment

"Mr./Ms. Business Owner, this is Joe Advisor from XYZ Financial. The reason for my call is that I know that as a successful business owner, you are always trying to improve your bottom line, and I specialize in helping business owners get more profits. I know you are successful, and if you give me the opportunity to meet with you, I am convinced that I can show you how I could add to your bottom line. Would you be available next Thursday to meet with me?"

"Mr./Ms. Business Owner, my name is Jane Advisor from XYZ Financial, and the reason I am calling you is that I specialize in working with successful owners of dry cleaners like you. I noticed you were recognized by the chamber of commerce as one of the top businesses in your community—congratulations. I understand your business, and I am convinced that if you give me the opportunity to meet you and find out more about your circumstances, I could show you some ways to improve your bottom line. I will be in your area next Thursday. Could we schedule a brief appointment?"

"Mr./Ms. Prospect, my name is Joe Advisor, and I work with XYZ Financial, and the reason for my call is that I used to do what you do now. If I had known then what I know now, I would have done better with my business and personal investments. I know you are successful and could benefit from someone like myself who understands the dynamics of your profession/business/industry. If you would give me some time, I know I could provide value. Would you be available next Thursday for a brief introductory meeting?"

The script above assumes you were a former business owner in that particular industry.

"Mr./Ms. Executive, my name is Jane Advisor, and I work with XYZ Financial, and the reason for my call is that I specialize in working with successful and highly compensated executives like you. I understand that there is a lot of complexity in your deferred compensation, stock options, and retirement plans. If you would be willing to give me the opportunity, I know I could provide you with valuable information on how to maximize your benefits and minimize your taxes. Would you be available for a brief introductory meeting on Thursday?"

"Mr./Ms. Past Contact, this is Joe Advisor, and I wanted to have the opportunity to reconnect with you. I have always respected you professionally and personally. I am currently working with XYZ Financial and have been very impressed with the training I have received and the unique wealth-management process that we offer our clients. I would like to have the opportunity to visit with you to find out more about your circumstances and see if I could provide some value. Would you be receptive to meeting with me and taking the opportunity to reconnect?"

"Mr./Ms. Prospect, my name is Jane Advisor, and I work with XYZ

Financial. My firm has asked me to cover your town/suburb. You have the reputation of being a successful business owner/professional/individual, and I would like to meet you and get your opinion on how I should best approach your town/suburb. I also could provide you with a contact with our firm and all the resources we have. Would you have time for a brief introductory meeting when I am in your area next Thursday?"

"Mr./Ms. Investor, my name is Joe Advisor, and I am with XYZ Financial. The reason for my call is that I know you are a successful investor and I wanted to offer to be a contact for you with our firm. We have excellent research, a good inventory of bonds, and a very broad product line. I know that in the long term I would be an excellent resource for you, and at the very least, I could offer a second opinion. I am going to be in your area next Thursday and was hoping to schedule a brief introductory meeting. Would you be available?"

"Mr. /Ms. CPA/Attorney, my name is Jim Smith and I am with XYZ Financial. I am in the process of getting to know the best CPAs in my market with whom to develop a professional relationship. As I continue to build my practice, it is among my highest priorities to build a network with the right professionals. I also believe there is a possibility that in the future we could share mutual clients. I would like the opportunity to meet with you and find out more about your practice. When would be a convenient time for us to get together for an introductory meeting?"

THE FOUR ELEMENTS SCRIPTS NEED TO HAVE

These scripts all have four things in common:

1. **Specialization.** The advisor draws a connection between the prospect's needs or situation and the advisor's specialization, expertise, and experience.

2. **Recognition.** The advisor compliments the prospect on her success or reputation.

3. **Value.** The advisor quickly states how he can provide some value to the prospect given the prospect's current situation.

4. **Commitment.** The advisor asks for a commitment to having a brief introductory appointment.

These are the four elements most initial contacts should have in order to get the appointment. Please note that some mar-
ket action plans require a softer, longer-term approach; examples of these are action plans that involve right place–right people net-working through organizations and nonprofit leadership.

If you include these elements in your con-
tacts, with experience and practice you should average one appointment per ten contacts. This will be an average of the blend of techniques you use. For example, the Rolodex technique delivers about five appointments per ten contacts, while cold calling delivers one per twenty. Using a mix of techniques, as you will in real life, you will average around one per ten.

The more experience you have getting initial appointments, the higher your success ratio will be. In our business, as in everything else, practice makes perfect. With experience comes skill and flow. The advisor who makes many contacts seeking appointments will naturally become more relaxed and more comfortable asking for, and getting, appointments. It is important to remember the low-percentage/high-payoff dynamic of this business (see Chapter 2). It is okay if you get only a ten-to-one contact-to-appointment ratio based on a combination of your different niche market plans; it takes eight appointments with new prospects per week to build the foundation for a million-dollar practice, and at a ten-to-one ratio, you need to make eighty contacts per week, or sixteen to twenty per day, to build a million-dollar practice.

A CONFIDENT STYLE GETS BETTER RESULTS

One of the reasons that practice and experience improve results is that your confidence will increase over time and create a more fluid style. These phone contacts should be friendly, relaxed, and filled with "give and take" and, when possible, humor. A confident style projects experience, and experience is what the prospect wants. A tight, scripted-sounding, nervous style projects inexperience and insecurity, which is not what the prospect wants in a future advisor. The only way to be relaxed and confident is to practice and gain experience.

For most advisors, if you practice diligently and make several hundred contacts, you will have the right level of confidence within three months. If it takes eighty effective contacts a week to build the foundation for a million-dollar practice, in three months you will have made about a thousand contacts, in six weeks almost five hundred.

HANDLING OBJECTIONS

You need to know how to overcome objections. You should be like a black belt martial arts master who anticipates his opponent's moves in advance and has a practiced move to deflect them—in your case objections. Prospects object in predictable ways, and you can prepare in advance how to handle them.

"No" is an overall objection that you will encounter in many different forms. The response that most people give to a stranger asking for their time is no. It is like walking into a store and the clerk asks, "Can I help you?" Our first reaction is, "I am just looking," even if we want help. Initially contacting a prospect in this business is the same. In many cases, the prospect will reflexively respond with, "No, I am not interested," whether she has a need or not. The key is to be prepared for the objection and build a case for why it is to her advantage to spend time face to face with you in as short a time as possible.

In some cases, prospects have trouble saying no, so delay saying it by sidetracking you: They will ask you to send something or to call them back. All the prospect is doing is delaying the "no" response. The trap the advisor falls into is that he wastes precious time following up with an uninterested prospect who will never commit to an appointment. You should either get an appointment or move on to a prospect you can get an appointment with. Here are the most common forms "no" takes, and how to respond:

Prospect: I don't have the time to see you right now.

Advisor: I understand you are busy. Most successful people are. Because meeting with you is a high priority for me I will work around your schedule, tell me a date and time and I will do my best to arrange my schedule to accommodate yours. What date and time works best for you?

Prospect: I don't have any money to invest right now. It would be a waste of your time.

Advisor: I did not expect you would have anything to invest immediately. My only intention is to have a brief introductory meeting so that we can meet each other and so that I can find out more about your circumstances. Over time I hope I can earn a portion of your business if you feel that I offer you value and if you feel that there is a good fit.

Prospect: I am taken care of. I have an advisor.

Advisor: I would be surprised if a successful investor like you did not already have an advisor. My intention is just to have a brief introductory meeting so that we can make a connection face to face, and so that I can find out more about you and see if I could potentially add value to your current situation. At the least it's prudent to have a second opinion on your current investment situation and I could provide that for you. I can also provide the considerable resources and intellectual capital of our firm, so I am confident that I could provide value to your current investment situation.

Prospect: I am not interested in seeing you now.

Advisor: My only intention is to make a quick connection and find out more about your circumstances so that I can provide you, at no cost, my time and our resources, research, and intellectual capital. I am confident that over time I could add value to your current investment situation.

These responses will cover 90 percent of the objections you will receive. Prospects do not think about objections in advance; this is simply a reflex response. By being prepared and practicing the objection responses, you can often overcome the objection and improve your appointment ratio by 25 percent. If the prospect responds negatively to your objection response, close the call by asking the prospect if she knows anyone else who might be interested in getting to know an honest, hard-working advisor.

Returning to our example of the retail store clerk and applying the principles described in the objections section, imagine a scenario where a customer walks into a store and the clerk asks, "Can I help you" and the response is, "No, I'm just looking." The clerk knows in advance this is the response that 99 percent of the walk-in customers will have. With that knowledge that clerk is prepared for that response and says, "Please take your time, but if you would be interested I could show you our items that are marked down and are on sale." The customer says yes and the sales clerk has the opportunity to engage the customer in a conversation and increases the odds that a sale will occur.

RECONTACTING A PROSPECT WHO WON'T MEET WITH YOU

If, after you try to overcome her objections, the prospect is not interested, you should ask for a referral and then move on. After you make a well-rehearsed contact in which you offer value with a minimum time commitment, if you cannot convince the prospect, she is no longer a prospect and you should recycle her name to be contacted several months later. You can contact her again later because her circumstances may have changed and the law of receptivity (which is that as circumstances change, the same prospect may become much more receptive) may apply; thus, there is good reason to recontact the prospect in several months and to ask for an appointment again. Qualified names are too scarce to discard a good potential prospect.

What will not work, however, is to follow through with a prospect who will not commit to an appointment. Sending an uncommitted prospect a follow-up mailing or doing any other follow-up activity before you have an appointment is a waste of time. The only exception to that is if the prospect indicates an interest in the appointment but physically cannot make an appointment in the next several weeks. Under those circumstances, it is a good idea for you to recontact the prospect to schedule an appointment at a more convenient time (within thirty days). There are so many prospects who will meet with you that you cannot waste time on those who will not. Move on.

KEEPING THE APPOINTMENT

Between the time you make the appointment and the time the appointment occurs, many prospects will have second thoughts, but because an appointment has been made, most prospects will keep it—they committed to doing so. Once a prospect commits to seeing you face to face, in most cases he will keep that commitment.

Do not reconfirm the appointment because that gives the prospect an easy out, and he may cancel.

HOW MANY PROSPECTS TO MEET WITH

You should expect that 50 percent of the prospects you meet with will convert to qualified prospects, i.e., meet, commit to a second appointment, and/or return calls. Qualified prospects are your future clients, and if you follow up with them at the right frequency, 25 percent of them should become clients within twelve months.

The total number of qualified prospects in your pipeline should never exceed one hundred. You cannot properly contact and service more than one hundred prospects. Once you have one hundred prospects in your pipeline, you should replace the smallest and least likely to do business with more qualified prospects. If you are an experienced advisor, your prospect pipeline can include a total of only fifty prospects, because they will typically be more qualified and you will have a higher minimum qualification.

In your first two years, you should meet a minimum of eight new prospects a week. This is a challenging but completely achievable goal, and there is no excuse for not meeting it. As I stated earlier, at a ten-to-one contact-to-appointment ratio, it takes fifteen to twenty contacts (not calls) each day to reach this goal.

Advisors in their third to fifth year should set a goal of four new prospect appointments per week, and senior advisors with length of service of six years or more should set a goal of one to two new prospect appointments per week. At a ten-to-one ratio, you can achieve these goals with approximately ten contacts per day and five per day, respectively.

It is important for you to understand that many affluent investors are underserviced and many are not completely satisfied with their current advisor. Your goal is to get an appointment to start building a case for why the investor is better off with you and how you can add value to her current investment situation. You want to position yourself as a "strong number two." Even if you do not open the account in the short term, you are positioning yourself to be the next in line for the account, right after the prospect's current provider. Be aware that there is little competition for the number two spot.

Now that you have the appointment, what do you do in the appointment? This is your golden opportunity, where you can create a connection with a prospect that will lead to his becoming a client. How do you do this? See the next chapter for the answer.

SUMMARY

+ From the first day of your career, make as many new appointments with new affluent prospects as you possibly can, with a goal of at least eight per week.

+ You cannot build the right relationship with affluent investors without meeting them face to face.

+ Your first priority in prospecting is to get an appointment.

+ Any marketing activity that delays an initial face-to-face appointment is a waste of time.

+ You will get a much higher contact-to-appointment ratio if you focus right away on getting an appointment.

+ Most prospects are underserviced. The key first step is to get a foot in the door through an appointment, and position yourself as number two in line for their business.

+ Before you make the contact, spend time prequalifying your prospects. If that is not possible, or if you want to verify their qualifications, you can do so during the initial contact.

+ Do not get sidelined by anything other than getting an appointment. If you cannot convince a prospect to meet, recycle the name and move on.

+ The minimum qualification for a prospect should be assets greater than your one-hundredth client or $100,000, whichever is greater.

+ Cold calling for appointments can be effective, but it has one of the lowest contact-to-appointment ratios of any direct marketing approach.

+ Every initial contact with a prospect should have four elements: specialization (with the prospect's situation), recognition (of the prospect's success), value (what benefit the prospect will derive from meeting with you), and commitment (to meet).

+ You should anticipate and have ready responses to objections that prospects may raise about meeting with you. If the response does not work, ask for a referral and move on. There are plenty of prospects who will see you.

+ A relaxed, confident style is essential to success in getting an initial appointment. This comes with practice and experience.

+ Weekly appointment goals:

  Length of service zero to two years: Eight appointments per week, minimum.

Length of service three to five years: Four appointments per week.
Length of service six years or more: One to two appointments per week.

♦ About half of your meetings will be with contacts who meet your qualification minimums and agree to a second appointment. These are true prospects.

♦ You should never have more than one hundred qualified prospects in your prospect pipeline. (That's for advisors with zero to two years of service; those with three to five years of service need seventy-five, and those with six years or more need only fifty prospects in their pipeline.) After your pipeline is full, you can add a prospect to it only if you also drop one from the bottom of the pipeline.

CHAPTER 6

The Appointment

THE INITIAL FACE-TO-FACE APPOINTMENT IS LIKE GOLD: It is hard to get, but it is extremely valuable. Because of the potential value of every face-to-face appointment, you must maximize this golden opportunity; in order to do so, you should know exactly what you need to cover in the initial appointment:

- You should make a positive connection by building rapport.
- You should gather all the information possible about the prospect. You will use this information in the important follow-up.
- You should get a commitment for a second appointment.

You can achieve all these objectives with the same technique: by asking a lot of questions.

START OFF RIGHT

You are a guest of your prospect, and you are asking for the privilege of asking her questions, so you should begin with a brief introduction that will let your prospect know your agenda. Here are some examples of how to set the stage:

> "Mr./Ms. Prospect, thank you for taking the time to see me. The purpose of the appointment from my standpoint is to get the chance to know you better and to find out as much as I can about your current investment situation. Hopefully, by understanding your situation better, I can follow up and provide some real value to you. As I mentioned on the phone, I am confident that I can add value to your cur-

rent situation. The best way for me to accomplish that is to ask you some questions. It is clear to me that you are successful—could you share your story with me?"

"Mr./Ms. Prospect, it is clear to me that you are successful, and I know your time is at a premium. By finding out more about your circumstances, I am confident that I can add value to your current financial situation. The best way I can accomplish that is to ask you some questions about your current situation. Could you share your story with me?"

"Mr./Ms. Prospect, I know that you are a successful individual and that you are busy. I hope that over time I can earn a portion of your business by offering you my time and the resources of our firm. The best way for me to get started is to ask you as many questions about your current financial circumstances as you are comfortable with. May I ask you about your story and how you have been so successful?"

"Mr./Ms. Prospect, I appreciate your time today. I know that since you are a successful individual, your time is at a premium. My intention is to position myself over time as a strong number two in line behind your current advisor, and to earn the right to a portion of your business by providing you with access to me and to the resources of our firm at no cost. I can best accomplish that by asking you some questions about your current financial circumstances and long-term objectives."

It is important that you use an approach that does not appear to be an interrogation. Start with softer, more general questions and gradually become direct. Be sure to be aware of the dynamics during this process and "give and take" as needed. Let the prospect set the pace. If the prospect wants to expand or elaborate, give him plenty of leeway to do so. Stay engaged throughout the appointment, and keep a relaxed, confident style. This comes only with practice and experience.

When appropriate, ask for a tour of your prospect's business or operation. The prospect will usually accept the offer and will show you her operation with pride. This is a great rapport-building, fact-finding technique that you should use whenever possible. If the appointment goes well, ask the prospect if she knows anyone else you should be talking to, and ask if she could possibly introduce you personally if that person works at the same location.

ASK QUESTIONS

The appointment should be a fact-finding mission. The facts you gather will become the basis of the all-important follow-up process. You will build rapport and gather the facts you need if you focus on asking the prospect questions. If the prospect talks, he will like you; if you talk, the opposite occurs. Most successful people like to tell their story, but too often no one is really interested in their story, and they do not get the opportunity to tell it enough. Think about the 80/20 rule as a guideline: 80 percent the prospect talking and 20 percent you talking. This is your chance to make a good first impression, and you can best do that if the prospect believes you are experienced and confident, and at the same time empathetic and sincere. You can accomplish all this by becoming a master of asking questions.

Note that the first two objectives of the first appointment are to build rapport and to gather information on which to set up the follow-through. If you use as guidelines the fifty questions I recommend (at the end of this chapter), you should be able to develop a sense of whether you have a qualified prospect or not and what his highest priority investment needs are. Use your own judgment about how specific you should be on the first appointment—if the rapport you have created seems particularly strong, you may be in a good position to be more specific.

If this is not the case, however, your opportunity comes a bit later. Note once again that the third objective of every first appointment is to get a commitment to a second, follow-up appointment; if the prospect agrees to the second appointment, it is at that appointment that you will present your wealth-management process and explain how different it is from the way the prospect is probably investing. If you do this properly, in most cases you will have created doubt in the prospect's mind about his current situation and caused him to consider whether it might make more sense to work with you. In this case, I recommend that as part of the second appointment you outline the next steps and ask for permission to get much more specific about the dollar amounts, the specific investments the prospect has, his net worth, his statements from other investment firms, and agreement to go through your planning process.

ASK ABOUT THE PROSPECT'S PERSONAL SITUATION AND INTERESTS

Remember the three objectives I stated at the beginning of this chapter: rapport, information, and commitment. One way to achieve all three is to gather as much information as possible about the prospect's investment situation and personal interests. This provides essential information to use for the later follow-up process. Gather information about the prospect's family, her marital status and her spouse, how many children and grand-children she has, and the interests and activities of those offspring. Gather information about her hobbies, such as performing arts, cooking, hunting, golfing, fly fishing, or tennis. All of this information will be useful during the follow-up stage. The personal information is as important in the follow-up process as the investment information.

As the questions progress, I strongly recommended that you pay attention to the prospect's surroundings. Pictures, trophies, and awards are important clues to the prospect's interests. You can build rapport by referring to these areas of interest throughout your questions; this will also help the prospect relax and feel more open. Everyone likes to talk about his personal interests and passions. You cannot give too many sincere compliments throughout the appointment. Some of the best rapport building happens when you and your prospect share interests.

PITFALLS

If the prospect asks you for your opinion about the markets, make your answers general and brief—this is not the time to impress the prospect. Be sure to get back to your goal of gathering information about the prospect. If the prospect persists and asks a question you do not know the answer to, offer to get back to her after you have had time to research or think about the answer.

One of the fears all new advisors have is that the prospect will ask about their level of experience. The best response is to be truthful but to emphasize the resources, research, intellectual capital, and training of your firm and its unique wealth-management process, and to emphasize your commitment to, and the time you can provide for, servicing the prospect. Remember, most senior advisors are short on time and long on accounts; the newer advisor has plenty of time to provide the much-needed service that the prospect is often not receiving.

If you discover during the appointment that the prospect does not meet the minimum qualification (despite your best efforts to prequalify), you should politely make the appointment as short as possible. There is no value to either you or the prospect in having a long appointment if he is not a qualified prospect.

HOW LONG TO MEET

A good appointment can last from thirty minutes to an hour or more. Never cut short an appointment with a qualified prospect; the opportunity is too valuable, and there is too much information that it is impossible to get otherwise.

Make sure that if you have multiple appointments in a day that you give yourself a buffer between appointments in case the appointments go longer than expected. You should never be late, but if you schedule appointments every hour, you may have to choose between being late and having to cut short a good appointment (or even end up doing both).

CLOSE THE APPOINTMENT

The best way to close the appointment is to thank the prospect for her time and her willingness to share information. Restate the purpose of the appointment, which was to find out as much information as possible so that you can tailor your advice and the resources of the firm to add value to the prospect's situation. Restate your confidence that over time, you will add value and hopefully earn a portion of the prospect's business—again, your objective is to be a strong number two in line, at no cost to the prospect. Before you part, suggest a second appointment at which you will present your preliminary thoughts and recommendations. Remember that one of your primary objectives at the first appointment is to get a commitment from the prospect to a second appointment, in which you can present your wealth-management process tailored to that particular prospect. If you cannot schedule a second appointment, try to set up a follow-up call.

When you get back to the office, be sure to enter the prospect into the contact management system for the follow-up process.

THE BAD APPOINTMENT

You should expect that about half of your appointments will not be good ones. In a bad appointment, the prospect will be abrupt and will not give you the time to ask the questions you need to ask or to build rapport, or may not be a good fit for your practice. But only 50 percent of the appointments need to be good ones to make the process work; if you have a bad appointment, you should be willing to cut your losses and move on to a potentially good appointment as soon as possible. The best tactic to use on a bad appointment is to thank the prospect for his time and then leave.

If the appointment is a no-show, leave your card, go to another appointment, then drop by again to catch the prospect. No-shows give you the right to drop in any time that day. If you miss the prospect throughout the day, call the next day and try once more to reschedule.

FOLLOW UP RIGHT AWAY

Send a follow-up letter the next day. Thank the prospect, restate the purpose of the appointment, and reconfirm the follow-up appointment.

Follow-Up Letter

Dear Mr./Ms. Prospect:

I wanted to sincerely thank you for taking the time to see me on Thursday. I was impressed by you and your accomplishments. I know your time is valuable, but by your giving it to me, I was able to gain some insights into how I might help you in the future.

I appreciate your willingness to meet again, to give me the opportunity to share with you some of my recommendations and thoughts on how you might improve your current investment situation. My objective over time is to earn a portion of your investment business by providing you valuable ideas and outstanding service.

Thank you again for giving me the opportunity to visit with you. I look forward to our next meeting.

Sincerely,
Joe Advisor

Follow-Up Call

Use this script in the event you could not get a commitment to a second appointment during your first meeting.

"Mr./Ms. Prospect, this is Joe Advisor with XYZ Financial. I wanted to thank you again for seeing me yesterday. Based on the information you gave me, there are a couple of suggestions I want to give you that I believe make sense."

Immediately after you say that last sentence:

+ Offer to do a complimentary plan for her.
+ Share the top one or two action steps that are most timely.
+ Suggest another appointment to review her situation in more detail.

Most prospects will not become clients during your first meeting with them. You have set the best possible conditions for them to become clients, but then you must do the proper things after that to finally convert them. I will cover what those things are, and how and when to do them, in the next chapter.

FIFTY SAMPLE QUESTIONS

The following questions should serve only as guidelines for questions that you might ask during the appointment. You can and should modify them to suit your own style and to the circumstances of the first appointment. Think of these questions as a "pool of questions" you can draw from depending on the situation of the prospect you are having the appointment with. I recommend that you memorize the questions you are going to ask, although it is not necessary—if you ask your questions spontaneously, it can seem less formal and more relaxed. Feel comfortable writing down notes on the information you gather.

I recommend that when you ask questions, you use the different categories in the order given; personal questions are easier to answer and can help build rapport, making it easier for the prospect to answer financial questions later on. I also recommend that within any particular category, you ask less personal and more general questions first, then move on to more personal and more specific questions.

Feel free to add more specific questions based on the circumstances and your prospect. It is okay to ask fewer questions if the prospect is getting impatient or seems pressed for time. You need to rely on your expertise in your target market to develop additional, more specific questions. Markets that could require additional questions could include business owners, executives, retirees, and professionals.

Personal Information

1. Where did you grow up? How did you get to [this town/city]?
2. Where do you live? How long have you lived there?
3. Where did you go to school?
4. How did you end up in this line of work?
5. Are you involved in any community, service, or charitable groups?
6. Do you belong to any social organizations (e.g., a country club)?
7. What do you do in your spare time (outside interests)?
8. Do you have a CPA and an estate planning attorney you are comfortable with?

Investment Information

9. What keeps you up at night regarding your investments?
10. What are your personal long-term investment goals?
11. What are your short-term goals?
12. What do you like about your current investment situation?
13. What would you change if you could about your investments?
14. How would you describe your risk tolerance?
15. What is your highest priority for your investments?
16. What do you consider an acceptable long-term rate of return (annual percentage rate)?
17. What does your current asset allocation look like?
18. Have you had a financial plan done? Have you followed it? How do you feel about your most recent financial plan?
19. How have you invested for your short-term cash flow needs?
20. How satisfied are you with your investments?
21. What could your current advisor do better?

Family Information

22. Tell me about your family.
23. Are you married?
24. Do you have children? Grandchildren?
25. How old are they?
26. Do you anticipate that your children/grandchildren will go to college?

Where would you like to see them go?

27. Have you set up funding for their education? Do you have an idea of the cost?

28. Are your parents still alive? Do you anticipate having to support your parents?

29. Do you have any gifting strategies for your children?

30. What is your spouse's involvement in your investments?

31. Does your spouse have the same goals and risk tolerance as you?

Retirement Information

32. When do you anticipate retiring?

33. What plans do you have in place to prepare for your retirement?

34. Does your company have retirement plans? Do you participate?

35. Do you contribute to an IRA or a Roth IRA? Does your spouse?

36. Are you on track with your retirement goals?

37. What rate of return do you expect to have in your retirement that will keep your principal intact?

38. How much money do you expect to need every year to support your retirement lifestyle?

Insurance and Estate Planning Information

39. What type of protection do you have in case of death or disability?

40. What type of life insurance do you have?

41. When was the last time you had your life insurance reviewed?

42. Have you made plans for the transfer of assets if something were to happen to you or your spouse?

43. Have you established a trust or will? When was the last time you had it reviewed?

44. How long has it been since you reviewed your beneficiary designations on your life insurance policy and retirement plans?

45. Do you or your parents (if living) have long-term-care insurance?

46. Do you have a charity you are committed to, and if so, have you developed any charitable gifting strategies?

Liability Information

47. Do you have a mortgage? What are the terms? How long has it been since you refinanced?
48. Have you established a home equity line of credit? What is the interest rate?
49. Do you have any other lines of credit? What rates are you paying?
50. Do you have a second home? If not, do you have any goals to purchase one?

Optional: Net Worth

51. Would you be comfortable sharing your net worth with me?
52. How much of that is investable assets (equities, fixed income, cash)?
53. What is your real estate equity value?
54. What is the value of your other types of investments?
55. What are your liabilities and their amounts?

Finally, ask the prospect if there is anything else you haven't talked about that he would like to discuss.

SUMMARY

+ The objectives of the appointment are to build rapport, make a connection and gather personal and investment information, and get a commitment for a second appointment.
+ The best way to accomplish the objectives of the appointment is to begin with a simple framing statement followed by questions.
+ A relaxed, spontaneous, confident style is important for the appointment. You will achieve this with practice and experience.
+ Expect 50 percent of the appointments to be good ones and accept that bad appointments do occur. Be prepared to leave politely but promptly if the appointment is a bad one.
+ Under no circumstances should you make a presentation on the first appointment. The second appointment is when you can present your wealth-management process and indicate what an investment experience with you would be like.

+ Ask for a tour of the operation if appropriate.

+ Pay attention to the surroundings—they are clues to the prospect's main interests. Try to make a connection to these interests and refer to them during your questions.

+ Personal information can be as valuable as investment information and can uncover important areas to follow up on.

+ A good appointment will last from a half hour to an hour. If it goes longer with a qualified prospect, do not rush through the appointment.

+ If a prospect is not qualified, minimize appointment time.

+ Get a commitment to follow up within a week to share your thoughts and provide preliminary recommendations based on the information you gathered.

+ Send a letter the next day. Thank the prospect for her time, review the purpose of the appointment, commit to follow through, and remind the prospect of the follow-up appointment.

+ Enter the prospect in the follow-up contact management process.

+ Have your fifty questions prepared and memorized whenever possible. This permits a more relaxed approach.

CHAPTER 7

Turning Prospects into Clients

IN CHAPTER 6, I EXPLAINED THAT ONE OF YOUR OBJECTIVES during the appointment is to get a commitment for a second, follow-up appointment. If you have built good rapport and have asked questions, you have set the stage for the second appointment.

THE SECOND APPOINTMENT

The second appointment is where you share how you can improve the prospect's investment experience. In the second appointment, you use all the information you gathered in the first appointment and give the prospect a customized presentation on why he is better off working with you. Keep these points in mind:

- The presentation should not be long—the ideal time is about an hour.
- The presentation can be as informal or formal as you think appropriate for the particular prospect.

In the presentation, give a brief overview of:

- Yourself and how you work with your clients.
- The value you offer your clients and how you are different.
- Your wealth-management process.
- The tools and resources you have that will improve the prospect's investment experience.
- The potential next steps, which in most cases should include the completion of a financial plan. The financial plan enables you to begin the

deep discovery process and make the important emotional connection that sets the stage for a long-term relationship of trust.

In addition, whenever possible, request statements of their investment accounts. You have now set the stage for either opening an account with the prospect or positioning the follow-up process. Clearly, not all prospects will commit to the next steps and open a new account. In fact, the majority will not, and that is when you will use the process I outline in this chapter for turning prospects into clients. The cornerstones of this process are the monthly contact and the drop-by. I should warn you, however, that you need to be patient: When this process is done properly, it can take from six to twelve months to convert 12 to 25 percent of your prospects into clients.

WHAT IS A QUALIFIED PROSPECT?

I tell new advisors that prospects should have at least $100,000 to invest, with a target prospect of at least $250,000. The more business you currently have, the higher this minimum should be; a rule of thumb for experienced advisors is that every new prospect should have more assets to invest than the advisor's one-hundredth largest client has, but the opportunity to transfer at least $100,000.

> **FUNDAMENTAL TRUTH:**
> A qualified prospect will become a client if she trusts you and likes you and if she believes that you will do a better job than her current advisor.

A prospect will become a client when you provide better service and build a stronger relationship with him than his current advisor has, and the objective is to do so in the shortest time possible. You will achieve this if you make a minimum of two contacts with each prospect per month.

Contacting each prospect once or twice a month is enough to build a relationship, but not so frequent as to be overly aggressive. There will be times when the prospect asks you to follow up or talk with her more than once monthly; if a prospect is ready to take action immediately, then more frequent contact is appropriate. One of the two contacts each month with each prospect is a monthly prospect contact, and the other is a drop-by.

THE MONTHLY PROSPECT CONTACT

The monthly prospect contact is probably the most important part of the marketing process. Before going into the mechanics of these contacts, it is important to spend time understanding the proper mindset and what the objective is.

The objective of these contacts is to build a relationship with the prospect and to create the perception that you will provide a higher level of service and be more attuned to his needs than his current advisor. The contact is either a phone call or an e-mail or mail piece followed by a phone call. (Personal visits are the drop-bys.)

As you have met with the prospect, you have determined what his investment and personal objectives are. As an example, let's say that on the initial appointment with a prospect, you discovered the following:

Your prospect is a male executive employed by a publicly traded company, he has an interest in retiring within five years, he has three teenagers for whom he has not set up a college education fund, he is an avid skier and golfer, and he loves baseball. With this basic information, you can set up an effective twelve-month contact system tailored to him. After the second appointment, you could call him and say:

- ◆ "I'm calling you with the latest earnings forecast our firm has on your company."
- ◆ "I'm calling you on a new research report or opinion upgrade/downgrade of one of your equity positions."
- ◆ "I'm calling you to encourage you to engage in our financial planning process and to do a financial plan with us."
- ◆ "I'm calling to invite you to a seminar titled 'Retirement Checklist— What Does It Take?' Do you know anyone else who might be interested in attending?"
- ◆ "I'm calling to tell you about a college funding idea: the 529 plan."
- ◆ "I'm calling to invite you to a major league/minor league baseball game next week."
- ◆ "I'm calling you about an article in *Golf* magazine that I am sending you that I thought you might be interested in."
- ◆ "I'm calling to congratulate you on your son's making the honor roll and on his being recognized in the community paper for that."

- "I'm calling you with an idea that I am sharing with my best clients, and I thought you might be interested."

Each of these calls provides valuable information and acknowledges the prospect's interests. Relationships are built by listening to and understanding the prospect and by responding to his needs and interests. Unless the prospect's existing advisor is one of the best, she is no longer taking the time to do these things, if she ever did; she takes most of her clients for granted. You, on the other hand, have made the commitment to the prospect, and your mind is "tuned into" your prospect's needs all the time.

Any time you see something or think about something that will be of interest to your prospects, send it to them, call them, or drop by. Over time, usually within six to twelve months, many of your prospects will come to the obvious conclusion that they would be better off with you than with their current advisor. You have earned this trust through the attention and service you provided.

As an advisor who is committed to growth by taking the time to follow up with your prospects, you are capitalizing on another fundamental truth.

> **FUNDAMENTAL TRUTH:** Most affluent investors know that there is little difference between competitors when it comes to the products and services they offer.

Portfolio performance matters, but it is not all that matters. Service and relationships matter too: Good performance without a strong relationship and good service isn't enough, and good service and a strong relationship without good performance are also not enough. It takes all three.

Most financial advisors manage investments in similar ways, and affluent investors tend to know this. The biggest difference, then, is in the strength of the relationship (trust) and in personal service. The combination of a strong relationship, excellent service, and good performance can give the prospecting advisor an edge.

The most successful advisors I have worked with were the ones who recognized that it was trust and service that set them apart and who made these their highest priority. Make no mistake, these advisors had established a wealth-management process and followed it in a disciplined way, but they understood that the fundamental difference was not in their wealth-management process, but in the depth of the relationship and the level of service they provided. Most advisors do not give the relationship and service a high enough priority; this weakness works to the advantage of the prospecting advisor who focuses on these aspects through the monthly prospect contacts and drop-bys.

What these two fundamental truths are saying is that you will have a higher success rate if you provide better service and develop better relationships than the prospect's current advisor does. This concept is particularly true for the new advisor who is long on time and

> **FUNDAMENTAL TRUTH:**
> Most advisors do not spend enough time servicing their accounts.

short on clients. By spending time with a manageable number of prospects, the new advisor is capitalizing on his strength (time) and the current advisor's weakness (lack of time). This dynamic is the engine that drives the prospecting process, and it will greatly increase the rate of converting prospects to clients. The more experienced advisor may not have as much time, but focusing on a manageable number of affluent prospects still allows this process to work.

THE DROP-BY

The drop-by is dropping by the prospect's home or office with some research or printed material that would be of specific interest to the prospect, and hand-delivering the information to her. Do this once a month for each prospect. This takes perceived service to the highest level. I recommend that advisors look for reports, articles, and other interesting information to use for drop-bys. Do the drop-bys when going to or from an appointment or to or from work. Highlight, underline, or make notes on whatever materials you are dropping off to show that you have customized the drop-by to your prospect.

Organize your prospects geographically so that when you are in a particular area, it is convenient to drop by. If the prospect is in, deliver the information to him by hand with a brief acknowledgment: "I was thinking of you and wanted to deliver this timely information personally." If the prospect is not in, then attach a note stating essentially the same thing and give this to his assistant to give to the prospect. The impact is the same: The prospect sees that you took the time to think about him, you found useful information connected to his interests, and then you personally delivered that information to him. This is a powerful message regarding the level of service you provide your clients. The prospect will compare the level of interest and service you are providing with the interest and service he is currently getting; over time, this will convince him that you are the better provider and that it is time to change.

My experience has shown that in addition to changes in circumstance, service and the relationship are the most frequent catalysts for change. The prospect cannot compare investment performance because she does not have an account with you yet, but the service you provide and the relationship you build are tangibles she can measure her current advisor against.

I recommend doing drop-bys once a month for each prospect in your pipeline. This will be more of a challenge for the experienced advisor, in which case I recommend that you do a drop-by whenever it is practical. This can be a challenge if you are prospecting someone long-distance. In that case, mail or e-mail the information but be sure to customize to that prospect and add a personal note. E-mail or mail is not the same as a personal drop-by and whenever practical the drop-by is preferred.

HOW MANY PROSPECTS TO HAVE AT ANY ONE TIME

A key here is to focus on a manageable number of prospects. To build your practice as quickly and strongly as possible, you must have enough prospects at one time so that ten prospects could be converted to clients each month, but not so many that you cannot follow through enough to build a strong relationship.

To have ten potential opportunities and actually convert at least one prospect to a client each month, you need one hundred prospects in your pipeline all the time (this applies mainly to new advisors—experienced advisors should have at least fifty). Remember that you need to contact each prospect twice a month, one drop-by and one monthly prospect contact. Reaching all one hundred prospects with both a drop-by and a contact each month requires averaging five phone calls and five drop-bys per day. One hundred prospects is the number I recommend because that is the most an advisor can handle. There simply is not enough time to do everything for more than one hundred prospects: contacts for new appointments, calls to existing clients, follow-up calls to prospects, and drop-bys to prospects.

It should take approximately six to eight months for the new advisor to build his prospect pipeline to one hundred. The more experienced the advisor, the fewer the number of prospects he can handle because the client service demands are higher; also, the experienced advisor can afford to be more selective. I recommend, however, that under no circumstances should the total number of prospects be less than fifty at any time.

Once you have one hundred prospects, you can drop the weakest prospects as you add new ones. Over time, you will upgrade your prospects by raising the minimum qualification; this will further accelerate the growth of your practice to a million-dollar business.

In my experience, an advisor has room for 100 to 150 client and prospect relationships. Fifty to one hundred of these relationships should be your clients, and 50 to 100 should be your prospects.

WHEN AND WHY YOUR PROSPECTS WILL SWITCH TO YOU

> **FUNDAMENTAL TRUTH:**
> Money is easy to transfer, and there are many opportunities for
> the current advisor to make mistakes; if you are a strong number two in line,
> over time you will have a chance to become number one.

The prospect's current advisor is number one, and you, as the one wanting her business, are number two. If you are a strong number two and you have no competition for the spot, you will have the opportunity to replace number one for all or a portion of the prospect's assets when the inevitable problems occur. By following the prospecting process I recommend, you will have been doing all the things that will allow you to take over the relationship. This requires patience and an organized process, two things the majority of your competitors don't have. This should also serve as a strong motivation for the established advisor to always continue to prospect; client attrition is inevitable.

Unlike in other industries, in financial services it is easy to transfer an account from one firm to another—in most cases it is as simple as signing transfer forms. This works to the advantage of the prospecting advisor: If you are able to establish that the prospect is better off working with you, the ease of transferring makes it easy for that prospect to give you a chance.

The very nature of financial services leads to perceived mistakes, which means it is impossible for the current advisor not to lose some of his affluent clients over time. The most common reasons are:

- Operational problems exist in every organization, and sooner or later a client will experience them.
- Client associate turnover is high in our business, and the quality of the associate will affect the client's experience, good and bad.
- The firm itself can experience bad publicity that can affect the relationship.
- Fee increases can weaken the relationship.
- The current advisor can change firms, retire, or leave the business.
- The attention the client receives can be less than satisfactory.
- Investment performance can be less than desirable.

All these factors can lead the prospect to have some level of dissatisfaction with her current advisor.

If you make yourself a strong number two with fifty to one hundred prospects at any given time, you will at some point have a chance to replace number one. With most prospects, there are no competitors for the number two spot because the other prospecting advisors have long since given up. You, on the other hand, through your monthly prospect contacts, drop-bys, and constant attention to your prospect's needs, will be in a strong position when number one makes a mistake.

SERVICE YOUR PROSPECTS LIKE CLIENTS

You should think about prospects the same way you think about your clients, and you should treat them the same way too. Your prospects are your future clients; the only difference is that they have not yet done business with you. Ask your prospects for referrals, such

> **FUNDAMENTAL TRUTH:**
> Treat your prospects
> as if they were already
> your clients.

as who their CPAs are, just as you do your clients. Ask them all the same questions you ask your clients. Seeing prospects as clients is the basis of your monthly prospect contacts and drop-bys.

One of the most effective calls you can make to a prospect is calling him to offer the same idea that you are offering your clients:

> "Mr./Ms. Prospect, I had an investment idea that I am sharing with my best clients, and I thought of you. The idea is [give details], and I was wondering if you would be interested."

THE RIGHT ATTITUDE

This leads to the important question of "style" or attitude when dealing with prospective clients. From the beginning of the relationship, it is important that you come across as confident, professional, empathetic, and responsive. Your prospects will respond best if they sense that you are confident. No prospect wants to work with an advisor who seems desperate for business or who shows little confidence.

Remember that your objective is to have fifty to one hundred prospects. Once you have reached this objective, no single prospect will make or break your career. This will give you the confidence to come across as the kind of professional a prospect wants to work with.

This same confidence will carry you when a prospect does not call you back after the second try. If you are able to reach this prospect, it is important to confirm in a friendly, professional way whether or not she is still interested in your calling her. If a prospect does not return your calls, or if she tells you that she is no longer interested in hearing from you, drop her from your list of one hundred and replace her with a new prospect. With one hundred qualified prospects, you are never dependent on any one prospect; if a prospect is not qualified or doesn't return your calls, it is okay to drop her.

The psychology of converting prospects to clients is very important. After the initial appointment, there is an excitement about adding another prospect and about what a good client this prospect will eventually become. Most advisors in this business are optimistic by nature and believe that good things will happen. It is easy, however, to get discouraged after a few follow-up calls when the prospect has still not become a client. At the initial point of discouragement, most advisors give up; that is why it is so easy for those who follow the process I am recommending to be in the number two position.

It is nearly impossible to build a strong and trusting relationship quickly. Most prospects will unconsciously, and in some cases consciously, test you in order to answer these critical questions:

- Can I really trust this person?
- Will he follow up reliably?
- Would I be better off with him?
- Is he willing to be patient?
- Is he willing to earn my business?

Rather than getting discouraged, your thoughts should be that you are laying the foundation that will convert your prospect to a client. If you lay this foundation properly, then you should convert 12–25 percent of your prospects to clients in six to twelve months.

REPLACING PROSPECTS

If it is taking longer than twelve months and you have been following the process of monthly prospect contacts and drop-bys, you need to decide whether or not to replace this prospect with a new one. Remember, the limit is one hundred prospects; once you have reached one hundred, one of two things must happen before you can add more:

1. You convert the prospect to a client.
2. You drop the prospect.

I recommend that you drop a prospect:

+ If she no longer returns your calls, or returns them infrequently
+ If you determine that you do not want to work with her
+ If you discover that she is not qualified
+ If it has been more than twelve months since your first appointment

In some cases, you may decide that the prospect is worth keeping beyond twelve months. If you feel that he is very qualified and you like working with him, then he is probably worth keeping. But if you have other qualified prospects that you believe are more likely to do business with you, then it makes sense to drop the prospect after twelve months.

If you are considering keeping a prospect longer than twelve months, you can find out if it's a good idea with one of three questions:

> **"Mr./Ms. Prospect, we have been working together for over a year, and I hope I have shown you how committed I am to earning your business as a client. If you were me, how should I approach you going forward?"**

> **"Mr./Ms. Prospect, I have been working toward earning your business for over a year, and I know I would do a great job for you as your financial advisor. What will it take for us to do business together?"**

"Mr./Ms. Prospect, I have enjoyed working with you for the past twelve months, and I am sure you can tell that I would very much like to have you as my client. I would like you to be candid with me. Do you see us working together, and if so, in what time frame do you see that happening?"

These questions are all appropriate after you have been building the relationship for twelve months. If you have been following the process for twelve months, you have built the kind of relationship that has earned you the right to be candid and ask these questions. How the prospect answers will determine whether you will keep him beyond twelve months.

CUSTOMIZING THIS PROCESS FOR NEW ADVISORS AND EXPERIENCED ONES

This process can be applied by any advisor at any stage of her career as long as she is willing to prospect. The numbers, however, change based on the advisor's experience level.

1. An advisor who is just starting in the business (and through his second year) should be having eight appointments per week with new prospects who have at least $100,000 to invest, with the target prospect having at least $250,000. This should result in acquiring four new prospects each week. After the first six months, the advisor should be adding between twelve and twenty-five new client relationships per year.

2. The advisor with between three and five years of service should be having four appointments per week with new target prospects having at least $250,000 to invest, or more than the advisor's one-hundredth largest client, whichever is greater. This will result in acquiring four new prospects and one new client relationship per month (twelve new client relationships per year).

3. The advisor who has six or more years of service has less time to devote to prospecting because of the time needed to service existing clients. Nonetheless, she should be having at least one, and ideally two, appointments per week with new prospects who have at least $250,000 to invest with a target prospect that has more assets than their average client. This will typically lead to twelve new affluent relationships per year, eight with investable assets of $250,000 or more and four with

$1 million or more; this will result in $12 million in new assets and $100,000 in new business. Note: A number of these new affluent relationships will come as the result of upgrading nonaffluent existing client relationships.

An experienced advisor can spend less than half the time prospecting that a new advisor spends and have less than half the number of appointments, and still open twelve new affluent relationships. This is for three reasons:

1. In general, the more experience an advisor has, the greater his skill in closing.
2. Experienced advisors' new prospects tend to come from referrals from clients and influencers, and these kinds of prospects have a much higher closing rate.
3. An experienced advisor can upgrade a lower-asset relationship into a higher-asset one by bringing in assets held somewhere else (see Chapter 11), which is essentially the same as bringing in a new high-asset relationship.

Prospecting in financial services is a low-percentage/high-payoff business. The prospecting process I describe will raise the percentage of success in converting prospects to clients. There is no magic in the process; it is just based on building good relationships, working with a manageable number of qualified prospects, and positioning yourself as a strong number two. The process will work and should result in 12 to 25 percent of your prospects being converted to clients within twelve months. Over time, these results should lead to a million-dollar-plus practice.

What you are actually selling in financial services is a wealth-management process. For new advisors, wealth management can be an area of uncertainty. This is unnecessary. In Chapter 9 I will show you how to turn wealth management into an organized process that you can have confidence in.

EXAMPLES OF MONTHLY PROSPECT CONTACTS

Letter (first follow-up contact)

Dear Mr./Ms. Prospect,

I wanted to sincerely thank you for taking the time to see me on Thursday. I was impressed with you and your success. I know your time is valuable, but by giving it to me, I gained some insights into how I might help you in the future.

I look forward to our second appointment, where I can share some of my initial thoughts and recommendations with you.

Thank you again for giving me the opportunity to visit with you. I look forward to talking to you shortly.

Sincerely,
Joe Advisor

Planning Contact

"Mr./Ms. Prospect, this is Jane Advisor at XYZ Financial. I am calling to encourage you to let me do a complimentary planning session with you. I am convinced that the most successful investors know where they are and where they want to go, and have a clear plan for getting there. This preliminary planning session is a great way to start that process (even if you have done one before, it makes sense to update it). If I could spend some time asking you some questions, I can share the results with you next week. Would you be interested?"

Research Contact 1

"Mr./Ms. Prospect, this is Joe Advisor with XYZ Financial. I hope things are well with you. I recently sent you some research I knew you would be interested in. What do you think? [Let the prospect answer.] Is there any other information I could provide you with? Has anything changed in your investment circumstances? Is there any service I can provide that you are not getting? [Let the prospect answer.] By the way, I have been contacting my best clients with an idea you might be interested in. [Give details, for example: "It is a muni-bond fund paying X percent tax free and has an average duration of X years."] Would you like the details?"

"Mr./Ms. Prospect, you know that my objective is to one day earn a portion of your business. I would appreciate your letting me know of anything I can do to help you. Thanks for taking the time. I will talk to you next month."

Research Contact 2

"Mr./Ms. Prospect, this is Joe Advisor with XYZ Financial. I want to offer you the opportunity to get a weekly research report from one of our top investment strategists. He offers a great perspective on the markets. It comes through e-mail and would be with my compliments. Are you interested? [Let the prospect answer.] By the way, I have a great idea I want to share with you. [Provide details.]"

Event Contact

"Mr./Ms. Prospect, this is Joe Advisor from XYZ Financial. I want to invite you to [fun event, date, time]. I thought it would be a great way to get to know each other better. I am also inviting some of my good clients and friends. Would you like to join us?"

Seminar Contact

"Mr./Ms. Prospect, this is Jane Advisor with XYZ Financial. I am hosting a seminar for my good prospects and clients to provide an update on XYZ Financial's view of the current investment environment. I know we will touch on some areas that you are interested in. [Give time, date, and place.] Would you like to attend?"

Portfolio Analysis Contact

"Mr./Ms. Prospect, this is Jane Advisor with XYZ Financial. The purpose of my call is to offer you a free analysis of all the equities/mutual funds we cover in your portfolio. XYZ Financial provides broad research coverage, and I thought you might be interested in what our best people think of your current holdings. Would you be interested? [Let prospect answer.] By the way, I want to share an investment idea I thought you might be interested in. [Give details.]"

Retirement Analysis Contact

"Mr./Ms. Prospect, this is Joe Advisor with XYZ Financial. We have a pre-retirement/retirement analysis available that serves as a progress check to make sure you are doing everything you can to take advantage of the current tax laws and benefits. This analysis will also include reviewing your beneficiary designations to make sure they are set up to your best advantage. Do you have a few minutes where I could ask you some questions? I will be glad to provide you with the analysis after I complete it. Would you be interested? [Let the prospect answer.] By the way, I want to share an investment idea that I thought you might be interested in. [Provide details.] Is there any other information or service I can provide you? My objective is to give you the best service possible."

Send a Book Contact

"Mr./Ms. Prospect, this is Joe Advisor with XYZ Financial. I have sent you a book I thought you might enjoy, as it puts a great perspective on successful investing. Let me know what you think after you read it. By the way, I want to share an investment idea that I thought you might appreciate." [Provide details.]

Suggested books (available at www.amazon .com):

1. *The Intelligent Investor*, by Benjamin Graham
2. *The Snowball*, (about Warren Buffett), by Alice Schroeder
3. *Stocks for the Long Run*, by Jeremy Siegel
4. *Animal Spirits*, by Robert Shiller
5. *The Number*, by Lee Eisenberg

SUMMARY

+ Prospects should have at least $100,000 to invest, with a target prospect of at least $250,000, or more than your one-hundredth largest client, whichever amount is greater.
+ The key to conversion is focusing on building the relationship and providing better service than the current provider.
+ The ideal number of prospects is between fifty and one hundred, depending on your experience and the number of clients you service.
+ Most clients are underserviced by their existing advisor; you should take advantage of this.
+ As a new advisor, turn a weakness into a strength: Your lack of clients translates into more time to service prospects.
+ The second appointment is your opportunity to make a presentation

that shows the prospect he would be better off working with you. It also sets the stage for follow-up prospecting. Recommend a financial plan as a follow-up from the second appointment.

♦ Drop-bys are invaluable in demonstrating to the prospect your commitment to a high level of service.

♦ Listen closely to your prospect's objectives and interests. Follow up constantly by connecting to her objectives and interests.

♦ You will convert prospects to clients through relationships and service, not by competing on investment performance.

♦ Your actions speak louder than words. Show the prospect your commitment to service by serving his needs before he is a client.

♦ Contact the prospect at least once a month by phone and, when possible, once a month via drop-by.

♦ Position yourself as a strong number two in line. You will have no competition for the spot. The number one in line will in many cases make a mistake.

♦ Treat your prospects like your clients. Be confident, and provide leadership in an uncertain investment environment.

♦ This process should provide at least twenty-five new $100,000-plus high-potential clients annually to advisors with zero to two years of service, of which twelve are new $250,000+ clients.

CHAPTER 8

Time Management for New Financial Advisors

"TIME IS MONEY" is nowhere more true than in financial services. How you spend your time determines how successful you are. There are so many distractions and so much information in this business that it takes a deep level of motivation and discipline to focus on the right activities. Those advisors who focus on the right activities are well on their way to building a million-dollar business. The right activities are:

♦ Appointments with new, qualified prospects
♦ Prospect follow-up calls and meetings
♦ Prospect drop-bys
♦ Client calls
♦ Client appointments

You should spend the majority of your time doing these tasks. It takes both courage and a deep level of motivation to spend time doing them because, to some degree, they expose you to rejection, and rejection is painful. This is especially true for the new advisor, who, if he wants to succeed, must spend the majority of his time making new appointments and following up with prospects—activities that have a high potential for rejection.

MAKE A DAILY AND WEEKLY SCHEDULE

Building a daily and weekly schedule that puts you in the position of maximizing your marketing time is essential to building the foundation for a million-dollar business. Marketing time is time spent executing marketing tasks, not preparing to do so. It is the time you spend executing your marketing plan. The following are four key elements of this schedule.

1. Do the Most Difficult and Most Important Things First

The first step in building the daily and weekly schedule is to recognize that the hardest and most important tasks should be done before anything else. If you do this, you create momentum that sets the pace for the entire day. When you have completed the highest-priority activities, you have a feeling of accomplishment and the knowledge that whatever else happens during the day, you have already done the most important things. For that reason, start the day doing those activities that will result in getting new appointments.

2. Keep a Time Log

Keep a time log of how you spend your time each day. This is an invaluable tool for effective time management. The log will keep you honest because it will show clearly how you are actually spending your time, which may not be how you think you are spending it. I recommend that at the end of the day, you record what you did during each hour. You should have spent at least 70 percent of your 7:30-to-5:30 working day marketing, which would include executing your market action plans, setting appointments with new prospects, going on appointments, doing drop-bys, and handling prospect pipeline follow-up.

3. Block Your Time

If you do the same activity for a period of time, you build momentum, you get better at the activity, and the hard activities actually get easier. These periods are called time blocks, and they also protect you from interruptions that disrupt your momentum.

One-hour uninterrupted time blocks are ideal. During those time blocks, don't let anything interrupt your activities. Allow no other activity during a time block except the marketing contacts you are making. It takes a lot of discipline not to be distracted from the task at hand, but you must have that discipline and motivation to succeed.

Time blocks work because if all you do during a time block is make marketing contacts with no distractions, you will make a maximum number of contacts and make a maximum number of appointments. Between time blocks, take a break and do other things that need doing.

4. Prepare in Advance

A great deal of preparation is required to make time blocking work: You should have, in advance, all the prospects and telephone numbers you are going to contact, you should have written and memorized all scripts, and you should know exactly what you are going to say to the prospects before the time block begins. This can be accomplished by building the market action notebook that I recommend in Chapter 4.

A SAMPLE SCHEDULE FOR THE NEW ADVISOR

For the new advisor, I recommend that you have three one-hour marketing time blocks, with ten- to fifteen-minute breaks in between. The following is a sample morning schedule for what I am describing:

7:30–8:30	Marketing contacts for new appointments
8:30–8:45	Break
8:45–9:45	Marketing contacts for new appointments, client contacts
9:45–10:00	Break
10:00–11:00	Marketing contacts for new appointments
11:00–11:30	Callbacks, catch up on administration
11:30–1:00	Appointments, drop-bys, or nonmarketing activities; try to schedule a lunch appointment every day

In the afternoon, spend the majority of your time following up with prospects, getting more appointments, and going to appointments. Use the same time-blocking principle. The following is a sample afternoon schedule:

1:00–2:00	Prospect follow-up contacts
2:00–2:15	Break
2:15–3:15	Appointments and drop-bys, prospect follow-up contacts or marketing calls for new appointments
3:15–4:30	Appointments and drop-bys, callbacks, catch up on administration
4:30–5:30	Appointments and drop-bys, or marketing calls for new appointments

In this sample schedule, you are spending at least four hours on marketing to get new appointments, two to three hours on actual appointments and drop-bys, and one hour on prospect follow-up. If you follow this schedule, you will spend between 70 and 80 percent of your time on the essential marketing activities. This is using your time effectively.

During an entire day, this schedule should result in your scheduling at least two new appointments, going on two new appointments (and drop-bys on your way to and returning from appointments), and making five prospect follow-up contacts. Also, keep in mind that you often need to schedule more than eight appointments in order to see eight new prospects. The appointments that are no-shows or that cancel can often be carried over to the next week to help meet the objective of eight appointments with new prospects that week. There will also be some time required to have follow-up appointments with existing prospects, and I would recommend doing these whenever possible in the afternoon, or set up a lunch appointment.

Scheduling up to one hundred drop-bys in a month can be challenging. I recommend trying to fit them into your existing schedule. For example, you can accomplish this goal if you do a drop-by every time you go on an appointment, drive to work, or drive back home. A drop-by should take less than ten minutes, so fitting them in while you are on your way to doing something else makes the drop-by schedule feasible. In many cases the prospect will not be available and you will be dropping off information with a handwritten note.

This schedule also gives you two to three hours of time for callbacks, breaks, and other essential but nonmarketing activities. In the evenings, in the early mornings, and perhaps on the weekends, do things such as writing investment proposals, education, administrative work, organizing your day, and preparing to do marketing. This means that if you are committed to building a million-dollar practice, this job requires fifty to sixty hours or more a week in the early years. While this seems like a big-time commitment, it is no more than any successful business owner must put in to launch a business. You are, in effect, starting your own financial services business.

It is impossible to follow this schedule every day, because you will have meetings, training, and a variety of other necessary activities that will require that you be flexible. You should, however, make up the marketing activities at another time during that day or on another day.

The bottom line: It is important that you have eight appointments per week with new prospects throughout the first two years of your career to build a million-dollar foundation. These first two years of your career are the time to build, which means spending the majority of your time marketing. This means that you should spend a minimum of thirty-five hours a week making calls to get new appointments, setting new prospect appointments and client appointments, making prospect follow-up calls, and doing drop-bys.

CLIENT CALLS

As you convert prospects to clients, you should contact these clients at least once per month. The goal is for you to have fifty client relationships (each with a minimum of $100,000 in investable assets) by the end of your second full year. If you contact three clients per day (fifty clients per month), that means spending between one and two hours each day doing that.

I recommend that you allocate up to two one-hour time blocks to client calls, between 9:00 A.M. and 11:00 A.M. This should replace some of the marketing calls for new appointments when you have enough clients. During your first year, however, you will probably not have enough clients to spend more than one hour on client contact, which means that you will require only one one-hour time block for this. During the second year, you will be more effective at getting new appointments, and it will take you less time to make the necessary eight appointments—by then, you will have established networks and referrals from existing clients, which makes getting appointments easier.

FRIDAYS

If you keep the schedule I have recommended on Monday through Thursday, then in many cases, you will have scheduled eight new appointments and all prospect follow-up calls. This means that you can use Friday as a catch-up day. Friday mornings can be an excellent time for actual appointments and drop-bys.

AN ALTERNATIVE SCHEDULE: APPOINTMENTS ALL AT ONCE

Another way to schedule the week is to dedicate one day a week just to appointments. The advantages of doing this are:

+ You get into an "appointment zone," and in many cases, this makes your appointments more effective.

- It provides more flexibility so that you can complete the maximum number of appointments.
- It makes prospect drop-bys easier to incorporate throughout the day between appointments.

It is more efficient because you minimize the amount of time it takes to actually get to your appointments. If your appointments are spread out among all five days, you must leave your desk, drive to the appointment, and then drive back to the office. If the appointment is a no-show, the travel time is wasted and the daily schedule is disrupted.

Having all your appointments on one day does require more preparation. I recommend that you plan your appointment-only days in detail and in advance:

- Make only morning or afternoon appointments whenever possible. This gives you the flexibility to allow good appointments to go longer if required.
- Schedule the appointments for that day close to one another so that you spend your time in one area. When you call for the appointments, call prospects in a similar geographical area so that the appointments will be closer together.
- Review all your existing prospects to see which ones are in the area so you can drop by between new appointments.
- Consider scheduling Thursday as a day for appointments because this gives you Monday, Tuesday, and Wednesday to make the Thursday appointments. It also leaves Friday free to be a flexible, catch-up day.
- If an appointment is a no-show, you can go to another appointment and revisit the no-show appointment throughout the day.
- Keep an appointment log, including the times you expect to see the new appointments, directions (written in advance), and a list of potential drop-bys. You can have eight new appointments and do four to five drop-bys during a ten-hour appointment day if you are well-organized.

ADMINISTRATIVE TASKS

Because most new advisors generally do not have good client associate support, you should be prepared to do much of your administrative work yourself. You must be very organized in order to do this. In the earliest stages of your career, you will probably be required to do some of your own basic operations and account-opening tasks, so you will need to learn how.

I recommend the following system for easily organizing your administrative tasks:

1. **Set Your Priorities.** Anything related to servicing your accounts should come before all other administrative tasks.

2. **Assign priority letters.** Assign a priority letter to each task:

    A: Most important, must be done that day

    B: Important, must be done that week

    C: Not important, can be done that month

3. **List and file.** Each week, make a list of your A, B, and C tasks, and put all the corresponding paperwork in file folders labeled A, B, and C. You or your client associate will work through each of these tasks. Maintain a separate pending file folder with A, B, or C written on each *pending* item. This can all be done electronically if that is your preference.

4. **Review and delegate.** Review with your associate the tasks you need to delegate to her or him at least every week—and possibly daily. Assign each task, explain the deadline, and give a copy of the corresponding paperwork to your associate. When you meet with your client associate, review the pending tasks to determine the status of those tasks.

It is ideal to have these meetings once a week, but you might need to have a daily meeting occasionally. If you don't assign a task to your client associate or don't have a client associate, you should do the task yourself, according to its priority, during nonmarketing time blocks. If Fridays are a flexible day, then this is an ideal time to catch up on the B and C items.

TELEPHONE COVERAGE

Telephone coverage can be a challenge, and using voice mail effectively can help, especially during marketing time blocks when sales support is not available. Incoming callers generally accept reaching voice mail, but be sure to check your voice mail between marketing time blocks so you can return phone calls in a timely fashion.

The new advisor should consider developing a "buddy" relationship with another new advisor: Each buddy can cover the other's phones (if you lack sales support) if the two of you alternate marketing time blocks. If you alternate appointment days, your buddy can also cover your phone when you are on appointments.

PREPARATION TRAINING

The training period between when you are hired and when you begin production is the ideal time to determine which market action plans you will use and to develop them. Note: New advisors who are already licensed can do this same preparation during the evenings and weekends. Collect all the names for these initial market action plans and do all the prequalification research. Practice and memorize the appointment scripts, the objections responses, and the appointment questions.

Additionally, develop your wealth-management process, build a presentation for the second appointment, set up your prospecting follow-up contact process, start to develop your niche market expertise, and learn the basics of operations and opening new accounts. Organize all this information in your market action plan notebook (as described in Chapter 4). If you use this training time to set up your practice, you will have a head start—all you will have to focus on from day one is executing your marketing plans.

SUMMARY

+ To build a million-dollar practice, it is essential that you use good time management from the beginning of your career.
+ Spend the majority of your time every day on the right activities: calling for new appointments, doing drop-bys, meeting new appointments, making prospect follow-up calls, follow-up appointments with existing prospects, and calling and seeing clients.
+ Do the marketing activities first every day.
+ One-hour time blocks are a key time-management technique.
+ You must prepare in order to make marketing time blocking work. A marketing time block is for the execution of the plan, not its preparation.
+ The new advisor should have three one-hour marketing time blocks before noon every day, and at least two one-hour marketing time blocks in the afternoon (these include appointments).
+ If you follow the sample schedule, each day you should get two to three

new appointment commitments, two appointments that you go on, one follow-up prospect appointment, five prospect follow-up calls, two to three client contacts, and several drop-bys.

- The new advisor should spend 70 to 80 percent of his time each day on marketing activities. There should be at least thirty-five hours per week spent on these activities.

- You will keep yourself honest about how you really spend your time if you keep a time log every day.

- If you follow the sample schedule, Friday can be more flexible—a catch-up day. Friday morning is ideal for drop-bys.

- Having one day per week dedicated to appointments can be very effective. You must organize the day well for it to work. You can do eight new appointments and five to ten drop-bys (five minutes each) in one appointment day. Thursday is an ideal appointment day.

- Sometimes the new advisor must take care of her own administrative and operational activities. The new advisor must have an organized way to handle administrative items in a timely manner.

- Drop-bys are an invaluable marketing technique, but the new advisor must be very organized to fit them into a busy schedule. They are best done on the way to another appointment.

- The preproduction period is an ideal time to set the stage for execution once the new advisor gets his production number.

As a new advisor, you now have all the elements you need to build the foundation for a million-dollar practice. If you follow all the steps I have outlined in this first section of the book, you will have done everything you need to do to be ready for the next step on your way to the million-dollar level. That next step is to balance clients and prospects as your client list grows. The experienced advisor needs to understand this balance as well. We will look at this issue in Part 2.

TAKING IT TO THE NEXT LEVEL

PART 2

TAKING IT TO THE
NEXT LEVEL

CHAPTER 9

Balancing Clients and Prospects: The Next Step

BUILDING THE FOUNDATION consists of developing one hundred qualified prospects and at least fifty client relationships, all with assets over $100,000. Ideally, at least twenty-five of those client relationships will be over $250,000. The total assets under management for the foundation should be $15 million to $20 million. If you follow the process outlined in Part 1 of this book, you can build this foundation in two years or less, and during this period you will most likely have spent at least 70 percent of your time marketing.

It is important for the advisor who has built the right foundation to reflect with pride on the accomplishment of having developed one hundred qualified prospects and fifty client relationships with $100,000 or more, with twenty-five of the fifty having $250,000 or more. Few advisors ever reach one hundred qualified prospects, and that achievement alone is golden.

Once you have built the foundation for a million-dollar practice, you are ready to take on the next set of activities that will take you there. You now need to shift your focus from primarily marketing to a combination of marketing and servicing the clients you already have. If you make this transition effectively, it will be much easier for you to actually reach the $1 million level, and you will reach it more quickly. This is not as difficult as it may sound. In this chapter, I will outline how to organize yourself to do this.

IF YOU HAVEN'T BUILT THE FOUNDATION, FILL IN THE GAPS

If you are an experienced advisor and you have not built a foundation of one hundred prospects and fifty relationships over $100,000, with twenty-five of the fifty over $250,000, you must fill in the gaps. Count all the client relationships over $100,000 that you have, and count all those under $100,000 that have the *potential* to reach $100,000 within the next twelve months. This is the total number of relationships that meet the requirements for your foundation. For now I will call these your *qualified relationships*.

If you have a length of service of three or more years, then your goal should be to build a pipeline of fifty prospects with $250,000 or more. The reason the number of prospects is less for the more experienced advisor is that the minimum qualification level is higher. The target prospect should be higher than the minimum prospect and should be at least $250,000 no matter what your length of service.

Subtract the number of qualified prospects and clients you have from the recommended foundation numbers, and the difference is the number of prospects and clients you need to fill in your foundation properly. To get these relationships, you must make a commitment to spend time marketing. There really isn't any other way.

HAVING GOOD CLIENTS MAKES GETTING MORE EASIER

It is important that you remember that the total number of client and prospect relationships should stay the same—no more than one hundred each. Over time, however, the asset minimums of both prospects and clients should increase. To reach a million-dollar practice, you will need at least thirty $1 million-plus client relationships, at least seventy client relationships that are between $250,000 and $1 million, and at least fifty prospects in the pipeline with a qualification level of $250,000 or higher. A base of at least twenty-five affluent client relationships ($250,000 or more) gives you an extraordinary opportunity you did not have before because you can leverage these relationships to bring in more assets and new clients.

The advisor with at least fifty client relationships can use most of those relationships to help her develop her prospect pipeline. This is leveraging your client relationships, and this leverage doesn't exist until you have built the foundation because you don't have enough clients to make it work. You must

> **FUNDAMENTAL TRUTH:**
> Servicing your clients properly will bring in more assets and new clients.

still work hard, but your job is easier now; it is easier to build upon the foundation than to build the foundation itself.

There are four ways to leverage your client relationships:

1. Bring in the assets your clients hold at other institutions.

2. Acquire new prospects that your clients introduce you to.

3. Broaden the range of products and services that each client uses.

4. Build a relationship with your clients' CPAs and attorneys as potential referral sources.

In order to be able to leverage your client relationships, however, you must build rapport and trust and be sure that you are taking care of their needs properly; in other words, you must service your clients well. The cornerstone of a strong service model is a consistent client-contact process.

THE CLIENT-CONTACT PROCESS

The client-contact process involves regular client contacts with specific objectives. It will allow you to get maximum leverage from your current client relationships in order to deepen account penetration, capture more assets, and develop new prospect opportunities. In Chapter 15 I will cover in detail the frequency (once a month) and the content of each client contact.

ORGANIZE YOUR TIME

If you are to contact each of your fifty to one hundred relationships and fifty to one hundred prospects once a month, then you need to contact two to five clients and two to five prospects each day. By the end of your third full year, you should have one hundred client relationships and one hundred prospects and you should contact five clients and five prospects each day. If you have six or more years of service, you should have one hundred client relationships and fifty prospects, and you should contact at least five clients and two prospects per day. If you can contact an average of two to three clients or prospects per hour, then it takes at least three hours per day to make the necessary contacts.

Keeping the principle embodied in this Fundamental Truth in mind, I recommend that you make these contacts between 8:30 and 11:30 A.M. or between 9:00 A.M. and noon,

> **FUNDAMENTAL TRUTH:**
> Do the most difficult and most important things first.

depending on the time zone you work in. Spend time during the first hour of every working day deciding which clients and prospects to call and determining the content of each call. There is no more important task for the advisor than contacting her clients and prospects every day, using this schedule.

If you have any time left during the first hour after organizing the prospect and client calls, then work on the highest-priority nonsales tasks. If you do this, you will have contacted five clients and five prospects and completed the highest-priority nonsales tasks by lunchtime every day. You can then spend lunchtime and the afternoon on at least one client and one new prospect appointment (for more senior advisors, one to two new prospect appointments a week is fine), marketing for new appointments, and high-priority administrative tasks. This is the ideal day for the experienced advisor.

If you are well-organized, your contacts and appointments should take five hours. This should represent 50 to 60 percent of your day. Delegate as many of your other tasks as you can to administrative staff. Do your reading and research outside normal office hours.

The result of following this schedule is that you will contact all fifty to one hundred clients and fifty to one hundred prospects at least once per month. If you contact them any less often, you will be underservicing both clients and prospects. This is another reason why it is not feasible to have more than one hundred client relationships and fifty to one hundred prospects. These numbers should stay the same, but you should consistently upgrade both clients and prospects.

It is challenging to balance marketing and client contact, but it is absolutely achievable. If done right, good client contact can improve your marketing results.

An Example of a Typical Client Monthly Contact

"Mr./Ms. Client, this is Joe Advisor. How are you? I hope all is going well with your family. How is your son doing at XYZ University? I am calling to give you a quick review of your portfolio [give details]. I also wanted to make a recommendation that you consider transferring those assets that you have at ABC Firm that are earning a low interest rate and invest with our firm in the following recommendation [give details]. While I am talking to you, I also wanted to ask your permission to introduce myself to your CPA—it would be helpful for both of us, I believe, to get to know each other. Is there anything else on your mind you would like to talk about? Is there anything else you would like to talk about that we haven't covered?

This call should take between fifteen and thirty minutes. Notice that it includes all four components that I mentioned earlier.

If you follow this schedule diligently, you will be a long way toward reaching the goal of a million-dollar practice. If you keep this schedule, the following should take place:

- You should add at least $12 million in new assets.
- You should add six to eight new $250,000-plus relationships to include at least two new $1 million-plus client relationships
- You should upgrade four to six current client relationships that are under $250,000 to over $250,000 to include at least one new $1 million-plus client relationship.
- You should increase your business by $100,000 each year.
- You should increase your business as a result of good contact frequency and deeper account penetration.
- You should have excellent retention and develop loyal clients.
- You should constantly upgrade your prospect pipeline, adding new potential clients to the practice each year.

As you develop more client relationships, you will have less time to spend marketing, as you will need to spend more time servicing clients. This doesn't mean, however, that you slow down growing your business. On the contrary, the more relationships you have, the bigger they are, and the more trust they have in you, the more business you can do. There are four ways to grow your business through your existing client relationships, and Chapter 11 will cover the first of them.

SUMMARY

- It takes a different focus to turn a good foundation into a million-dollar practice.
- A good foundation to build on is fifty relationships (with at least $100,000), of whom twenty-five have at least $250,000, and one hundred prospects (with at least $100,000). Most experienced advisors should have fifty prospects.
- The number of client relationships and prospects should not exceed one hundred of each, but should always be upgraded.

+ You should leverage existing client relationships to bring in more assets and provide introductions to nonclients.
+ Contact each client and each prospect once a month. This should be done in the mornings. With fifty to one hundred prospects and fifty to one hundred client relationships, this means that you should contact three to five clients and three to five prospects a day.

There are four components of each client call:

Part 1: Connection
Part 2: Portfolio review
Part 3: Marketing
Part 4: Offer of help

+ The monthly contacts should include three quarterly reviews and one annual review.
+ Organize and prepare for each client and prospect contact in advance to get the maximum impact from each call.

CHAPTER 10

Wealth Management

THE ROLE AND JOB OF THE FINANCIAL ADVISOR HAS EVOLVED DRAMATICALLY over the past thirty years. In 1980 the same job was given the title "account executive" and the job was a "sales" job. Today, these same men and women are called "financial advisors" and their primary job is educating and guiding each client to the fulfillment of their lifetime financial goals. The job is much more complex and is more akin to the relationship a patient has with his physician. In the best scenario, a financial advisor is an indispensable confidant who can have a profound influence and impact on the lives of her clients.

As both the affluence and sophistication of well-off clients have increased, so has their aversion to being "sold" something. The only sale a financial advisor makes is the "selling of trust," which is done through actions, not words. What affluent clients expect from their advisors is a deep understanding of their investment goals, understanding of their risk tolerance, and provision of both expertise and empathy in guiding them to the fulfillment of all their financial goals.

If the new advisor understands and builds his practice from the beginning of his career based on the understanding that affluent clients expect expertise, empathy, and guidance, he will thrive now and for the remainder of his career. The best advisors today are teachers for their clients, taking the complex, emotional, and ever-changing world of investments and distilling it into a wealth-management process their clients understand and have confidence in. Clients are willing to delegate the investment of their assets to a trusted advisor but they want and need to understand the wealth-management process.

Affluent clients also expect leadership from their financial advisors, and these skills come when the advisors have achieved a high level of expertise. The best advisors in our business start as "students" and evolve into teachers of the wealth-management process. As wealth managers they never quit in their pursuit of knowledge and the accumulation of experience that allow them to successfully guide their clients. New advisors start with a base of knowledge and resources that their firms provide and their genuine concern about the best interests of their clients. This "base" must be built upon throughout each advisor's career, because as the affluence of investors increases, so does their expectations and requirements for solutions to meet their more complex needs.

This chapter is the result of interviews with some of the most successful financial advisors in the industry and is intended to provide a "gold standard" of the wealth-management process. Whether you are brand-new to the business or an industry veteran, this chapter is designed to provide an outline of the wealth-management process that when implemented will fulfill the needs of the affluent investor and position you as her "trusted advisor," allowing you to grow your practice to the highest levels.

The following is an outline of the "gold standard" wealth-management process that will be covered in this chapter:

1. Trust—where it all starts.
2. Value Proposition—how are you different?
3. Investment-Management Process—the mechanics of investing.
4. Wealth-Management Services—holistic approach.

Wealth management, according to Andrew Rudd, is "a holistic financial advisory relationship that is broad based and attempts to deal with all aspects of the financial life of the household that one is trying to serve." According to Rudd, the best financial advisors are knowledgeable, personable supporters of the household. The wealth-management process starts with developing a trusting relationship between the advisor and client.

TRUST

One of the most important questions an advisor need to understand is, "How do clients choose their financial advisor?" The selection process is really based on the level of trust the affluent investor has toward a particular advisor and the perceived value the advisor will provide. Everyone knows the phrase that "clients do business with people they like and they trust."

The "like" part is easy. The "trust" part is more complicated than most realize. You can work and develop terrific business-development processes, but to be effective in attracting new affluent clients you must first be able to answer one basic question: "What do affluent investors want from a financial advisor?" The answer to the question is simply "the ability to completely trust you."

Based on my research and experience, the answer to that question is based on a variety of components that include competency, ethical behavior, and being a personal stakeholder in clients' lives.

Competency

The affluent investor must believe that the financial advisor is technically competent enough for him to delegate the responsibility for reaching his financial goals. This belief comes from the advisor's ability to articulate the wealth-management process, share her experience, inform clients of her professional designations, provide references, and demonstrate leadership and confidence. This can only come by establishing a foundation of knowledge at the beginning of her career and continuing to be committed to ongoing professional development. The best advisors are teachers who have honed their skills to the point that they can transfer their knowledge in such a way that affluent investors are confident and trust the advisor's ability to guide them on the fulfillment of their lifetime goals. The more affluent a client becomes, the higher his expectations that his financial advisor is among the most competent.

Ethical Behavior

Most successful people have developed a strong intuition about the ethics of people they know and work with. I believe this is based not on what a person says but rather on what a person does. In many cases the small actions that a person may not even be aware of are the clues that people use to make a judgment about whether or not they trust someone. Some examples could include failure to disclose all fees, not following up on promises made, and overpromising.

In the financial services industry there have been many intelligent, well-spoken individuals who have taken advantage of investors, and their numerous and well-published stories have contributed to a skepticism that many people have about our industry. Most affluent individuals are more interested in the actions taken rather than the words spoken by financial advisors. These actions include investing in the relationship and being patient during the process, following up on promises, providing references, having a clean FINRA (Financial Industry Regulatory Authority) compliance record, and providing transparency of pricing. In particular, explaining fees in a straightforward and clear way is especially important to affluent investors. The subject of fees and pricing will be add-ressed specifically later in this chapter.

Personal Stakeholder

The highest level of trust comes when an affluent investor believes the financial advisor has a deep stake in his life and cares at the deepest level about the investor's reaching his personal and financial goals. The most successful advisors are committed to developing the deepest relationships with their clients. To achieve the highest levels of trust, the financial advisor–client relationship has to transcend giving professional financial advice to having a personal stake in the client's life.

The best financial advisors know their client's children. These advisors are invited to the weddings, funerals, baptisms, bar mitzvahs, etc., of their clients and their loved ones. They visit their clients and family members in the hospital and call them on their birthdays and other special occasions. They spend time together doing activities the clients enjoy doing—building deep personal relationships in the process. The financial advisor is elevated into the client's circle of most trusted people and is one of the first persons called when good things happen in the client's life or when the client needs personal advice or consolation during setbacks.

This can only occur when the advisor puts the client's interest ahead of his own and demonstrates that through his actions every day. It also requires a major time commitment, but in the end the time is well spent because once the advisor becomes a personal stakeholder, he gets everything. The advisor gets all the client's assets, business, referrals, and loyalty, the result of the highest level of trust the client has with her financial advisor.

Fees

Affluent investors are often suspicious of how financial advisors and their firms price their services. This is especially true since the financial meltdown of 2008. The gold standard of the disclosure of fees is complete transparency from the beginning of the relationship, before any investments are made.

In my experience clients are willing to pay for value, but absent of value price is the only consideration. In the "wealth" business, financial advisors are often the higher-priced option when compared to the other popular discounter's model. But the affluent have demonstrated a willingness to pay a premium for perceived value in all industries. One of my favorite examples is the hotel industry. The hotel industry provides basically the same service: a safe and comfortable room to sleep in. But there is a wide range of hotel experiences and prices. It can range from the Hilton Garden Inn, which provides the basic room, to the Ritz-Carlton, which provides a special overnight experience. Affluent people have demonstrated that they are willing to pay a significant premium for a Ritz-Carlton stay because of the perceived value they get for the hotel experience. Financial advisors like the Ritz-Carlton example can charge a premium if affluent investors feel they are getting a premium value.

In interviewing some of the industry's most successful advisors I have asked them how they price their services. In general terms there was a concensus that in today's environment it is a 1 percent business. For smaller relationships it's higher and for the most affluent clients it's less. It should be noted that 1 percent fee is for actively managed assets. The actual ROA (return on assets) is typically less than 1 percent when cash equivalent and passive assets are blended together with the actively managed assets.

One of the industry's most successful advisors, however, charges the following and makes no exceptions to his pricing:

- Under $10 million—1.5 percent
- Over $10 million—1.0 percent

He feels justified in his pricing because of his track record for long-term performance. He believes he has provided his clients with superior long-term returns and exceptional service and that this justifies what many would consider a premium-pricing model. According to this advisor pricing is never an issue with his clients. The important lesson in his example is that affluent investors will pay a premier price for the premier value he provides.

The gold standard pricing model is full disclosure, simplistic and fee-based. The fee-based model has replaced the transactional pricing model that defined the industry twenty years ago. It aligns the client's and financial advisor's interests and also provides transparency, which is a cornerstone of trust. Through fee-based pricing the advisor's compensation is more aligned with her actual responsibility, which is to provide the most objective advice and guidance toward the fulfillment of the client's lifetime goals. In many cases that means not making a change or moving assets to the most conservative asset classes if warranted. It could also involve making frequent changes. Clients' best interests are served by the fulfillment of their objectives and shouldn't be dictated by how much a product pays or by how many transactions are required to achieve their goals.

The Value Proposition

In interviewing and observing many of the most successful advisors in our industry I realized that as their success increased so did their confidence in their ability to make a positive difference in the lives of their clients. This wasn't a false sense of confidence; it was backed by their experience, expertise, and continued professional development. In sum, this was their value proposition.

The most successful advisors I have worked with are able to articulate their value proposition. The most successful advisor I interviewed for this book, who is currently in the *Barron's* Top 50 Financial Advisors in the United States (and has been for the past ten years), provided me with great insight into the importance of the value proposition. When I asked him how much time he had given to his value proposition, his answer was, "You know, that's pretty much all I think about. I think the most important question that a financial advisor can answer is how they bring value, and it's essential that they can articulate their value and convince the client of the value they bring. So I think about it all the time and for me there are four distinct categories where I bring value."

I believe his value proposition can serve as a template for most advisors as they organize and develop their own value proposition:

1. Experience—describes his experience in the industry and the experience levels of his team members.
2. Credentials—describes his professional designations and industry recognition.
3. Client Service—describes his commitment to client service and the service experience a client should expect to get if she works with him.
4. Wealth-Management Process—describes the process clients experience when they work with him. He places emphasis on his investment process and the performance of his model portfolios. He places

particular emphasis on his cash-flow delivery, providing clients with the cash flow needed to maintain their desired lifestyle when they retire.

Not only has this highly successful advisor given much thought to his value proposition, his ability to articulate it is flawless. I would challenge any affluent clients who heard his value proposition not to be tempted to invest all their assets with him. During his presentation to me he described himself as a "financial missionary" because he knows that if a client works with him, he can and will make a positive difference in that client's life. This ties in directly with how advisors who have committed to providing a high level of value to their clients are also successful at acquisition of new affluent clients and assets—they become financial missionaries.

For the motivated financial advisor to take his practice to the next level, he must provide a strong core offering to his clients that provides a high level of perceived value. That core offering must include a high level of service, a deep commitment to the client, an investment process that provides good relative performance, ongoing advice and guidance on reaching the client's lifetime goals, and the highest ethical standards. Once the core offering is developed the advisor must be able to articulate through his value proposition how he is different from his competitors and the value he brings to his clients.

It is critically important that the sequence of this process be completed in the right order: core offering (wealth-management process), value proposition, business development tactics. In many cases too much time and emphasis is placed on the business development tactics and not enough time on the development of the core offering (wealth-management process) and the value proposition. The core offering and value proposition are what drives business development and are required for the successful growth of a financial services practice. Based on my research and experience I have found there is a direct correlation between the best wealth managers and best asset gatherers; they are usually one and the same.

New financial advisors may be intimidated about the value proposition process, but they don't have to be. Early in an advisor's career she must rely on the resources, intellectual capital, and reputation of her firm. She should also delegate the management of assets to professional asset-management firms and proven model portfolios. I have often heard the expression that you are either an asset gatherer or asset manager but you can't be both. I couldn't disagree more with that statement: You must be able to successfully do both. Asset management can be delegated to full-time asset managers, but the oversight and selection process cannot.

VALUE PROPOSITION MECHANICS

In developing your value proposition there are a number of different components that need to be brought together. These components include:

1. Establishing Self-Knowledge—describing your practice, what the client experience is like, why people should do business with you, and how you are different.

2. Organizing Your Value Proposition—taking the different elements of your practice and organizing them into distinct components of value to your clients.

3. Communicating Your Value Proposition—how you can summarize your identity and then condense it further into a two-sentence introductory statement. This is often referred to as an "elevator pitch" because it should take no longer than an elevator ride to explain your proposition.

4. Implementing Your Value Proposition—ensuring through your established business processes that you deliver what you promise.

5. Sharing Your Value Proposition—communicating your value proposition through your marketing materials and business development activities.

Self-Knowledge

This can be accomplished in a combination of ways. Interview your best clients and ask them to describe your practice from their point of view. What do they think you do best, what do they think you could do better, honestly, how do you compare with other advisors they have worked with, and, most important, how are you different? Write down the feedback you collect and, if appropriate, review it with other team members. Then answer the following questions. The answers to these questions and the information from your clients will provide you with the information you need to organize the different components of your value proposition.

1. How are we different or how would we like to be different?
2. What does the ideal financial services practice look like?
3. Who is our ideal client?

4. What are our core values (what do you believe in and stand for) as a financial advisory team?

5. What value do we currently deliver?

6. What is our long-term vision?

7. When our clients think about our team, what are their first thoughts?

8. What do our clients need most from us?

Organizing Your Value Proposition

Think back to the *Barron's* Top 50 advisor I featured earlier in this chapter. He had organized his value proposition into four distinct components: experience, credentials, team and investment process, and results. The following are some categories or components that can help you organize your "defining exercise" into your value proposition:

1. Experience
2. Credentials
3. Investment process and performance
4. Team
5. Service
6. Specialization
7. Ethics
8. Resources
9. Expertise
10. Focus on goals and plans
11. Holistic approach
12. Intergenerational planning
13. Cash flow and income planning
14. Communication
15. Fair pricing—fee-based
16. Your firm

Communicating Your Value Proposition

The objective is to take the components you chose to be part of your value proposition and pull them together into a formal value proposition that is a summary of how you are different and the value you bring to the clients who work with you. This summary should be used during your first meetings with your prospects to describe your practice and what they should expect to experience when they work with you. This value proposition is also what you should use in all your marketing materials (printed materials and website). The value proposition summary is also what your two-sentence introductory statement is drawn from. The following are examples of value proposition summaries and introductory statements derived from the extended value proposition.

Value Proposition Statement: Example #1

"Our team embraces and advocates a deep discovery process that leads to a comprehensive planning-based approach that covers all aspects of our client's financial needs. We also help our clients with their intergenerational planning needs so that they are able to create a legacy for their families.

"Our team has more than fifty years of combined experience, and members of our team have made a commitment to the highest level of expertise by obtaining the Certified Financial Planner professional designation. Not only does our team have the experience and credentials to help our clients reach their goals but we also have the highest commitment to providing exceptional client service.

"Most important, we work with our clients as if they were family members, building relationships based on trust and the highest levels of integrity."

The introductory statement that is derived from the value proposition statement:

Introductory Statement: Example #1

"I focus on a holistic, planning-based approach guiding my clients to reaching their financial goals and provide intergenerational planning. Our team's combined experience, expertise, and commitment to service are the cornerstones of the value that we bring to our clients."

Value Proposition Statement: Example #2

"We provide an institutional investment experience for a limited number of very wealthy families in the context of the optimal trust and estate structure for helping clients achieve their financial, nonfinancial, and philanthropic goals.

"We have twenty years of investment experience through some of the best and worst years in modern financial history, and we have invested well for our clients, providing reasonable returns during that span of time. We have channeled that experience and our expertise together with a high commitment to service to optimize the risk-adjusted returns for our clients."

Introductory Statement: Example #2

"We provide an institutional investment experience for our clients to achieve their financial goals. We have accumulated a high level of experience and expertise that we have used to optimize the risk-adjusted returns that we provide for our clients."

Value Proposition Statement: Example #3

"I have developed a high level of expertise and experience in working with successful senior executives. I provide financial solutions for the unique and complex needs senior executives face, including concentrated stock options, restricted securities, deferred compensation, and estate planning strategies.

"My team is dedicated to providing a concierge level of service for my executive clients. Our primary objective is to help them generate the necessary income to maintain their desired lifestyle during their retirement years and help them preserve and grow their assets for future generations."

Introductory Statement: Example #3

"We have the experience and expertise to help senior executives with their unique and complex needs. Our goal is to ensure that they have the cash flow needs to maintain their desired lifestyle in retirement."

Value Proposition Statement: Example #4 (New Advisor)

"I have developed an expertise in helping affluent individuals transition from the accumulation of wealth to the distribution of wealth in preparing for their retirement years. I have associated myself with the firm that has all the resources, intellectual capital, and services to enable me to guide my clients to the fulfillment of their financial goals and help them plan for the cash flow needs they will require in retirement.

"We are committed to building long-term relationships and earning our clients' trust through our actions. Every day, we treat our clients' assets as if they were our own."

Introductory Statement: Example #4 (New Advisor)

"We help our clients determine their future cash flow needs to maintain their desired lifestyles during their retirement years. My greatest satisfaction comes from seeing my clients reach their financial goals."

Implementing Your Value Proposition

Your value proposition is only as good as your ability to deliver on it. For example, if one component of your value proposition is the high level of service, you and your team must be committed to providing a world-class service model. You must define what a world-class service experience is like and develop a checklist of service practices that your affluent clients will experience. Examples could include the following:

1. Clients never get voice mail, always a human voice by the fourth ring.
2. Calls are returned within an hour.
3. Problems are resolved within forty-eight hours.
4. There is monthly contact from the advisor.
5. Proactive service calls come from client associates.
6. Notes are taken on client conversations and are shared with the team every day so whoever answers the phone is up to speed.
7. There is a time deadline on e-mail responses.
8. There are team meetings to discuss potential problems that clients might have.
9. Timely research and market updates are provided to clients.
10. Advisor conducts in-person reviews at least twice a year.

This same exercise should take place for every component of your value proposition so that your clients experience the "value" they signed up for and that expectations are met and exceeded. Without the highest commitment to delivering on the value proposition, it becomes just an empty promise, and the lack of delivery will be worse than if the promise was never made.

An important exercise is to solicit feedback from your clients to see if they feel you are consistently delivering on your value proposition and to get their suggestions on how you might improve on your delivery. This feedback will give you an ongoing indication of whether you are delivering on your value proposition and, if not, what changes you need to make to ensure you are delivering. The mindset of the best financial advisors is an insatiable appetite for self-improvement and underpromising and overdelivering.

Sharing Your Value Proposition

Taking your value proposition together with the confidence that you can execute on it becomes the cornerstone of your marketing strategy. The final step is to effectively market yourself so that your target market is aware of your competitive advantages, the value you bring, and how you are different. Your value proposition becomes your professional identity and is pervasive in all aspects of your practice. It becomes the foundation on which your website, printed materials, and all other marketing activities are based.

Pitch Books

The feedback from the best practitioners was mixed on whether or not to use a pitch book and, if used, the best way to use one. Most of the advisors agreed that if the pitch book was used it should be used more as a reference and not as a book to be read through page by page.

One of the best practitioners gave the best description I have ever heard of how to use a pitch book: "The whole point of the pitch book is to facilitate dialogue. The best meetings feel like conversations with a lot of give and take, and the only point of the pitch book is to establish credibility so that when you get to a concept, you can flip to a page and quantify the concept as being true. It's almost like a lawyer arguing a case where you're making your argument to the judge and you'll put a few exhibits on the table to quantify and establish your points as valid. But if all you did as a lawyer was just point the judge to charts without making an argument that probably wouldn't go very well."

My view is that the concept of the pitch book is largely overworked. The fifty-page-plus pitch books that are used by some financial advisors completely miss the mark. What seems to be the most effective is a PowerPoint presentation that outlines the unique value proposition that you bring. This can most often be summed up in a five- to ten-page document.

THE INVESTMENT PROCESS

The actual investment process is the core or foundation of wealth management. It is the part of the job that most advisors focus on and spend the most time with. In my experience, though, there is a big disparity in how different advisors invest assets for their clients. The objective of this section of the wealth-management chapter is not to get into the details of how to invest money for clients, but rather to provide an investment process framework that most of the successful advisors I have worked with and interviewed have in common. I consider this the investment process "gold standard" that when employed will guide their clients to their financial goals.

The following is an outline of the wealth-management investment process:

1. Goal-Based Investing—funding of future liabilities
2. Discovery—establishing the baseline
3. Planning—investment policy statement
4. Asset Allocation and Rebalancing—risk management
5. Model Portfolios—selection of investments
6. Performance Reporting—monitoring and communicating returns

ON BECOMING A SUCCESSFUL INVESTOR

I find that the most affluent individuals have the intellectual skill set to manage their own investments, but they recognize that they want to spend their time and life in other ways. They may be running their own business, enjoying time with family, or pursuing a particular hobby. Most realize that developing and managing a world-class investment process is a full-time job.

As one of the best practitioners I have interviewed and worked with explained, there are four characteristics most successful investors share.

1. They are natural savers.
2. They have an interest in their money—they pay attention to their portfolio.
3. They have a portfolio dominated by quality.
4. They understand the importance of diversification.

GUIDELINES FOR INVESTMENT SUCCESS

One of the most successful advisors in our industry shared with me his six guidelines for long-term investment success:

1. Buy equities when most investors are showing high levels of pessimism and fear.

2. Reduce exposure in equities when most investors are overly optimistic and overly confident.

3. Over time, higher-yielding stocks outperform lower-yielding stocks with less risk.

4. Common stocks of companies that raise their dividends perform considerably better than those that don't.

5. Common stocks of companies that deliver better than expected earnings (earnings surprises) perform significantly better than those that don't.

6. Low price/earnings ratio stocks, known as P/E stocks, outperform high P/E stocks over a complete market cycle.

INVESTMENT PROCESS: GOAL-BASED INVESTING

The most important question an investor can be asked is, "Why do you need money?" The correct answer is to realize and accomplish specific goals. This is where all the best practitioners start their serious conversations with prospective clients and separate themselves from other financial advisors.

According to the renowned professor and author Andrew Rudd, the financial goals of each investor are the most important component of the investment process. Rudd believes that the reason that people invest money is to fulfill their goals, which he defines as the sum of all of their current and future liabilities. He believes their investments and their personal capital should be managed with respect to these future liabilities. For example, funding retirement is the largest liability for most households. Other major liabilities that need to be funded may be children's education or the goal of being debt-free before retirement.

Most successful financial advisors focus on the cash flow that their clients need to maintain their desired lifestyle during retirement. They understand that the most important goal an affluent investor has is having enough money to maintain this standard after retirement. The goal then is to determine how much the clients will need and in what time frame they will need it to make sure their cash flow needs are funded. It is also important to take into consideration that purchasing power needs to keep up with increased levels of inflation. Once the cash-flow funding needs are satisfied, the assets left over are excess assets and can be used for other priorities, which could include gifting and estate planning strategies.

While the cash-flow goal is typically the most important, there are other goals that could include:

1. Helping children buy a house
2. Funding grandchildren's college education
3. Purchase of a second home or acquiring other discretionary lifestyle assets
4. Setting up an endowment for an alma mater or other charitable giving
5. Supporting children in starting up a business
6. Paying off a home mortgage
7. Being debt-free

DISCOVERY: UNCOVERING RISK TOLERANCE

Just as important as uncovering the clients' goals is determining their risk tolerance and time frame in which they want to achieve their goals. All of this should be determined during the discovery process.

The discovery process provides the baseline from which a financial plan is built and on which the investment process is based. It uncovers the goals, the risk tolerance, the current investment situation, and the other financial needs (asset protection, educational planning, liability management, and estate planning). The gold standard is to make sure you have addressed discovery in the very first meeting with a prospective client. This conversation should be done in person whenever possible.

I have found that on average, the first discovery meeting lasts about one hour and in some cases up to two, and all the advisors I interviewed agreed that the best meetings are when the clients are fully engaged, answering and asking questions. If the discovery meeting turns into a presentation, it is unlikely to have a successful outcome. One of the objectives of the discovery meeting is to make sure the fit works both ways; the financial advisor is determining if the potential client meets her criteria as well as the prospect determining if the financial advisor is right for him.

One of the best practitioners I interviewed shared the following insight:

> "If we are not the right fit for a client, meaning that the client is looking to indulge in recreational investing, looking to be entertained, looking for very high returns without any particular assessment of the risks, they seem to have unrealistic risk/reward expectations, if we sense any of that, we'll be very candid in highlighting where we think their expectations may differ from our capabilities and if necessary admit that what they're looking for isn't what we do, and politely end the meeting."

The most important objective of the discovery meeting is to determine the client's goals and if those goals are realistic. One of our best practitioners put it well by explaining, "Our discovery process is to identify what our clients' goals are and how much risk they need to take to reach their goals."

Asking questions that enable you to determine your prospective clients' unique needs and determining their goals and risk tolerance are the primary objective of the discovery meeting. The following are examples of some of the questions that could be asked:

1. Why do you have money?
2. What are your financial goals?
3. Give me an example of something that has gone wrong with your investments in the past.
4. What's important to you?
5. What are you trying to accomplish?
6. How are you currently investing? What's your strategy?
7. What's causing you to think about exploring another relationship?
8. Describe the perfect advisory relationship.
9. In twelve months, what are the things we would have done for you to give us an A+ and say this was the best decision you have ever made?
10. What would you say twelve months into our relationship that would cause you to say working with us was a mistake?
11. How many liquid assets could you actually invest today?

THE POWER OF DISCOVERY

The best financial advisors understand how powerful a highly successful discovery meeting can be. It can provide the advisor with the knowledge she needs to control the client relationship. If for example a prospect shares deep feelings on financial security or risk aversion, the financial advisor will be able to respond by diversifying the prospect's portfolio away from a popular concentrated position. In this way she can tailor her advice to be consistent with the client's deep-seated psychology and personal goals.

One of the best ways for prospective clients to participate in discovery is by sharing their current financial statements. One strategy that some of the best practitioners shared was asking for copies of investment account statements so they could review them and set up a follow-up meeting. Once they are in possession of these statements, most successful advisors find that it is much easier to convert the prospect to a client.

After the discovery portion of the first meeting, or during the follow-up meeting, you need to make your presentation on your value proposition so it is clear to the prospect why he should do business with you. You can then describe your investment process, how you work with your clients, and the importance of identifying the right fit. You can then share a sample portfolio and provide references of other clients whom you currently work with.

PLANNING PROCESS

The planning stage in the investment process involves taking the information that was gathered during the discovery stage and, once the prospect has agreed to work with you, developing a wealth-management plan. The plan takes into account the goals, time frame, and risk tolerance, and it provides a personalized asset allocation. The plan should also incorporate the other aspects of the wealth-management process to include, if appropriate, liability management, cash management, asset protection recommendations, and estate planning and gifting strategies. The plan can be formal and comprehensive or simply an outline of the recommendations made during the presentation stage of the process, depending on your style, the sophistication and affluence of your client, or both.

ASSET ALLOCATION AND REBALANCING

Most investment experts agree that the success of any portfolio is dependent on asset allocation. Asset allocation is really about risk management, and there is no component in the investment process that is more important than risk management. The most successful financial advisors are likely to be the most conservative. In terms of the investment process, from the perspective of a successful financial advisor, the most important thing is to be the least wrong. One of the best practitioners once told me, "I would rather have a conversation eighteen months into a relationship where a client tells me that he or she is ready to take more risk and is ready to be more aggressive to get higher returns. I would much rather have that conversation than having to deal with the fallout of losing someone else's money."

Determining the right mix of different asset classes and the diversification within those asset classes and the quality of investments within those asset classes will define the amount of risk that the portfolio is subjected to. At a minimum you should have asset-allocation models for the most conservative, moderate, and aggressive investors. One of the best practitioners framed the importance of asset allocation very well by explaining, "The most important part of the investment process is the asset-allocation decision. Then, within each asset class the investment style decision is the most important, and the least important decision is security selection. We explain to our clients that what is really going to drive positive long-term investment results is the asset allocation of your portfolio."

Dynamic rebalancing is another important component of determining a portfolio's success. As one asset class inevitably outperforms another the need for rebalancing the asset classes is essential to ensure the integrity of the asset-allocation process. For example, suppose the client is a conservative investor and the initial asset allocation is 30 percent equities, 60 percent fixed income, and 10 percent cash. If the equity markets do very well and three months later the equity portion of the portfolio is now 40 percent, then you must rebalance the portfolio, reallocating 10 percent of the equity portion of the portfolio to the fixed income and cash portions of the portfolio. The frequency of rebalancing is recommended to be quarterly if a significant move in any of the asset class occurs.

The complexity of the asset allocation depends on the individual advisor. Some advisors incorporate active and passive management styles (index funds), international, alternative investments, and currency and commodity investing into the asset-allocation mix. However complex or simple you make the asset-allocation process is less important than making it the foundation from which your investment process is built.

MODEL PORTFOLIOS

Using model portfolios with individual securities or outside asset managers is the gold standard that our best practitioners all followed. Advisors either employed model portfolios they constructed or models that were provided by their firm's research departments or other asset managers. These portfolios don't change by client, but each client, depending on his or her risk tolerance, will have a different percentage risk allotted to the portfolios. An example of one of the best practitioner's model portfolios included the following:

1. Dividend growth
2. International dividend growth
3. Blue chip
4. Aggressive
5. Value
6. Fixed income

Almost all of his clients have one of the dividend growth portfolios and fixed income, and many clients have a combination of the three growth portfolios (blue chip, aggressive, and value).

The number of different model portfolios could increase or decrease, but the important factor is that these portfolios are established in advance and that each client would have a percentage of his assets invested in the appropriate model portfolio customized for him. Whether the individual equities are invested by you or delegated to an asset-management firm is an individual preference. Our best practitioners were mixed, with some favoring managing the individual security selection themselves and others favoring delegating the management of the securities to an asset-management firm.

CLIENT REVIEWS AND PERFORMANCE REPORTING

The gold standard of client reviews and performance review frequency is quarterly, with two of those reviews performed in person if possible. The more affluent the client, the more important it is to have frequent reviews. These reviews serve as an important communication opportunity between you and your best clients. You want to make sure they know the performance of their investments, but just as important, the reviews can serve as a chance to educate and interpret the investment results for them. Clients, no matter how affluent, can be confused or distracted by the Standard & Poor's, Dow Jones, and Russell 1000 indexes or even by how their friends' portfolios are performing. If an affluent client has 50 percent fixed income and she is frustrated because she is not achieving S&P 500 returns, she needs to be reminded that only 50 percent of her portfolio is in equities and can be expected to match or exceed the S&P 500. Clients also are bombarded by headline news about the investment markets and need to be assured that they are invested according to a long-term plan and are on track. The most frequent complaint affluent clients mention is lack of communication from their advisor, particularly during volatile markets. The best practitioners never allow this happen to their clients because they use the quarterly reviews as an opportunity to update, educate, and communicate with their clients on their investment portfolios.

WEALTH-MANAGEMENT SERVICES: A HOLISTIC APPROACH

The gold standard of the wealth-management process is for the financial advisor to provide holistic, comprehensive advice in guiding clients in reaching all their financial goals. Successful wealth managers have expanded their role to include comprehensive planning, advice, and guidance beyond asset allocation and trade execution. The best practitioners I interviewed and have observed are providing their clients with sophisticated advice on areas beyond just their investment portfolio. The advisors were not always experts on all topics involved in the comprehensive planning process, but they either had people on their team or had access to specialists in their firm who were experts. The most important thing was that they could provide expertise on all areas that were related to all aspect of their client's financial lives.

Oftentimes the need for advice is related to investments but also could include liability or asset-protection strategies to provide investment solutions, and having the expertise to provide these solutions increases the advisor's value to clients. The best practitioners also understand that the ideal role they can provide to their clients is to be viewed as the coordinator and overseer of their entire financial situation. This type of comprehensive relationship not only helps the retention of their best clients but could also significantly increase their business. They aspire to the role of being the client's indispensable advisor who coordinates and is involved in all aspects of his or her financial life.

The discovery and planning stages of the wealth-management process become the foundation from which the holistic approach is built. During the discovery stage you should address all areas of the client's financial situation and in the subsequent planning stage provide solutions when appropriate in these areas. The plan sets the stage to position you as the advisor who can help the client with all financial needs in the most comprehensive way.

In Chapter 13 of this book, tactics are provided on how to expand relationships with existing affluent clients. A recommended best practice is the use of a strategic review for each affluent client analyzing what he is doing with you now and what he needs. Some of the additional areas where you can provide advice and guidance include:

1. Retirement plans
2. Liability management
3. Estate planning and gifting strategies
4. Asset protection
5. Education plans
6. Cash management
7. Long-term health care
8. Charitable planning

Note—for new financial advisors, taking the time to develop a wealth management process is essential to attracting affluent clients. As a new advisor you must be confident in your ability to help your clients reach their investment goals and be able to articulate exactly how you will do that through your value proposition. This is your core offering and taking the time to develop your wealth-management process is a critical step to reaching a million-dollar practice.

CHAPTER 11

Getting More Assets from Existing Clients

THE EASIEST WAY FOR AN ADVISOR TO GET MORE ASSETS is from existing clients. My experience shows that most clients have as many assets somewhere other than with their advisor as they have with him. In some cases these assets may be held in 401(k) or retirement plans, but at some point these assets become available. If you have built a relationship of trust with your client, he will be open to discussing consolidating at least a portion of those assets, provided that you ask. These are the easiest new assets to get because a relationship of trust already exists.

If you are an experienced advisor and have built the foundation, you can expect to achieve up to 50 percent of your new asset goal by bringing in outside assets from existing clients. Let's say that you have one hundred client relationships with a total of $50 million in assets. This $50 million is likely to be only half of these clients' investable assets because they hold another $50 million somewhere else. If you bring in a total of $25,000 of clients' assets held away each day you will bring in $6 million in a year. This is half of a $12 million goal. The more assets you have under management, the more assets there are that are held elsewhere that you can bring in.

THE AWAY-ASSETS PROCESS

The primary reason most advisors do not get more assets from existing client relationships is that they do not have a process for discovering those assets, acquiring them, and tracking them.

The process I recommend has four elements:

1. **Discover.** Determine exactly what assets each client has that are held elsewhere.

2. **Acquire.** Have a strategy to bring in assets that are held elsewhere.

3. **Track.** Keep track of the assets that are held elsewhere and how many of those assets you acquire each year.

4. **Update.** During the annual review verify if there are any assets held away and update any new assets that the clients has accumulated in the past year that are held away.

The way to use this process is to incorporate it into the overall client-contact process that I outlined in the previous chapter.

Discovery: The Annual Planning Session

Discovery is the key to making this process work, and the best way to discover these other assets is through an annual planning session, which should be part of your annual review with each client. This planning session can include a formal investment plan, planning questions you have developed, or a planning update. The objective is to complete a balance sheet of all the client's assets both with you and held away. This balance sheet will prompt a discussion about asset allocation and how the asset allocation for the entire portfolio needs to be coordinated. This sets the stage for you to provide oversight and help to coordinate the entire portfolio, not just what is held with you.

The planning session can be as detailed or as simple as is appropriate for each client. You could include the following elements and incorporate them together on an agenda for the planning session:

1. Re-verify the client's long-term goals and objectives.
2. Assess or reassess the client's risk tolerance.
3. Review the performance of the portfolio.
4. Review asset allocation and adjust if needed.
5. Review the client's liabilities (margin, mortgage, and business credit).
6. Review the client's protection (life insurance, disability insurance, long-term care insurance).
7. Review the client's estate plan.
8. Evaluate expected assets (sale of business, bonus, inheritance).
9. Discuss assets held elsewhere.
10. Get feedback on service quality.
11. Discuss referrals.

Item 9: Discuss Assets Held Elsewhere

In order to acquire additional assets from existing clients, you must discuss these assets each year at the planning session (Update). This establishes a baseline of just how many other assets the client has. If you do not do this, your client may add more of these assets without your knowing about it as her circumstances change from year to year.

The best way to position yourself for asking about these assets is to share with the client the role a true wealth manager should have. The following is an example of how you can do this:

> "Mr./Ms. Client, if I am doing my job correctly, my relationship with you should go beyond just advising you on the assets you have at our firm. As you know, asset allocation is a core part of our wealth-management process, and I am comfortable with the way your assets that you have with me are allocated. But I need to have an idea of how the assets you have with me relate to the asset alloca-tion that you have at other places. It gives me the perspective and context that enables me to do the best possible job I can for you. Let's take a minute and allow me to build out your complete balance sheet so that I can see the asset allocation of all of your investments.

If you conduct a conversation like this with each client during his annual review, you will discover many other assets held by existing clients. Without a doubt, this discovery process is the most important step in acquiring new assets from existing clients. Most advisors have not done this.

Acquisition

Keep a balance sheet (a hard copy file or an electronic one) for each client with the details of all the assets held at other institutions and update this at least annually as you discover new assets. Start to look at all the client's assets as if you were managing them and incorporate those "away assets" in your investment conversations with clients. Develop a specific strategy for bringing in these assets and put the strategy in each client's file. Elements that strategy might include are:

+ Finding ways to reduce fees
+ Coordinating the asset allocation for all assets the client has
+ Incorporating these assets into the client's overall plan
+ Coming up with ideas for better performance

- Presenting innovative ideas—alternative investments, structured products, annuities
- Simplifying the client's life by having all her assets in one place
- Simplifying paperwork and having one consolidated statement
- Moving company retirement assets

Refer to this file as part of your client-contact process: As you contact the client each month, refer to the file and, if appropriate, share ideas on why the client should bring in all or a portion of these assets. The following are some examples of how to do this:

"Mr./Ms. Client, I am glad we had a chance to review your port-folio today. I would like to add to our conversation an idea about holding your IRA accounts at XYZ Financial. XYZ charges no account fees for retirement assets over [give amount]. If you transferred your assets to me, you would not only save your IRA account fees, but we could include these assets in our overall plan and simplify your paper-work. Would you consider making the transfer?"

"Mr./Ms. Client, I enjoyed visiting with you today. I also wanted to talk about the retirement plan you have with your company. You may not be aware that at a certain age, you can roll over all or a por-tion of those assets into an IRA rollover account through an in-service withdrawal. I am convinced that I can do a better job of managing those assets for you while incorporating those assets into our total plan. Would you be interested in the details of how we could move those assets into an IRA rollover at XYZ Financial?"

"Mr./Ms. Client, I am glad we had a chance to review your portfolio. I would also like to let you know that we have an investment avail-able that I believe would fit with the equity portion of your portfolio. It is a structured investment that is tied to the performance of the S&P 500 index and will have most of the upside, but the principal would have limited downside. My suggestion is that we use the money (or a portion of it) you have invested with ABC Firm for this investment. What do you think?"

"Mr./Ms. Client, I feel good about our conversation today regarding your investments. However, there is something I would like to add to your portfolio. To supplement your retirement income I would like to recommend an annuity that I believe would fit well in our retirement-planning strategy [then provide details]. My recommendation is that we take a portion of the assets you have with ABC Firm and invest in the managed futures recommendation that I am making."

"Mr./Ms. Client, you mentioned when we reviewed the assets that you have away from us at XYZ Financial that some of those assets were invested in bank certificates of deposit earning a very low rate. I made a note that those bank certificates you referenced were coming due next month and I wanted to suggest that you consider investing a portion of those CDs in the following investment (provide specifics) that have limited risk but are paying a higher rate than your CDs."

The point of all these examples is that during the monthly contact, you should execute the strategy you have developed to bring in all the client's assets. Most affluent investors want their lives simplified, and if you have built a strong relationship and offer a good rationale for consolidating their assets with you over time, they will.

Tracking

The advisor who wants to maximize the opportunity to bring over more assets from existing clients should track the money each client holds at other institutions and track the progress he is making toward bringing it in. I recommend that you use a spreadsheet to keep track of these assets. List each of your one hundred client relationships by name, and beside each name list the assets held elsewhere. Total these assets at the bottom of the column to give you an idea of how big the opportunity is. As you bring this money in, list those amounts in a second column, and list the difference in a third column. This spreadsheet is a good way for you to know at all times how much money your clients are holding at other institutions and how you are doing at acquiring it.

You need to realize that the easiest assets to bring in are those from existing clients. The key to acquiring these assets is discovering how much money each client holds at other institutions during your annual planning session with each client. If you have etablished the foundation for a million-dollar practice, you can expect to bring in at least $6 million in new assets each year, and in some cases much more, by developing a strategy to do so and using the monthly contact system to execute the strategy. Keep track of where these assets are, how much they are, and the progress you make at bringing them in.

Annual Update

Every year during your annual review update, share with the client the balance sheet that you developed on all that client's assets both with you and away from you. Explain to the client that every year you need to update his balance sheet to make sure it is current and incorporate any additional assets he may have added that are not with your firm. You will be surprised how many additional assets can come into a client's life in a year, such as inheritances, bonuses, real estate and business transactions, and accumulated savings.

Capturing the assets your clients hold at other institutions is just one of the four ways you can build your business using your existing clients. The second way is to use the trust you have built in them to get new clients. I will cover how to do this in the next chapter.

SUMMARY

+ The easiest new money to bring in is money that your existing clients hold at other institutions.
+ An experienced advisor who has built the foundation can reach at least 50 percent of her annual new asset goal and bring in a minimum of $6 million in new assets by bringing in clients' outside assets.
+ Discovery is the key to making this process work, and the best place for discovery is in the annual planning session.
+ Create a file for each client on the details of the assets she holds elsewhere.
+ Develop a strategy for each client for capturing these assets and put it in the file.
+ Execute the strategy through the monthly contact process.
+ Use a spreadsheet to keep track of the total assets held at other institutions and to track the progress you make toward bringing them in.
+ Update the client's balance sheet every year to include new assets held.

CHAPTER 12

Leveraging Clients to Get New Ones

THE MOST EFFICIENT AND EFFECTIVE MARKETING you can do is to leverage your existing clients to get new ones. This gives experienced advisors a real advantage, but many experienced advisors miss this opportunity. Once the advisor has built a foundation of fifty to one hundred client relationships (each with investable assets of more than $100,000), leveraging existing clients is likely to take the advisor close to the goal of acquiring ten to twelve new affluent client relationships of $250,000 each and $12 million in new assets each year.

To be effective in leveraging clients to get new ones, you must be very organized and consistent in your approach. This chapter focuses on four methods to leverage current clients to get new ones:

1. Referrals
2. A CPA and attorney network
3. Speaking opportunities
4. Client events

REFERRALS

There is no marketing activity that is more effective than a proactive, organized referral process. If you had to engage in only one form of marketing, a proactive referral process should be it. Eighty percent of most advisors' new affluent households come from referrals.

If you are in frequent contact with your clients, have a disciplined wealth-management process, and provide great service, you are in the right position to have a referral discussion. High client satisfaction will occur if you contact clients frequently, have a portfolio performance that is consistent with client goals and expectations, and provide great service. This is the prerequisite for effective referral marketing. As an advisor who is committed to having a million-dollar practice, you should have these client-satisfaction fundamentals in place.

Too much emphasis in much of the industry's training is focused on referral mechanics and scripts, and not enough emphasis is placed on developing loyal clients. If your clients are receiving the highest level of satisfaction they will provide you with referrals, but only if you have the conversations and help them to help you. The client surveys I have reviewed reveal that the majority of loyal clients have indicated they would provide a referral to their financial advisor. If your clients aren't loyal there is not a good enough script or process that will generate referrals.

In Chapter 15, I describe the different elements that should be incorporated into your practice to develop loyal clients. A recent study titled *Anatomy of the Referral*, created and conducted by Advisor Impact, that looked at why affluent clients refer validated the point of having loyal clients. According to this study, one of the primary reasons affluent clients refer is as an "act of reciprocity" for the good work their advisor has done for them. Another reason is that their advisor "reminded them" periodically that they were growing their business and had a referral conversation with them.

There are three primary factors that when applied will increase your referral rate to at least ten referrals a year (when applied to one hundred affluent clients):

1. The right referral mindset.
2. A consistent referral process.
3. Helping your loyal clients help you.

The Right Referral Mindset

The most common way most experienced advisors acquire new clients is through a referral from another client. Most of the advisors I have worked with and surveyed, however, don't have a consistent proactive referral process. When I asked advisors why they don't have a consistent referral process, the most common answer I received was a general discomfort in asking. Many of the top advisors still felt like they were "pressuring" their clients or felt as if they were "crossing the line from professional to salesperson." One top advisor told me, "My doctor never asks me for a referral, and if I consider myself a professional like a doctor, why should I ask for a referral?"

I don't agree with this way of thinking. When I ask these same advisors if there is any other advisor they know that would do a better job with their clients than themselves, the answer is always, "No one would do a better job for my best clients than me." Based on that response I then ask them, if you feel so confident about the good job you do with your clients, then why are you reluctant to have a conversation with them about how you could help other people they know and care about? The point I want to make is that if financial advisors believe they are offering or helping their clients rather than asking or selling, the referral conversation is much easier to have.

Another way of looking at this is to think about all the wealthy individuals who lose their money through the incompetent and dishonest advisors who exist in our industry. Think no further than Bernard Madoff and all the investors who trusted him to invest their assets and whose lives he destroyed. Too many good financial advisors in our industry make the assumption that affluent investors are taken care of properly. But the right referral mindset instead makes the assumption that most affluent investors are not taken care of, and it is your professional mission to make a positive difference for investors.

If you had an outstanding doctor that you had a strong relationship with, wouldn't you refer him or her to your friends? What if your doctor was opening a new concierge medical practice? Your doctor asks you if you would be interested in joining his new practice and then asks if there is anyone you know who would be interested. Would you, as his loyal patient, be willing to brainstorm with him about potential new clients? Would you resent that he asked? The answer to the questions is that if you liked and respected your doctor you would be glad to help him, and the same would be true for your clients.

It is also naïve to assume that your best clients will naturally refer you to their friends and colleagues. Loyal clients are willing to help their advisors, but it's seldom on the top of their mind. When loyal clients think of their advisor they think about a professional who manages their investments, and they have no idea about the growth component of their advisor's practice or even if it is accepting new clients and what type of clients it is looking for. An advisor will never get as many referrals from loyal clients by relying on just unsolicited referrals.

There is, however, a balance between periodically reminding loyal clients and inundating them with referral requests.

Consistent Referral Process

I recommend that you create a list of your core affluent clients (top fifty to one hundred) and commit to having at least one in-person referral conversation once a year. I would also recommend that you keep track of these referral conversations by placing a check mark next to each client's name after you have had the referral discussion. I recommend once a year because I believe is the perfect balance between reminding loyal clients without inundating them. It is recommended that these referral conversations be done as part of a client review and whenever possible in person. Having it part of a client review session helps to build the goodwill that most clients feel toward their advisor after she has committed her time with the client.

Formally put the referral on the agenda so that the client can see in advance that the subject of referrals will be covered and also so that you have no excuses not to cover the topic.

Helping Your Loyal Clients Help You

If loyal clients were asked if they had a person to refer to their advisor, the percentage would be much lower than if they were asked if they were willing to provide a referral. The most common response a client will give his advisor when asked for a referral is that he will "think about it—no one comes to mind right now." The reason for that response is that most loyal clients don't spend a lot of time thinking about referrals they can provide to their advisor. These loyal clients are willing to help, but if you want to increase your referrals you must help them help you.

You can help your loyal clients provide referrals by sharing with them examples of the kind of people you would like to add to your client list. You can also provide them with specific names of people they know that you would like to be introduced to. The more specific you are with your loyal clients the more likely you will get a referral or at the very least have a discussion about a potential introduction. Remember if you have loyal clients and you make it easy for them, in most cases they will help you and provide a referral.

There are three primary ways I recommend you generate specific names to provide to your clients. In all these cases you are doing some detective work to find specific names of people your client knows that you would like to be introduced to.

1. Google your client's name. In many cases affluent people they know or work with will come up in a Google search.

2. Visit the website of their business or professional practice.
3. Connect with them through LinkedIn (see Chapter 22 for details of generating potential referrals through LinkedIn).

I have provided some specific scripts that incorporate the factors of the referral process that has been described in this chapter.

Referral Agenda Technique

Here are some specific scripts that incorporate the factors of the referral process discussed in this chapter.

"Mr./Ms. Client, even though we have gone through some challenging markets, I feel good about the work I have done for you. You may be aware of other individuals who if they knew about the kind of work that I do, might be interested in working with me. I wanted to make an offer to help anyone who you think would benefit from the way we work with our clients.

Specifically, we work best with nice people like you [state minimum if you are comfortable] who are going through a change of circumstance in their life—as an example someone who has recently retired, is about to retire, had a major transaction, gone through a divorce or lost a spouse. Does anyone in those circumstances come to mind?"

If the answer is "Yes, I can think of one person":

"Thank you, could you let him know in advance that I will contact him next week and introduce myself and share that we work together; would that be okay? Does anyone else come to mind?"

If the answer is "No, I can't think of anyone":

"I understand, but I wanted to mention to you that Joe Jones is on my marketing list and I noticed that he works with you at your firm. Would you feel comfortable providing me with a favorable introduction to Joe or could I use you a reference when I call Joe?"

Or "I was reviewing my LinkedIn connections and I saw that you were connected to David Jones, and David has the ideal profile of the type of new client that I am looking for. Would you feel comfortable brainstorming with me on the best way to meet David (or would you feel comfortable providing me with an introduction to David)?"

WORK WITH THE CLIENT'S EXISTING CPAS AND ATTORNEYS

Another excellent technique for leveraging current clients is to ask for introductions to their CPA and/or their estate attorney. According to Thomas Stanley, author of *The Millionaire Mind*, many millionaires find their financial advisor via referrals from their CPA or attorney. This is why you can benefit from a strong network of CPAs and attorneys.

You do not need to have a large number of CPAs or attorneys in your network in order to make it effective. For example, a strong network can be made up of three to five CPAs and attorneys who consistently refer potential affluent clients. Note, however, that the follow-up and relationship-building time required to have an effective network will limit the number of relationships you can maintain—most advisors cannot adequately manage more than a total of six CPA and attorney referral sources.

The first step is to contact each client once a year, ideally during a quarterly review or annual planning session, and ask if she is satisfied with her current CPA and if she has an estate planning attorney. If the client is satisfied with her current CPA, you should ask for permission to call the CPA for the purpose of getting acquainted; make the same request if she has an estate attorney she is satisfied with. Explain that you are asking to get acquainted with these people because a good relationship between you and the CPA or attorney can be very helpful, as there is a degree of overlap among you. Once the client gives you permission, call the CPA or attorney and suggest an informal appointment to get to know each other for the client's benefit.

If the client is not satisfied with either his CPA or his attorney, he is an excellent candidate to refer to your existing CPA/attorney network.

The following are examples of the initial call asking permission to call the client's CPA/attorney and the initial call to the CPA/attorney:

Client Call

"Mr./Ms. Client, I am committed to doing a better job this year of collaborating with my clients' other advisors, specifically your CPA. Are you currently satisfied with the work your CPA has done for you? If you are comfortable I would like to contact him/her and introduce myself so that we can establish a professional working relationship for your behalf. Could you provide me with your CPA's contact information?

Initial Call

"Hello Ms. CPA, this is Mike Jones at XYZ Financial. Jane Smith is a mutual client of ours and I'd like to build a professional relationship with you for the benefit of Jane. I'd like to facilitate that relationship by inviting you to a lunch meeting. And by the way, Jane speaks very highly of you and I'd like to learn more about your practice. I'm always looking for top professionals to include in my professional network.

During the lunch meeting with the CPA or attorney, make your primary emphasis understanding the CPA's or attorney's practice, specialization, and experience. The following are some questions that can serve a guide for the kind of questions you can ask the CPA during the lunch meeting.

Professional Referral Source: First Meeting Questions

Background

- Where are you from? Go to school? How long have you been in this area?
- How did you get started as a CPA/attorney?
- What other firms have you worked with?
- What are your outside interests? Family situation?

Clients

- How many clients do you have?
- What is the profile of your typical client?
- How would you describe your role/relationship with your clients?

Firm

- How is your firm structured? Partners?
- What are the goals of your practice?
- Where do you see your practice five years from now?
- How long have you been with your current firm?
- Do you have a specialization?
- What are the biggest challenges that you face?
- What are your retirement plans? (if appropriate)

Marketing

+ How do you get new clients?
+ Do you have a marketing plan to get new clients?
+ How do you describe your practice to new clients?
+ How did you meet/acquire your top ten clients?
+ Who are your major competitors and what is your competitive edge?
+ How many new clients do you bring in in a typical year? What is your goal this year?

Resources

+ How do you stay current on tax law changes as they relate to investments?
+ Do your clients ask you investment-related questions?
+ What are your continuing education needs?
+ What information would be valuable to you from an investment firm?
+ Are you or anyone in your firm licensed to provide investment advice?
+ Do you have any financial advisors currently who are providing you with ongoing information, resources, and education?

Discuss your mutual client and how you and the CPA or attorney can work together for the benefit of that client. As you are paying for lunch ask the CPA/attorney if she would be open to having a second brief meeting with you in which you could share your value proposition, how you are different, and the value you bring to your clients.

End of First Appointment

"Thank you for your time today I have appreciated the opportunity to find out more about your practice and being able to develop a professional relationship for the benefit of our mutual client Jane. I would appreciate having the opportunity to share with you the unique and special way that we help our clients achieve their long-term financial goals. Many professionals believe financial advisors are all alike, and nothing could be further from the truth. Could we schedule a convenient time and place for me to share our wealth-management approach with you?"

The majority of your clients' CPAs/attorneys will be open to meeting with you out of professional courtesy: You have a mutual client, you asked about their practice, and you bought them lunch, and in the process you have begun to build a relationship with them. I believe it is important to separate the lunch meeting from the presentation meeting because when you invited the CPA/attorney to lunch you positioned it as a way to develop a professional relationship for the benefit of your mutual client. To make a presentation during the lunch would be disingenuous and would probably not make a good first impression. Also, by spending the majority of the lunch meeting talking with the CPA/attorney about his practice you are building a relationship with him before requesting a presentation meeting. Lastly, you don't want to feel rushed in giving your presentation, and both trying to get to know a CPA/attorney and making a presentation is too much for one meeting.

If the CPA is willing to meet you again, be prepared to give a brief and well-rehearsed description of your value proposition, the process of how you work with your clients, and any tangible reports or tools that bring to life your wealth-management process. In most cases if you have a well-organized presentation you will leave a favorable impression. Based on my experience, most CPAs don't have a very good idea of how advisors today work with their clients and are not aware of how far our industry has evolved regarding the wealth-management process, or even the resources an advisor has to help clients.

At the end of the presentation meeting I recommend that you position the continuation of your professional relationship and position the ongoing follow-up process.

End of Second Appointment

"I appreciate the opportunity you gave me to share our wealth-management approach with you. I would like to suggest moving forward that we develop a long-term professional relationship. I would like to become an important resource for your practice, providing you with an ongoing education on investment-related subjects and keeping you updated with the markets and resources available to help your clients. As you become more familiar and comfortable with our wealth-management approach if the occasion arises where you believe we could provide help to your clients we would be happy to do so. Would you be open to developing that kind of professional relationship moving forward?" [yes]

"As it turns out I'm going to be back in the area three weeks from now, and I would like to share with you some alternative minimum tax strategies as related to investments that I think you would find helpful to your practice; could we schedule a short meeting when I'm back in the area?"

The key to building a successful CPA/attorney network is to regularly contact and educate the CPAs and attorneys in your network. Here are my recommendations on how to do that:

◆ Meet with each CPA or attorney, ideally once per month.

◆ Try to add value each time you visit the CPA or attorney—provide her with information that will help her practice. Your priority is to educate her on areas that are of interest to her and to her clients. This is why it is critical that you understand her practice and the type of clients she has.

◆ During these visits, provide the CPAs and attorneys with examples of the type of clients you work with and how you help them. It is very important that the CPAs and attorneys know exactly what you do for your clients. This will raise the comfort level the CPA or attorney has with your practice and will make it easier for her to provide referrals.

◆ Invite the CPAs and attorneys to your office. This can be very helpful in building trust, because it shows them firsthand how your practice works. You can further distinguish your practice in the eyes of the CPAs and attorneys, and further raise their comfort level, by sharing the technology and wealth-management tools you use and by introducing them to your team members.

◆ Provide seminars for the CPAs and attorneys where they can get continuing education credits. I also recommend that you schedule fun events after such a seminar (or as stand-alone events) to develop these relationships further. These events could include golf, sporting events, or dinner.

◆ Contacting, educating, and offering value to the CPAs or attorneys regularly is more important than how many referrals you give them. If you have four total CPAs and attorneys in your network, you should expect to get eight referrals per year (two from each). If you close 80 percent of these referrals, you should get six or seven new affluent client relationships from your CPA/attorney network each year.

The bottom line is that developing a CPA and attorney network can be one of the most effective marketing techniques you can have. Building this network with existing clients' CPAs and attorneys is the best place to start. Regular follow-through (monthly contact) is required to build the kind of professional and personal relationships that will result in these influencers providing regular referrals. For more information on marketing to CPAs and attorneys, see Chapter 29.

SPEAKING OPPORTUNITIES

You can further leverage current clients by finding out what organizations they and their spouses belong to and offering to speak to those organizations. This technique can put you in front of several hundred new prospective clients each year.

Most clients and their spouses each belong to at least one organization. Some clients may belong to more than one organization, and some clients may not belong to any, but overall, your pool of fifty to one hundred clients probably has access to at least twenty-five different organizations. If these organizations have an average of twenty members and you get in front of twelve organizations each year, you will reach 240 potential prospects. If you follow up and set appointments with 10 percent of the attendees, this will generate twenty-four new appointments with qualified prospects, and if 25 percent of the appointments become new clients, this marketing technique alone would generate six new client relationships per year.

A key element of this marketing technique is that most organizations are looking for interesting topics and speakers. Your expertise on the current state of the economy and the markets is very interesting to many. Other potential topics could include:

1. How much is needed for retirement
2. The importance of financial planning
3. The wealth-management process
4. The state of the current market and what is ahead
5. The fundamentals of successful investing
6. Behavioral finance

To be effective, you must be very organized and ask each of your fifty to one hundred clients once a year for the opportunity to speak at their organizations; be sure to ask both husband and wife, as they most likely belong to different organizations. In most cases, your client will not be the person in charge of the organization's speakers, but he can put you in touch with the right person. You can ask the client to talk to the program coordinator ahead of time, or you can simply ask for the contact's name and number and call her directly.

Once you have given your talk to a particular organization, offer to speak to this organization at least once a year on a different, relevant topic. That way you can continue to market through these same organizations each year. As you develop new client relationships, find out what organizations they belong to and offer to speak to those organizations.

The following are examples of how you can introduce this idea to your clients and to organizations:

> "Mr./Ms. Client, I enjoy educating investors about XYZ Financial's view on the current investment environment. Are you a member of an organization that would be interested in this kind of talk? Who would be the best person to call about the logistics?"

> "Mr./Ms. Club Official, I was referred to you by my client [client name]. The reason for my call is that XYZ Financial encourages us, as a service to our communities, to talk to local organizations about the current investment environment. I would enjoy having the opportunity to address your group. Would you be interested?"

I recommend that when you speak to the organization, you do not bring any materials to hand out. A much better technique is to pass out response cards requesting information or a follow-up call. This provides an easy way for you to follow up with interested prospects. After the seminar, contact those who filled out response cards and offer them an appointment. The following is a script to do this:

> "Mr./Ms. Prospect, this is Joe Advisor, and you attended my recent talk at the ABC organization. I received your request for more information. I would be happy to mail that information to you, but I wanted to offer you my time to review your current financial situation and provide a second opinion. I would be glad to bring the information you requested to that meeting or mail it to you in advance. Would you be receptive to meeting with me?"

Make sure you ask the organization's program coordinator for permission to pass out the response cards. You want to reflect positively on your referring clients, and getting permission is professional and courteous. An example of a response card can be found in Chapter 20.

CLIENT EVENTS

Inviting clients to events they are interested in is another way to leverage current clients to meet new ones. The key concept in this marketing technique is to help clients help you. Typically, your clients' best friends are those who like to do the same things they do.

By organizing events around your clients' interests, you are providing your clients with an easy and nonthreatening way to introduce you to their friends who have the same interests. The first step is to survey your best clients to determine what their two favorite outside interests are, such as golf, fly fishing, wine tasting, fine dining, sporting events, or cooking classes. Educational seminars on topics of interest to particular age groups are another good idea for client events. The next step is to group clients by interests and invite them to these events. The key ingredients for making these events successful are that the events be tied to the clients' interests and that the events be fun and well-organized.

I recommend having a fun event (can be combined with a educational event) every month or at least ten per year. Ideally, you should invite each local client to an event at least once or twice a year. As a guideline 6–10 participants (clients and prospects) is ideal; you want to keep the group small in order to get to know the guests.

The leverage for meeting new prospects begins when you invite your client. Tie this invitation to your past requests for referrals. The following is an example of how to do this:

"Mr./Ms. Client, this is Joe Advisor, and I am calling to invite you to a golf event I am hosting for my best clients. It will be [provide details of time, date, location]. I really appreciate your being such a good client, and I know you enjoy golf, so I hope you can attend. This event can also be a relaxed way for me to meet prospective clients who like golf. I would really appreciate it if you could invite someone you enjoy spending time with and who you think I should meet. I hope you and a friend can attend this fun event. I will send you several invitations."

"Mr./Ms. Client, I want to invite you to a dinner we are hosting at our home later this month. [Give the date.] Can you attend?"

If the answer is yes:

"I also would like to encourage you to invite a couple you enjoy spending time with that you think I should meet. Can you think of anyone who might be interested?"

If sixty clients attend events throughout the year, and on average each client brings one friend, then you will meet sixty new people. If you convert 10 percent of the new introductions to clients, then you will acquire six new clients through this marketing technique.

The best way to follow up with these prospects is to invite them to other events or educational seminars. Over time, a relationship will grow, and offering them a complimentary discovery meeting will be part of the natural progression.

Clients will feel good about the event, which helps retention, and they are helping you in an easy, nonthreatening way; the client is simply inviting a friend to an event that you are hosting. Often clients are reluctant to provide referrals directly because they worry that doing so could jeopardize their relationship with their friend if you do not perform well. Inviting a friend to a fun event, though, is much less of an endorsement; it is up to you and the prospect to build the relationship through the event. If these events are well-organized, and if you follow through, you will get new clients. I know advisors who have successfully built their entire marketing efforts around client events.

The most effective way for you to get new clients is to use one or more of these leveraging techniques. Working through existing clients to meet new ones is much more effective than trying to meet new prospects "cold." An experienced advisor can meet at least 50 percent, and even 100 percent, of his asset and new client goals using these techniques. You must have satisfied clients, be well-organized, and have good follow-through to make this marketing technique work. If done correctly, however, this can be the easiest, most enjoyable, and most effective marketing you can do.

Now you know how to bring a client's assets that are held at other institutions to you, and you know how to leverage your current clients to acquire new ones. The next technique of growing your business through your clients is to expand the products and services that your current clients use. Read Chapter 13 to find out how.

SUMMARY

♦ The most effective and efficient way that an experienced advisor can market is through existing clients.

♦ A proactive referral process is the most effective marketing activity an advisor can engage in.

♦ To get referrals, the advisor must have satisfied clients and must ask for referrals.

♦ Ask each client for a referral at least once a year.

♦ Establish a network of referring CPAs and attorneys. This is among the most effective marketing techniques an advisor can use. The CPAs and attorneys your clients use are the place to build this network.

♦ Follow-up and relationship-building activities are the key ingredients for a successful CPA and attorney network (twelve contacts per year with each CPA and attorney).

♦ Offering to speak at clients' organizations is time-effective and can get the advisor in front of several hundred new prospects per year.

♦ To be effective with speaking engagements requires good follow-up of the response cards.

♦ Client event marketing is an ideal way to meet new prospects.

♦ Invite each local client to an event she is interested in and encourage her to invite a friend with a similar interest.

♦ Event marketing is a nonthreatening way for clients to get you in front of prospects they know.

♦ Follow up with prospects you meet at client events by inviting them to future events and educational seminars, and culminate by offering them a complimentary portfolio review.

CHAPTER 13

Expanding the Client Relationship

ONE OF THE MOST EFFECTIVE AND EFFICIENT WAYS to grow your practice is by doing more business with your existing clients. Most advisors are not organized enough to do this and generally do not expand their relationship with their clients as far as it can go or establish minimums for their clients. This is one of the most important fundamentals and levers of growth.

The successful advisors I have worked with understand that one of the most important leverage points in our business is to increase the affluence of the clients that they work with, and always work toward 100 percent wallet share with each of their affluent clients. Once you have established a strong relationship of trust with a client it is much easier to do more business with existing clients than to bring on new clients.

In addition to bringing in more assets, there are two reasons to expand your client relationships and increase business:

1. The more products and services a client uses, the more business you will do with that client. In my experience, clients who use five or more products and services do three times the business of clients who use two or fewer.
2. Raising the minimums for your clients is an efficient way to grow your business by working with individuals who can afford what you offer.

MINIMUMS

Each client should generate a minimum level of business in order to stay in your practice. This concept is consistent with the policy in many other professions. For example, a well-established accounting firm will charge a minimum fee no matter how simple the tax return it completes; if a client is unwilling to pay that much, the accounting firm will refer him elsewhere.

A successful advisor should handle her practice the same way. Each of your clients who have $100,000 in assets with you should generate at least $1,000 a year in business. This minimum amount of business could certainly be higher, but should not be much lower after an advisor has three or more years of experience in the business. This would be a 1 percent fee for a client who has $100,000 invested. Clients who have $1 million or more invested should be generating $10,000 or more per year in business, or at least a minimum of $5,000.

Whether the minimum amount is $1,000 or a higher number, you must run your practice like a business. Time is money, and the time you spend with clients who do not generate enough business is time taken away from clients who do. There will always be exceptions to the minimums stated, and it goes without saying that all investments recommended be appropriate and consistent with the client's goals and risk tolerance.

Adding products and services to your clients' relationships is an ideal way to increase your business from each one and raise clients' minimums.

ADD PRODUCTS AND SERVICES THAT DON'T COMPETE WITH THE PORTFOLIO

Most advisors have an established process for managing their clients' portfolios. Generally, once you have invested the assets and set up the management of the portfolio, a predictable amount of business is generated. The most obvious way to increase business at that point is to add more assets to the portfolio. This is especially true as fee-based pricing has become more popular. Most advisors do a good job of generating business through active portfolio management; the challenge is how to add more business without changing the way the portfolio is being managed.

The way to do this is to add appropriate products and services that do not affect the assets in the portfolio. The reason most advisors don't add these products and services is either that they are not organized enough to introduce them on a regular basis or that they are not comfortable enough with these products and services to introduce them.

Typically, these appropriate products and services do not compete with the assets the advisor manages through the wealth-management process. These are add-on products that generally require little or no additional assets, but still add business. Examples of additional products are:

- Retirement plans
- Liability management
- Estate planning and gifting strategies
- Asset protection
- Educational products
- Cash management
- Long-term health care
- Annuities

Services by themselves may not directly add business, but they can have a positive impact. Additional services of this type tie a client closer to you and significantly improve retention. These services are hard to unwind and will make a client think twice before leaving. They also make a client more comfortable with you in your role as manager of his entire financial life, a relationship that should lead the client to the inevitable conclusion that he should have all his assets with you.

Examples of additional services are:

- Credit cards and/or debit cards
- Direct deposit
- Online access
- Web bill paying

Clients who have more than $1 million in assets are your biggest market for additional products and services; not only do they have the greatest need for them, but they also have needs that clients with fewer assets don't have. For example, liability management can be just as important as asset management for very wealthy clients; they are generally more appropriate candidates for alternative investments; and they have need for asset protection strategies. The more complex strategies and products that your $1 million-plus clients need can generate significantly more business, and these products do not compete with the assets you are managing. This is why your goal should be to get at least $10,000 or more in business from each account of $1 million or more. By introducing these products and strategies, not only are you increasing the opportunity for more business, but you are also showing your clients the value you add.

Examples of additional products for $1 million-plus clients are:

- Concentrated stock strategies (liquidity, protection)
- Liability management
- Asset protection strategies
- Trust and estate strategies
- Alternative investments

Alternative investments should be included in a portfolio only in smaller increments and only if they are consistent with the client's risk tolerance. These investments can be noncorrelated assets that, in small quantities, can decrease risk and add to performance. Annuities are excellent products as well, especially for conservative investors; you can add them to the portfolio or replace existing assets with them to provide a guaranteed future income stream (in most cases). These products when appropriate can add significant business without the need to make significant changes to the portfolio.

HOW TO DO IT: BE ORGANIZED AND HAVE THE DISCUSSION

In order to be effective in adding these products and services, you need to do two things: You need to be organized, and you need to discuss them with each client.

Be Organized

My formula for obtaining 100 percent wallet share is simple:

$$P + D + E = 100 \text{ percent}$$

P stands for positioning yourself as being capable of handling all aspects of a client's financial life.

D stands for discovering those products and services clients are not doing with you that you can offer them.

E stands for exposing the client to those appropriate products and services that he has not used with you during each monthly contact with the client.

Strategic Client Review

Implementing the 100 percent wallet share formula can be accomplished through the strategic client review. Write a list of appropriate products and services for each client and then compare it to what each client is doing with you right now. This is really a gap analysis to determine what appropriate products and services they could be doing with you that they are not. Once you have determined the appropriate products and services that you offer that they are not doing with you, write a second list of those and put it in the client files. During your monthly contact with each client recommend one appropriate product on your list. The key to success with expansion is exposure. If the client knows you have a particular product or service and you can show how it will improve his current situation, he will most likely do it with you. I also recommend that you have your client associate recommend appropriate services to the client as she interacts with him. Your goal should be obtaining at least six different appropriate products and services with each significant client.

This simple organizing process ensures that you systematically discuss with each client the products and services that are appropriate for that client. This process will work whether or not the client is interested in each of the products and services you share with him; the only thing that counts is that you take the time to ask if he is interested in more information or details on the product you suggest, and that you provide this information. Just exposing your clients to more options and choices expands the products and services they have and will generate more business.

Have the Discussion

You don't need to make a separate contact to discuss these products and services. You can add these discussions to a portfolio review or a monthly contact.

One of the real values of this approach is that it makes every client contact more valuable to both you and the client. Many contact systems are good at organizing contacts, but few of them provide the content for the contact (see sample scripts below).

If you do this every year, you should add at least 10 basis points of business. For example, if you have $100 million in assets and are generating $600,000 of business from that asset base, then by systematically exposing your clients to additional products and services, you should add a minimum of 10 basis points to your practice per year, increasing your business from $600,000 to $700,000 the first year.

REASSIGNING CLIENTS

If you have diligently exposed a client to additional products and services over the course of a year, and she is still under your minimum business level, you need to give the account to a newer advisor who is willing to accept a lower minimum. One of the best expressions of this concept I have heard is that every client deserves to be in someone's A book. Giving a low-fee-generating client to a newer advisor ensures that the client is in someone else's A book and is being well-served.

The following script shows how you might handle reassigning a client because she is not meeting your minimum business level:

Advisor: Mr./Ms. Client, this is Joe Advisor from XYZ Financial, and the reason I am calling you is that I am going to reassign your account to another advisor. The reason for my decision is that I do not feel that I can provide you with the level of service you are entitled to, and I want to assign you to someone I trust who has the time to give you better service.

Client: I do not want to be reassigned. I am fine with your service. Can I stay with you?

Advisor: Since you have asked, I will tell you that to provide the level of service my clients should expect, I have a minimum level of annual business of $1,000. Since you have not done that much business with me in the past, I assume that you will not be willing to do it this year. But if you are interested in staying with me, I would be glad to discuss a fee-based pricing option and some additional products and services that I believe would be appropriate and would benefit you. Would you be interested in discussing these?

The approach of expanding the relationship with each client is consistent with what affluent clients are looking for. According to Russ Alan Prince, in his book *Cultivating the Middle-Class Millionaire*, 76.8 percent of clients with more than $1 million prefer to work with a wealth manager. According to Prince, the definition of wealth management is a "comprehensive, holistic approach to provide integrated solutions." This wealth-management definition ties in with the expansion approach I have recommended in this chapter.

EXAMPLE SCRIPTS FOR EXPANDING THE CLIENT RELATIONSHIP

IRAs: General Query

Your objective here is to transfer IRA assets held somewhere else.

> "Mr./Ms. Client, I was reviewing your account and wanted to ask you about your retirement assets. Do you have any retirement accounts held outside of XYZ Financial?"
>
> If the answer is no, then:
>
> "Then all your retirement assets [if the client has any] are with XYZ Financial? I appreciate your confidence in us, and I will continue to do my best in managing them for you."
>
> If the answer is yes, then:
>
> "It would help me to do a better job of allocating your assets if I knew where these retirement assets are and how they are invested. Could you provide me with the specifics? Would you mind sending me a copy of your most recent statement?"

IRAs: Beneficiary

Your objective is again to transfer IRA assets held somewhere else.

> "Mr./Ms. Client, the beneficiary designation on your retirement assets can have some important tax considerations. I would like to have a chance to review with you your beneficiary designations on your XYZ Financial account [if applicable] and to do the same on any retirement accounts that you have outside XYZ Financial. When would be a convenient time to discuss this? I would suggest sending me in advance your statements and plan documents on those accounts that are not with XYZ Financial so that I can review them before our appointment."

Business Financial Services

> "Mr./Ms. Client, I am calling you because I realize that you are a business owner, and I have never talked to you about your banking relationships. We have a very competitive offering that pays an attractive rate on cash balances with low fees and no compensating balances,

with an attractive credit line if you choose to use it. Would you like to know the details?"

If the answer is no, then:

"Thanks for your time. If the need does arise, let me know."

If the answer is yes, then provide specifics or offer to arrange an appointment where this offering can be discussed.

Annuities

"Mr./Ms. Client, with the volatility we have experienced in the equity markets, many of my clients have re-examined their risk tolerance, and in many cases they are looking for more conservative investments. One idea I would like to share with you is a variable annuity. It grows tax deferred, can be diversified, and will give you most of the upside of an equity portfolio, but the downside risk is limited. Would you like the details?"

If the answer is no, then:

"Thank you for your time. If your interests change, I can provide the details anytime."

If yes, then give the specifics of a particular variable annuity.

401(k)

"Mr./Ms. Client, do you currently participate in a 401(k) plan?"

If the answer is yes, then:

"You may not realize it, but under current tax law, you may be able to transfer all or a portion of your 401(k) to an IRA rollover account. The benefits include my being able to allocate the assets in keeping with your investment plan and reallocate them as the market dictates. Further, it would streamline your reporting and give you an open platform to invest your assets in. If you transfer your retirement account to me I also could provide you with more investment options than your current plan provides. With your permission, I can review your plan documents to see if you are eligible for this option. Are you interested?"

Mortgages

"Mr./Ms. Client, I am sure you are aware of the record volume of home refinancing occurring because of the current interest rate environment. XYZ Financial has some attractive mortgage products and very attractive rates. Would you be interested in the details?"

If the answer is no, then:

"Thanks for your time. Let me know if your interest changes."

If the answer is yes, then provide the details of offerings and rates.

Life Insurance

"Mr./Ms. Client, I find that many of my clients have older life insurance contracts (ten years or more) that can be replaced at a lower cost. The cost may be lower because life expectancy is increasing. If you would send me a copy of your policy and share how much it costs, I will do a complimentary review to see if I can save you money."

Long-Term Care Insurance

"Mr./Ms. Client, I have found that many of my clients have concerns about the rising costs of long-term health care. A sobering fact is that 60 percent of people who reach age 65 will need long-term health care at some point in their lives. Presently, the insurance to protect you and your heirs can be relatively inexpensive. It may also be something you should consider for your parents. Would you like to learn the details?"

EXAMPLES OF SCRIPTS FOR $1 MILLION-PLUS CLIENTS

Concentrated Stock

"Mr./Ms. Client, several of my clients who, like you, have had a successful career with a public company have been granted restricted stock and/or stock options. Would that apply to you?"

If the answer is yes, then:

"As you may know, you have alternatives in how you receive the options/stock, but all of them have tax implications. I would like to have the opportunity to review your restricted shares and stock options, and share with you our thoughts on what your best alternatives would be. Additionally, in some cases we can provide some liquidity and protection options for your restricted shares before they are released. Would you be interested in this kind of review?"

Lending

"Mr./Ms. Client, I have found that many of my clients who, like you, have significant net worth have unique lending needs. We can provide potential solutions for effective liability management. How do you currently handle your lending needs? [If appropriate] I would like to meet with you to discuss what we could offer you at XYZ."

Trust and Estate Planning

"Mr./Ms. Client, most of my clients who have a net worth similar to yours have spent time developing a long-term estate and trust plan. What kind of trust and estate planning have you done? We would be glad to give you a complimentary review and to update your plan as it relates to your trust and estate issues. Would you mind sending me a copy of your trust [if one exists] so that we can do a preliminary review to see if a follow-up meeting would be appropriate?"

Alternative Investments

"Mr./Ms. Client, several of my clients who, like you, have significant net worth have expressed an interest in private equity investments. A private equity investment can complement your existing portfolio, and, while the risks are greater, there are opportunities for significant upside potential. Private equities are companies you can invest in before they are public. It takes the kind of net worth that you have to even qualify for these investments. If you are interested, I would suggest that you consider a small percentage of your portfolio for private equities. Would you like to know the details of some current offerings?"

Expanding your business with existing clients takes discipline, organization, and a willingness to go beyond the comfort range most advisors have. As much work as it is, it is still less work than getting new clients. We now have three ways to work with your clients to build your business: leveraging clients to get new ones, bringing in clients' assets held at other institutions, and broadening your relationship with your clients. In Chapter 14 we will look at the fourth way to use clients to grow your business.

SUMMARY

- The more products and services a client is exposed to, the more business he will do.

- Clients who use five or more products and services can generate three times as much business as clients who use two or fewer.

- Clients who have six or more different products and services have a very high retention rate.

- Clients who have $1 million or more in assets have the greatest need for additional products and services.

- The most successful advisors are always working to achieve 100 percent wallet share.

- The formula for 100 percent wallet share is $P + D + E = 100$ percent.

- The best way to achieve 100 percent wallet share is through the strategic client review process.

- Most affluent investors want a wealth-management relationship with their advisor that offers a holistic, comprehensive approach.

- The result of the strategic client review process, if executed systematically, should be an increase of 10 basis points in your ROA (return on assets).

- You can make your discussions of additional products and services an add-on to your monthly contacts with clients.

CHAPTER 14

Your Natural Market

IF YOU ORGANIZE YOUR CLIENTS by age, occupation, or outside interests, you will see that they cluster into groups. For example, say that a large portion of your clients are retirees over 65, golfers, and business owners. You can then combine these groupings—combinations might be retirees over 65 who like golf, or business owners between 50 and 60 who fly fish or enjoy the performing arts. Or it may be that a large portion of your clients have different occupations but like golf, or a high percentage are in a certain age group but have different occupations and interests. The combinations can be endless.

These similarities among your clients—alone or in combination—represent your natural affinities, or your natural market, and can provide a significant marketing opportunity because these natural groupings show where you have been more successful in your past marketing.

Every advisor has a natural market or markets, and focusing on these markets is one of the best marketing opportunities you have, but most advisors have never taken the time to determine what their natural markets are or how to leverage them.

HOW THE NATURAL MARKET WORKS

The theory behind this approach is that clients associate with people they work with, who have similar interests, and who are of a similar age: "Birds of a feather flock together." There are three primary benefits to this approach.

1. It is a way to connect with your clients in a format that is fun for, and valuable to, those clients.

2. It gives clients a way to socialize with and offer value to their friends.

3. It allows you to meet prospects in a nonthreatening way.

Through natural marketing, you make it easier for your clients to introduce you to their friends, your prospects. Natural marketing is nonthreatening because it is generally easier for a client to invite a friend to a fun event or to a seminar than to make a referral. The client feels less of a commitment than when making a referral because a referral puts a client in the position of endorsing the advisor; the client fears that if the advisor loses her friend's money, her friend will blame her. With natural marketing, the client is making an introduction by extending an invitation to an event, not by giving an endorsement.

HOW TO DEVELOP A NATURAL MARKETING PLAN

Step 1: Organize Your Clients

Organize your top fifty to one hundred relationships:

+ By age range (in ten-year increments)
+ By occupation
+ By outside interests
+ By the source of the account (how you acquired the account)

This analysis is the basis for the natural marketing plan. Start your plan with the two largest occupations, age ranges, and outside interests (two groups in each of these three categories equals six groups in all). For example, say that your analysis shows that:

+ About 60 percent of your clients are retirees and business owners.
+ About 80 percent of your clients are either between 50 and 60 or over 70 years old.
+ About 75 percent of your clients are golfers or enjoy fly fishing.

Step 2: Make Lists

Once you have done the analysis, list the clients in each of these six groups. These lists are the foundation of the natural marketing plan.

Step 3: Organize Events and Seminars

Once you have analyzed your clients and made your lists, organize events and seminars for those clients with similar age ranges and interests. Later in this chapter there are examples of how to use natural marketing techniques for occupations, age ranges, and outside interests.

Step 4: Follow Up

You must follow up with new prospects you acquire through these events and seminars. You should call each new prospect following the seminar or event and either invite him to another event or seminar or, if appropriate, ask him if he would feel comfortable meeting with you to discuss the potential value that you might add to his specific investment situation.

HOW TO CREATE YOUR GROUPINGS
Same Occupations Natural Market: Referrals

People from the same occupation have strong connections and valuable information:

♦ People in a particular occupation have a good idea of the best way to market to others in that occupation.

♦ People in a particular occupation know others in their field and have a good idea of how qualified those people are (income, stock incentives, position, seniority, and so on).

♦ People in a particular occupation are aware of money in motion within their own firm and elsewhere in the industry: who is retiring, who has been transferred, who the new senior managers are, who the movers and shakers are, and other such information.

The best way to leverage the occupations groupings in your natural market is to ask for referrals from the clients in those occupations. Here is a sample script that demonstrates how you can ask a client for introductions to others in her occupation:

"Mr./Ms. Client, I have recently analyzed my business and determined that the majority of my clients do what you do. [State the occupation.] It is clear to me that I work well with people in this occupation, and I wanted to ask your help: Is there anyone you work with or know in your industry that I should be talking to? Examples might be someone who has done very well in your business, someone who is retiring or relocating to this area, or someone who has had a significant event occur in his or her life. If so, would you feel comfortable providing me with an introduction?"

Same Age Ranges Natural Market: Seminars

Clients who are of a similar age are usually at a similar place in the investment cycle. The investment cycle does not apply to all investors of the same age in the same way, but age is typically an important factor in determining an investor's financial needs. For example:

+ Investors in the 40 to 50 age range are most interested in funding their children's college education, setting up retirement plans, and perhaps purchasing a vacation home.
+ Investors in the 50 to 60 age range are focused on having enough money to retire.
+ Investors in the 60 to 70 age range are focused on estate planning, and on not outliving their retirement assets.

Most people are friends with other people their age. This is because they often share interests and family circumstances. The best way to capitalize on similar age ranges is to organize educational seminars that are of value to clients in a particular age range. When you offer educational seminars for particular age ranges, not only are you providing a valuable service to clients, but you are also giving them an opportunity to invite a friend of a similar age with similar interests—a prospective client. This is an excellent way to meet prospects. Be sure to ask your clients to bring a friend of similar age to the seminar.

Here are some examples of seminars you can offer that focus on the needs of people within a particular age range:

+ Seminars on 529 plans for forty- to fifty-year-olds who are concerned with funding their children's educations.
+ Preretirement issues seminars for fifty- to sixty-year-olds, covering how much money they need to retire, net unrealized appreciation, accelerated savings strategies, and other such information.
+ Seminars on topics such as estate planning, gifting strategies, and staying ahead of inflation for sixty- to seventy-year-olds.

Here are two scripts you can use to invite clients to such events:

> "Mr./Ms. Client, I wanted to invite you to a seminar that, based on your investment circumstances, I thought you would be interested in. The topic of the seminar is [give details] and the date and time is [give the date and time]. Would you be interested in attending?"
> If the answer is yes, then:
> "Is there anyone else you think I should meet who might be interested in this seminar? If so, I would encourage you to please invite that person. Does anyone come to mind?"

> "Mr./Ms. Client: The reason for my call is to invite you to a seminar that I am conducting on [relevant topic to appropriate age group]. In the past, I have found this topic to be very interesting and relevant to clients and prospects who are at a similar stage in their investment cycle. Would you be interested in attending?"
> If the answer is yes, then:
> "Good. Is there anyone else you think I should meet who might be interested in attending? It is a nonthreatening way for me to meet prospective clients who might have an interest in this seminar topic."

Same Outside Interests Natural Market

Your clients are likely to have friends who share similar outside interests; people like to be around other people who enjoy doing the same things. By classifying clients by their outside interests, you can organize events that appeal to these interests. Examples include golf, fly fishing, fine dining, wine tasting, cooking, and travel.

The best way to leverage your clients' interest groupings is to organize fun events. These events, focused on clients' outside interests, provide an excellent opportunity to meet new prospects. Invite clients to events they are interested in and ask them to invite a friend who shares the same interest. Your clients will appreciate being invited to an event they are interested in, and you will have a nonthreatening way to meet prospective clients.

A MARKETING BOARD OF DIRECTORS

Once you have grouped your best clients by occupation, age range, and outside interests, you can ask their help in finding prospects in those same groups. The idea is to create a "marketing board of directors," made up of clients who fall into a particular category, that will help you find and market more effectively to people in those occupations, age ranges, and interests.

The ideas I have presented so far focus on offering events that appeal to people with the same occupation, age range, or interest. Now you are asking people in these groups for advice on marketing to others in the same group. There are no better counselors than these people for telling you the best marketing technique to reach a certain group of people. You want to ask, "What advice can you give me on how to market effectively to people in the same field/age range/interest group as you?"

Here is an example of it:

> "Mr./Ms. Client, in reviewing my clients, I realized that most of them have the same occupation as you do. I wanted to ask your advice: I want to attract more clients like you, so what advice can you give me on how to approach individuals who do what you do?"

USE YOUR GROUPINGS TO UNCOVER YOUR BEST MARKETING ACTIVITIES

You can determine what marketing activities have been most successful for you with these groups by analyzing how you acquired your current clients. This is good information on which to base your future marketing efforts. For example, if you discover that your greatest source of clients and prospects is seminars, then this indicates that your primary marketing activity should be seminars. If you take the time to do this analysis, you can spend the majority of your marketing time doing those activities that produce the best results. In addition, if you want to develop a market niche(s) beyond your clients, your natural market is the best place to start. You have developed the expertise and experience necessary to market effectively to this particular niche.

NATURAL MARKETING FOR PROSPECTS

The same principles of natural marketing that apply to clients can also apply to prospects. If you categorize your prospects by age, occupation, and outside interest, you can invite prospects to attend events and educational seminars. Another benefit of this is that a new advisor with few clients can use natural marketing techniques before she has an established client base. By including existing prospects in the natural marketing process, you double the number of affluent clients and prospects you can build relationships with, and at the same time you create goodwill.

In Chapter 7, I covered how to gather information on the interests and details of your prospects. Now you will use that information. Organize the prospects the same way I described organizing your clients. Then list prospects by age range, occupation, outside interest, and source.

If you are organizing a client event around golf, invite existing prospects who like to golf to the event. Do the same with educational seminars that are appropriate for both clients and prospects in a particular age range. By including prospects, you can double the attendance at seminars and events and further develop your relationship with your prospects.

You can even take this a step further by asking each prospect to bring a friend who has a similar interest. You can also call prospects and ask for suggestions on marketing to other prospects in similar occupations, and you can ask prospects who else they know in their occupation that you should be talking to.

Natural marketing is one of the most effective and efficient ways to leverage clients and prospects for the purpose of finding new prospects. It is simply a method of organizing clients and prospects by age, occupation, outside interests, and source. This provides opportunities to recognize good clients and to help them help you in an easy, nonthreatening way. This is what effective marketing is all about.

NICHE MARKETING FOR EXPERIENCED ADVISORS

This part of the natural marketing process focuses on developing an expertise or specialization working with a specific occupation, professional, or type of investor. Many of the same principles that apply to the new advisor (covered in detail in Chapter 4 in Part 1) also apply to niche marketing as an experienced advisor. By focusing on a specific niche market the experienced advisor can achieve the "3 Rs" necessary to continue growing her business: reputation, referrals, and references.

The most successful advisors I have worked with have all developed a deep level of expertise and experience in working within a very specific occupation or type of investor. This makes complete sense because as the affluence of investors grows, so does their belief that they are unique and their desire to work with a financial advisor who is singularly qualified to work with people who do what they do. For example, if you are a senior executive you want to work with an advisor who has experience working with other senior executives; the same is true if you are a business owner, fiduciary for a retirement plan, lawyer, or doctor. There is also much less competition if you are a specialist within a niche market because most other advisors don't specialize. In addition, referrals are easier to get within a niche market because of your ability to relate to the specific investment needs of affluent individuals within your niche market. I recommend that all experienced advisors identify and commit to a niche market plan.

The first step is to identify the niche market that you can become committed to and put a "stake in the ground." Most likely that will be the natural market you have identified when you listed the occupations of your clients. The second step is to interview your clients who share the occupation you have identified as your future niche market. The following is a sample script and interview questions you can ask your clients in your selected niche:

"Mr./Ms. Client, I have done an analysis of my business and determined that many of my best clients share your profession. I have made a decision that in the future I would like to focus my business development activities around attracting new clients who are [state profession]. I have a great deal of respect for you and was hoping you could answer some questions that would be very helpful to me. Do you have some time to answer a few questions?"

1. If you were me, what recommendations would you make on how to best approach people who do what you do?

2. What trade publications/periodicals do people in your profession read? Are any of them local publications?

3. What associations or affinity groups do people in your profession belong to? Are any of them local groups?

4. Are there any speaking opportunities you are aware of that I can take advantage of?

5. Who are the centers of influence and leaders of your profession whom you think I should meet?

6. Are there any books you would recommend that I read that would contribute to my understanding of your profession?"

Once you have interviewed all your clients in your niche market you will have all the information you need to start your niche marketing process. I recommend that you supplement the information gained by these interviews with resources and specialists within your firm who can add to your expertise.

The third step is to develop a list of qualified individuals in your target niche market. In the resource section of this book I have provided sources of names for many different niche markets. I would recommend that you invest in a list of at least 500 prequalified names for your target niche market.

Now you are ready to take action. Join the industry associations, subscribe to the local and national trade publications, or offer to speak at the association meetings. You'll quickly find that everyone is interested in investments and insights you can provide about their industry from an investment point of view. Sponsor anything you can afford to show you are a "friend of their profession" and, finally, call your list.

The following is an example of a script you might use when calling individuals within your target niche market:

> "Mr./Ms. Jones, this is Joe Smith with XYZ Financial and the reason I'm calling you is that I have developed both expertise and experience working with successful [state occupation] like you. You deserve to work with someone who understands the unique and complex investment needs that people in your occupation are faced with. I believe we have a great deal in common, and there are a number of people in your profession whom I work with and can provide as references. I would like to suggest we meet at a mutually convenient time so that I can share my experience and expertise in helping you with your investments."

I have talked about getting new clients and getting more from your existing ones. But if you don't develop loyal clients, you will be missing an important business growth component.

SUMMARY

♦ Natural marketing is simply the classification of clients and prospects by age, occupation, outside interests, and how you acquired the client or prospect (the "source").

- Natural marketing gives you an opportunity to help your clients help you by introducing you to new prospects with common interests, age ranges, and occupations.

- Asking for referrals to others who have the same occupation is an effective natural marketing technique for clients and prospects with similar occupations.

- Educational seminars are the most effective natural marketing avenue for clients and prospects in similar age groups.

- Fun events are the most effective natural marketing avenues for clients and prospects with similar outside interests.

- A marketing board of directors is an effective natural marketing technique for getting marketing ideas from clients and prospects with similar occupations, age ranges, and interests.

- Organizing clients and prospects by source is the best way to determine what kind of marketing you do most effectively and how to spend the majority of your marketing time.

- Natural marketing techniques can work as well with prospects as they do with clients.

- Inviting a friend to a fun event or a seminar is easier than a direct referral for most clients to introduce prospective clients to their advisor.

- You must follow up with prospects you acquire through events and seminars. Schedule appointments with them as soon as possible after the event or seminar.

- Niche marketing for experienced advisors can lead to the crucial development of the "3 Rs": reputation, referrals, and references.

- Follow the four-step process outlined in this chapter and you will become a master niche marketer.

CHAPTER 15

Client Retention

RETENTION OF CLIENTS IS MUCH MORE THAN JUST KEEPING CLIENTS; it should be developing loyal clients. Having loyal clients can be the most important acquisition and growth strategy you can engage in. My definition of "loyal clients" includes those individuals who are "raving fans" of their financial advisor. These loyal clients experience a high level of satisfaction and are then interested in giving their advisors all their business, all their assets, and referrals for new clients, as well as their long-term loyalty.

The objective for any financial advisor who wants to reach the million-dollar level is to have as many loyal clients as possible. Based on my experience and research there are seven important factors that when incorporated into an advisor's practice will result in having many loyal clients:

1. The right number of client relationships
2. Developing deep client relationships
3. Frequent proactive client contact
4. Good performance
5. Effective problem resolution
6. A holistic and comprehensive relationship
7. Positive new account experience

THE RIGHT NUMBER OF CLIENT RELATIONSHIPS

Good client service is built on a single essential point: a manageable number of client relationships. If you have too many clients, it is difficult to provide the level of service required to both keep your clients happy and meet their needs.

The definition of a relationship is the sum of the time and energy you spend with an individual. Just spending time with an individual doesn't ensure a good relationship, but without a commitment of time it is hard to develop and maintain a good relationship. I believe the saying "the greatest gift you can give someone is your time and attention" applies to the development of loyal clients. In order to develop a loyal affluent client you must commit at least ten hours a year of your time to the client relationship. I further define hours spent to include proactive contact, appointments, and personal interaction, as well as fun and educational events. I do not include e-mails, reactive contacts, preparation, and service work.

In order to convert prospects into clients you need to treat your affluent prospects as if they were your best clients. That means you should be spending at least ten hours a year with each prospect. The result of this time commitment is that it becomes physically impossible for most experienced advisors to work with an affluent client base of more than one hundred client and fifty prospect relationships. The number of client relationships you have has a significant effect on your client associate, too. The client associate should make each client and prospect feel like she is getting Ritz-Carlton service, and for the client associate to provide this level of service, he must have a manageable number of relationships. The time a client associate spends with smaller, less affluent relationships is time he can no longer spend serving more affluent relationships. Advisors often underestimate how much time it takes a client associate to answer calls and service smaller relationships.

DEVELOPING DEEP CLIENT RELATIONSHIPS

Top advisors understand that constructing trusting relationships with their prospects and clients is essential to building a successful financial services practice. Once a good relationship is established, all good things come: more assets and referrals, and an increased wallet share.

In Chapter 9 I covered the importance of developing trust and outlined the three different levels of trust. Specifically, I said that the highest level of trust is when clients believe that you have a personal stake in their lives and the lives of their families. They believe you care at the deepest level about them and the fulfillment of their life goals. That same principle of achieving the highest levels of trust and becoming a stakeholder in the lives of your clients applies to developing and maintaining loyal clients through the deep relationships you have with your clients.

FREQUENT PROACTIVE CLIENT CONTACT

Clients want to hear from you: I cannot overemphasize the importance of this factor. Clients want to feel that you care and that you are paying attention to them and their assets, especially during volatile market conditions. There is so much competition for affluent clients that if they do not feel appreciated it is easy for them to transfer their assets to someone who does appreciate them. Based on my experience and the many affluent client surveys and client satisfaction research I have seen, the contact frequency that affluent clients expect and desire from their financial advisor is monthly.

My definition of client contact involves proactive contacts and appointments, not reacting to requests from clients or e-mails, letters, and other forms of communication. Three of these twelve contacts should be quarterly reviews, and one of them should be an annual planning or review session. The monthly contacts should last between twenty and thirty minutes each. The quarterly reviews should last between thirty minutes and an hour depending on whether or not they are in person. The annual review is more extensive than the quarterly review and is organized by an agenda. The annual review, in addition to a performance review, is also a planning session and should include an update on new assets and a formal referral discussion. The annual review, when possible, should be done in person, should include the spouse, and should last approximately one hour.

Each client contact has four parts:

♦ Reconnection
♦ Portfolio review
♦ Growth opportunity
♦ Closing question

The reconnection is a link to the last conversation and in most cases should be personal rather than investment-related. The portfolio review should be a review of the overall status of the investment portfolio, including any recommended changes. The growth opportunity is employing one of the concepts of the fundamentals of growth. Examples could include adding a product or service, referral discussion, asking for a CPA or attorney name, inviting a client to come to an event and bring a guest, or suggesting the transfer of away assets. Not every monthly contact needs to include the growth component; it's a judgment call that depends on a particular client at a particular time. The closing question is simply asking the client if "there is anything else on your mind that you would like to discuss." This ensures that free-flowing communication exists at all times and opens the door for the client to discuss anything she may be concerned about.

There are a number of other contacts you can make with your clients that can have a positive impact on retention. These contacts supplement, but do not replace, the monthly advisor contact. These can include:

♦ Mailings with personal notes attached.

♦ Client events or seminars. Holding events and seminars is an excellent way to demonstrate to your clients how much you appreciate them.

♦ Two movie tickets for her birthday. The client will feel good that you not only remembered her birthday, but also sent her a gift. Movie tickets are a nice night out, and your client will think of you during and after it.

♦ A call from your manager to the client thanking him for his business and offering him access to her if needed. Involving a full-time manager can go a long way in making clients feel important. E-mail the client's name and number to your manager and ask her to make a goodwill call. Because of the manager's time limitations, I recommend that you ask your manager to call only your best clients.

Providing outstanding, proactive service is as important as any job the client associate can do. Outstanding service involves asking clients if they have any needs before they call and ask. I recommend that the client associate call each client at least twice a year and ask if the client has any service issues. This gives the client the feeling that both the advisor and the client associate really care about providing great service.

Here is an example of a client associate script for doing this:

> **"Mr./Ms. Client, you are one of our best clients, and we are committed to providing you with outstanding service. I am calling to see if there is anything we can do to better serve you and to see if there are any service issues we can help you with."**

If you follow the client contact model that I have outlined then you will spend at least ten hours annually to develop and maintain loyal clients:

Four hours—eight monthly contacts

Two hours—three quarterly reviews (one in person)

One hour—annual review (in person)

Three hours—fun/educational event (at least one per year)

PORTFOLIO PERFORMANCE THAT IS CONSISTENT WITH THE CLIENT'S GOALS AND EXPECTATIONS

There are two sides to performance: what the client expects and how her assets perform. If these two factors are mismatched and the client expects better performance than she is getting, there is a problem.

Expectations

If a client's assets are performing as the client expects, or better, the client should be very satisfied. If you educate your client about the kind of performance he can expect given his goals and risk tolerance, then his expectations are likely to be in line with the long-term performance he will get. Educating clients is key to setting their expectations.

Performance

The keys to better portfolio performance are asset allocation, diversification, and a disciplined investment process. If you manage these components wisely, the long-term results will be good. Over the long term, a conservative approach with the right asset allocation will outperform a less disciplined, aggressive investment approach. Chapter 9 contains a more detailed discussion on the investment process as it relates to performance.

EFFECTIVE PROBLEM RESOLUTION

Operational problems are inevitable, and the majority of clients understand this. The key to good client retention is not to have no operational problems, but to quickly resolve the problems that occur. How many operational problems there are is a smaller factor in client satisfaction than how well these problems are resolved. Communication with the client about the status of the problem is also important. In my experience, affluent clients are less concerned about how quickly problems are resolved than the fact that someone is working on them and notifies them of the status. I have developed a problem resolution method I call "communicate and elevate." As the financial advisor, you should delegate problem resolution to your client associate, but don't delegate and then forget about the problem.

Once a client problem has been brought to the attention of the associate, resolving that problem needs to be the number one priority. If your associate runs into any roadblocks in the resolution of the problem, it needs to be elevated to the advisor within 48 hours. If the advisor can't work through the roadblock it needs to be elevated to management immediately. Communication should be made with the client if there is any delay, providing the status and time period in which the problem should be resolved. When the problem is resolved, this should be communicated to the client as well. Good communication can be as important as the resolution itself.

A BROAD RELATIONSHIP

Clients who use six or more products and services have a near-perfect retention rate. This makes sense, since the more products and services a client uses, the more she is tied to the advisor and the firm. In Chapter 9 I described the importance of wealth-management services and the value of a holistic, comprehensive relationship. In Chapter 13 I described a systematic process of expanding appropriate products and services to each core affluent client. If the recommendations in both of these chapters are followed, then a broad relationship with the client will be developed.

ENSURING THAT THE NEW RELATIONSHIP EXPERIENCE IS POSITIVE

The new relationship experience is important because it is the client's first experience with the advisor's firm. It sets the perception that the new client has, which in turn colors many of the experiences that the client has with the firm later on. A good first experience subsequently encourages positive perceptions.

The client associate and the advisor together should develop a checklist of all the things that need to be done to make the first experience a good one. One of these new account tasks should be a letter from the client associate introducing himself to the new client and offering himself as the person who will be responsible for the service side of the relationship. The client associate should follow up the letter with a personal call doing the same. The client associate or advisor should also call the client right after her first statement arrives and review the statement with the client so that she is comfortable reading it. These things will ensure that the new account experience will be positive.

Create a spreadsheet that organizes the client associate to ensure that the new relationship experience is a good one. Put the new client's name in the first column and list the tasks to be completed in the subsequent columns across the spreadsheet. As the client associate completes the tasks, he should place a check mark on the row for that client under each task. Each new client should have a check mark under each task within ninety days of opening the new account.

One of the tasks on the checklist should be sending the client a small gift of appreciation for starting a new relationship. I believe that the best type of gift is an investment-related book (see Chapter 7 for book recommendations). For those relationships that are large enough, have a manager call the new client and welcome her to the firm. This gives new clients the feeling they are appreciated at all levels of the organization, and they are often flattered that a senior manager would take the time to call.

SCRIPTS FOR THE CLIENT ASSOCIATE

Welcome Call

"Mr./Ms. Client, I am calling to introduce myself and thank you for opening a new account with us. Do you have any questions regarding your account that I may assist you with? I will call you when you receive your first statement to go over that with you. In the meantime, if you have any questions, you can call me at [client associate's direct line]."

Thank-You Letter

Dear Mr./Ms. Client:

Thank you for choosing [advisor's name] to help you reach your financial goals.

I am writing to introduce myself to you as part of [advisor's name]'s support staff. I am your primary service contact. I am here to assist you with any service requests and questions you may have.

Please do not hesitate to call me directly if any questions should arise. We take great pride in servicing our clients and look forward to a continuing relationship with you.

Sincerely,
[Client associate's name]
[Address]

By providing such a positive new client relationship experience, you are building the foundation for a long-term loyal client relationship. By starting the relationship on a positive note you are reaffirming to the new client that he made the right decision by investing his assets with you. By under-promising and overdelivering, you are incorporating an important element of trust, matching your words with your actions.

Developing loyal clients takes a great deal of time, energy, organization, focus, and commitment, but the value of developing a loyal client base is worth every bit of all those components. When clients are loyal not only do they stay with you but they can become the biggest factor in the growth of your practice.

Experienced advisors have a lot to do to retain clients, and they must also make time to market. It may seem overwhelming, but in the next chapter I will explain how to do it all by managing your time effectively.

SUMMARY

♦ Your client relationships should to be limited to one hundred for client retention to work.

♦ A good client-retention strategy is as important as a client-acquisition strategy.

♦ The client associate can play a critical role in the client-retention strategy.

♦ Incorporate the seven factors into your practice to develop loyal clients.

♦ Effective communication is the key to client retention.

CHAPTER 16

Time Management and the Client Associate

HOW AN ADVISOR SPENDS HER TIME WILL DETERMINE how likely it is that the advisor will become a $1 million-plus advisor. Time is all an advisor has, and how you use that time and your energy determines your success. You have only a limited amount of energy; how many hours you work each day is less important than how many of those hours are productive. The advisor who is committed to a million-dollar practice must devote his high-energy hours to the right activities, or else the opportunity for that day is lost.

One of my favorite expressions in our business is "the right activities lead to the right results." As a financial advisor there are many things that are beyond your control: markets, client behavior, whether a prospect agrees to open an account with you, whether a client provides a referral. But there is one thing as an advisor you have complete control over and that is how you spend your time and the activities that you do every day. I believe the right activities are the leading indicator of the right results.

FUNDAMENTALS OF TIME MANAGEMENT

You need to balance client contact, marketing time, and administrative time every day. To be effective, you must be organized and follow the four fundamentals of time management:

1. Prioritize
2. Delegate
3. Block your time
4. Prepare

If you follow these fundamentals, you can get everything done that is necessary to build a million-dollar business.

PRIORITIZE

Prioritizing daily tasks ensures that you perform the most important activities first, while your energy is high. Resist the temptation to spend high-energy hours on administrative tasks, reading, research, or preparation. Those tasks are easier but not as important as developing relationships with affluent clients and prospects.

1. Your first priority needs to be monthly contact with clients and the investment of their assets.
2. Your close second priority should be following up with existing prospects and getting in front of new ones.
3. Your third priority should be doing the one or two highest-priority administrative tasks daily that cannot be delegated.

Return calls and do lower-priority administrative tasks at the end of the day, when you have spent much of your daily energy. You must constantly prioritize, and you should spend the high-energy early hours of the day on the high-priority tasks so that no matter what comes up, these tasks are always done first.

Your First Priority Needs to Be Monthly Contact with Clients

Spending time contacting clients is your number one task. Every client survey I have ever seen shows that client satisfaction is tied to regular contact by the advisor. If you limit your number of client relationships to one hundred, and you are committed to contacting each client at least once a month, then you need to contact five clients each day; if each call lasts about thirty minutes, then you need to commit approximately two hours each day to client contact. Some of these client contacts could last fifteen minutes, and some could last an hour or more if they involve an annual review or in-person quarterly review. Three of these monthly contacts should be a quarterly review (in person if convenient), and one should be a yearly planning and review session (also in person whenever possible).

The bottom line is that you need to spend between two and three hours a day to provide the service level that one hundred clients require.

Your Close Second Priority Should Be Following Up with Existing Prospects and Getting in Front of New Ones

You must spend time marketing every day if you expect to achieve a million-dollar or multimillion-dollar practice. If you are not committed to a disciplined marketing process, there is little chance you will build a million-dollar practice. The most successful million- and multimillion-dollar advisors I have worked with have all had at least one thing in common: They never stop marketing and putting themselves in front of affluent individuals.

For an experienced advisor, marketing can take many forms. Some examples of very effective marketing techniques I have observed in million- and multimillion-dollar advisors are golfing at private clubs, fly fishing, hunting, charity work, network groups (their own), nonprofit boards, center-of-influence networks, client events, and client referrals. Additionally time needs to be spent contacting the prospects in your pipeline. In Chapter 7, on converting prospects to clients, I suggested that you should have fifty qualified prospects in your pipeline, and they should be treated like your best clients. This means contacting each prospect once per month (call or appointment), which means two to three contacts per day, or approximately one hour a day. This is not an exhaustive list, but it is a sample of the way many of the successful multimillion-dollar advisors I have worked with market every day.

I recommend that you spend a minimum of one hour a day, with a goal of two hours or more every day, contacting and building relationships with prospective clients. The most successful advisor I have ever worked with ($10 million-plus per year) marketed many hours every day. The bottom line is that you must build marketing time into every day.

Your Third Priority Should Be Doing the One or Two Highest-Priority Administrative Tasks Daily That Cannot Be Delegated

Even though you should spend most of your high-energy time each day on client and prospect contact, you need to spend time on administrative tasks in order to build and maintain a million-dollar practice. Problems that require your personal attention will come up, and they must be dealt with effectively and efficiently. If you prioritize properly, you should be able to personally handle ten high-priority administrative items per week. If there are more than ten that you need to handle, chances are you are not delegating properly.

Examples of administrative items you cannot delegate include resolving an operational problem that the client associate cannot, putting together an important client or prospect presentation, following up on an unresolved client problem, preparing a presentation for a meeting with a CPA or a client seminar, and preparing for a top-client portfolio review. You should do at least two of these high-priority administrative tasks each day, and you should schedule an hour daily to work on these issues.

DELEGATE

You must try to delegate everything that is not involved with building client relationships and with being in front of affluent clients and prospects. While you need to oversee portfolio management, client reviews, and high-priority administrative tasks, you do not have to do each task. Your priority should be to establish processes and follow-through checks, not to actually do these tasks. Think of yourself as a Broadway actor, focusing on the audience and the performance, and not spending time on the scenery, the music, and the makeup; for a great performance, the actor must give those tasks to someone else so that she can focus her attention on the performance. The advisor must do the same thing. Relationship building and marketing are the hardest things to delegate, but try to delegate everything else.

If you want to improve your delegation skills, focus on the "Big Three"— setting investment policy, strategy, and implementation; affluent client contact and appointments; and marketing—and delegate everything else. Keep a sheet of paper on your desk and every time you engage in an activity that is not related to the Big Three, write it down. These become the activities that need to be delegated to someone else on your team. If your support person is at capacity, these items then become part of the job description for an additional support person. I realize hiring an additional support person can be expensive, but when you can spend $30 an hour to free up time to do more $500 an hour work (time with best clients and marketing), that math makes sense every time.

BLOCK YOUR TIME

Time blocking is focusing your time on similar tasks for a period of time. One of the most effective time-management techniques I have worked with advisors on is what I call the BL/AL (before lunch/after lunch) system. I recommend that you do all the high priority (Big Three activities) before lunch. Have your support person screen your calls, suggesting to clients that you will call them after lunch. I would also recommend you avoid responding to and if possible not viewing e-mails before lunch. Our brains are programmed to respond quickly to opportunities and threats, and every e-mail that comes in is either good news or bad news (opportunity or threat). We can't help but look at incoming e-mails and respond to them unless we discipline ourselves otherwise. If we do not exercise discipline, one of the potential greatest productivity enhancers (e-mail) can become one of the greatest productivity distractors.

I also suggest using lunch for appointments whenever possible—a prospect appointment, a professional referral appointment, or a client review or meeting. Everyone eats lunch, so why not make this a natural time to have a meeting. For clients this could mean bringing in lunch for a review meeting.

I recommend spending time after lunch on those reactive activities that normally take time away from the proactive activities. Examples include the administrative tasks described earlier, presentation preparation, research, responding to e-mails, returning nonessential calls, meetings, and any other non–Big Three activities. The only exception to after-lunch reactive activities would be outside appointments that are better done later in the day than earlier. If you follow the BL/AL system you will find that you will be spending at least 50 percent of your day on those proactive activities that will grow your business and still get all the reactive activities done.

PREPARE

The objective is to have a process-based practice in which the machine is already built and during the day the power switch is turned on. Examples of processes that need to be established are monthly client contact, prospect's first appointment (questions developed), prospect pitch book, prospect pipeline management, new account checklist, problem resolution, professional referral network presentation and follow-up, client review preparation, and setting client event dates. Every day becomes an execution of the vision and all processes are in place to execute this as seamlessly as possible.

THE ROLE OF THE CLIENT ASSOCIATE

The work flow between the advisor and the client associate is critical to successful time management. There are four primary areas of responsibility for a client associate:

1. General administrative and operational duties
2. Client-service tasks
3. Screening calls
4. Preparing and customizing templates and template libraries

General Administrative and Operational Duties

As I mentioned earlier, delegate all non–Big Three activities to your client associate. Avoid giving your client associate piles of tasks to do because she could be confused about what she should work on first. Prioritize the work you give her by attaching a note to each task explaining what needs to be done, and be sure to include all corresponding paperwork. Prioritize all tasks with a 1, 2, or 3:

1. The task needs to be done that day.
2. The task needs to be done that week.
3. The task needs to be done that month.

Keep a task list of tasks you have delegated and indicate the date you delegated them. Keep this task list in a pending file. Each day, when you meet with your client associate, review the pending file and check the status of each item. This process helps the client associate prioritize what is most important to the advisor and also holds the client associate accountable to a date for completion. If the client associate is accountable, he will either work hard to meet the deadline or explain to the advisor why he cannot meet the deadline. I recommend that you assign tasks and review the pending file with your client associate once a day, as early in the day as possible. This meeting should not take more than thirty minutes. This keeps the advisor from interrupting the client associate throughout the day. This system can be set up through e-mail and electronic files if the advisor prefers.

Client-Service Tasks

The client associate can help the advisor not only with administrative tasks but also with providing the outstanding service that affluent clients expect. Most client associates do not have time to be proactive with service and instead react to problems as they arise; this merely shows a lack of organization. If the advisor wants her client associate to take service to the next level, she must help organize the assistant to do so. The client associate has four areas where he can take service to a very high level: the new-relationship experience, expanding the services that clients use, outstanding problem resolution, and proactive service.

Screening Calls

The client associate should screen calls for the advisor whenever possible. Clients should be trained to know that the advisor will not pick up the phone as soon as they call, but will always call back within a reasonable time. I have never worked with a professional in any industry who took my call the minute I called him. My expectation and those of clients should be that unless it is a market-related event, the advisor will call back by the end of the business day. This system allows you to call back after you have made the proactive client and prospect calls and appointments after lunch using the BL/AL system. A sample client associate script for screening calls may be as follows:

> "I am sorry, Mr./Ms. Client, Joe Advisor is [on the line, meeting with a client, away from the office]. Is there anything I can help you with?"
> If the answer is yes, get the details. If it is no, then say:
> "I would happy to interrupt Joe if it's a market action issue or an emergency; otherwise, could Joe call you back after lunch?"

Note that the client associate should always ask if she can be of service. In many cases, the advisor doesn't need to call the client back because the client associate can handle the problem. Also, the client associate has given the advisor the freedom to call back in the afternoon when it is most convenient for him. This allows you to call back after you have finished your calls to clients and prospects.

Preparing and Customizing Presentations and Presentation Libraries

For the most part, you can prepare client and prospect presentations and reviews well in advance of the meeting. With the help of your client associate, you can prepare a menu of different presentations on different topics and hold these presentations in a presentation template library so that, with minimum customization, they can quickly be ready for presentation. The key to making this work is for you and your client associate to take the time in the beginning to set up the presentation template library.

The same principles hold for quarterly and annual client reviews. The format of the reviews, the agendas, the performance data, and the planning information can all be prepared in advance. Like presentations, these review files and templates can be set up in advance; then, with minimal customization, they can be made ready just minutes before the review. To make this process work, the advisor must commit to setting up the format and to training the client associate how to customize it.

REWARDING YOUR CLIENT ASSOCIATE

A good client associate can be an invaluable asset to the experienced advisor in building a million- or multimillion-dollar practice. It is very important that you reward your client associate so that he feels like an appreciated member of your team. This reward should be in the form of both recognition and compensation. Recognition is easy to give but often is not given enough. Look for every opportunity to recognize your client associate's good work. Compliments go a long way, but so do flowers, movie tickets, and nice cards. These are easy things for you to give and will add greatly to the client associate's morale and good feelings about the job.

An outstanding client associate deserves outstanding pay. Unfortunately, the industry does not pay client associates well, and it is up to the advisor to supplement her associate's pay. Many advisors pay their client associates a percentage of their business; others give them a bonus at the end of the year. How you pay is less important than the fact that you are willing to pay extra for outstanding work.

Good recognition and compensation will keep a good client associate loyal for many years, providing the advisor with the support required to build a million-dollar business.

SAMPLE SCHEDULE

Taking into account the time-management fundamentals and the activities that the advisor must do every day to build a million-dollar practice, I would recommend the following daily schedule as a guideline:

8:00–8:30	Prepare for your client contacts, pipeline contacts, and marketing contacts.
8:30–10:30	Client contacts and inside appointments (5).
10:30–12:00	Prospect pipeline (2–3) and marketing contacts (4–5).

| 12–1:30 | Client, prospect, or professional referral source lunch meeting. |
| 1:30–5:00 | Client associate meeting, e-mails, return calls, administrative work, presentations, meetings, events, outside appointments. |

Thus at least 50 percent of your time is spent on client and prospect contact and on marketing activities. Also note that you may not be able to follow this schedule perfectly in a normal day. Unexpected events may occur that will make it impossible. But the principle of time blocking high-priority activities and doing them first is important for those advisors who are motivated to build a million-dollar business.

How an advisor spends his time will define his success in this business. Good time management is the critical difference between the advisors who achieve a million-dollar practice and those who do not. Prioritizing how you spend your time, delegating, blocking your time, and using your client associate effectively are all essential ingredients required to build a million-dollar business.

Time management is about productivity, and an important tool for increasing productivity is being part of a team. Chapter 17 looks at how teams work and how and if you should form or join a team.

SUMMARY

+ Good time management will determine whether or not an advisor will be able to build a million-dollar practice.

+ Spending the majority of your time building relationships with clients and prospects is required for a million-dollar practice.

+ Time-management fundamentals are delegating, prioritization, time blocking, and preparing.

+ Adopt the BL/AL (before lunch/after lunch) time-blocking technique to maximize each day.

+ Advisors must organize a good workflow process between themselves and their client associate.

+ Advisors should focus on the Big Three and delegate everything else.

+ Strong recognition and good compensation are required to motivate and keep a good client associate long term.

CHAPTER 17

Teams

TEAMS HAVE PROLIFERATED IN FINANCIAL SERVICES over the past ten years, and for good reason: Advisors who work in a team generally do better than those who work on their own. Some financial services firms have more than 50 percent of their advisors in teams. The team structure works well in financial services in large part because of the productivity and client-service (retention) improvements they afford. While being on a team is not a prerequisite for having a million-dollar practice, being on a good team can increase the probability of reaching $1 million and can reduce the time it takes to reach it.

Among the advantages of teams are:

Deeper Expertise: Teams often specialize so that each team member can be an expert in something without needing to be an expert in everything. This specialization can be in a particular product area, marketing, portfolio management, presentations, or some other element.

Better Client Service: Clients appreciate their advisor being part of a team because they feel that with a team, there is always someone there to take care of them who is familiar with their situation. This gives clients a sense of continuity should something happen to their advisor.

Deeper Motivation: Team motivation can be very powerful. Teams that have regular meetings where every team member is held accountable for his tasks and his results are teams that work harder. Many advisors feel a higher level of accountability to other team members than they do to themselves; this improves motivation, but it also improves productivity because each person's results should be transparent.

Better Ideas: Financial services can be a competitive business, and advisors can be very protective of their best practices and reluctant to share them with potential competitors, even within the same firm. Sharing ideas among and getting input from all members of the team is invaluable.

Pooling of Resources: There are many ways to enhance productivity, but many of them are expensive, such as hiring a fully paid assistant, upgrading technology, and purchasing marketing resources. A team can share in these extra expenses. Resource decisions are much easier to make when the team members share the costs.

Better Penetration: Better account penetration can occur, especially when one or more of the advisors on a team has a mature business. I have seen several examples of two senior advisors joining together and finding opportunities in each other's business that would not have been discovered otherwise. Better account penetration also can result when a senior advisor turns over her inactive or smaller accounts to a junior partner. In many cases the junior partner will find new assets and generate more business just because he is paying more attention to these relationships. An example of this is when a new advisor joins a senior advisor and completes a financial plan for every account assigned to him; the junior partner often finds significant new assets as a result. Another example is a team in which a partner brings a particular expertise to the team and uncovers opportunities that an advisor without that kind of expertise could never find.

Of course, there are also pitfalls when working in teams:

There Must Be a Good Fit: While the benefits of being on a team are numerous, the team will work only if there is a good fit between team members. In a team that has a good fit, the phrase "One plus one equals three" is true. Too often, however, advisors join or form a team as a way to increase productivity without thinking about team fit or synergy. Teams don't automatically increase productivity; if the fit is not good or synergy doesn't take place, or if team members don't have common professional values, teaming can actually hurt productivity. In that case, "One plus one equals one." It takes time to put a team together, to have team meetings, to measure results, and so on. If productivity is not higher, then all of this is a waste of time.

Hiding Behind the Efforts of Others: I have seen situations where a team did less business than the advisors had done on their own. This generally occurs when one of the team members hides behind administrative duties, relying on the other team members to do the work. This is why accountability is so important.

TYPES OF TEAMS

The majority of successful teams that I have observed fall into one or more of four general categories: 1. Specialization, 2. Inside and outside, 3. Vertical (or superstar), 4. Junior and senior.

Specialization

In this kind of team, each member brings an area of specialization or expertise that is different from those of the other team members. When the team works with clients and prospects, different team members are brought in as their expertise is needed. Examples of such areas of expertise are insurance and estate planning, retirement planning, investment planning, liabilities, and corporate services. These teams generally do well because the value of each team member is apparent, and each can be paid based on the additional products and services she provides to clients. This structure also gives the team the opportunity to differentiate itself because of its depth and its wide range of expertise.

Inside and Outside

In this structure, there is an outside advisor, who is primarily responsible for marketing and building new relationships, and an inside advisor, who manages the portfolios and handles the administrative and operational aspects of the team. The outside advisor can market the inside advisor's expertise. If the senior advisor has strong marketing and relationship skills, he will be the outside advisor; the outside (senior) advisor describes the wealth-management process, while the inside (junior) advisor implements the strategy and supports the outside (senior) advisor. In other cases, a junior partner will be the outside partner, marketing the experience and skills of the senior partner. The senior inside partner is brought in after the first appointment. The advantage of this partnership is that marketing, portfolio management, and organization can require different skill sets, and by consolidating them through a partnership, great synergy can occur.

Vertical

The vertical structure is sometimes described as the "superstar" structure. This type of team is completely centered on one very successful advisor. This advisor has it all: She is a great marketer and has a strong wealth-management process, and all she needs is administrative support to handle the details of the practice. All business goes through the superstar, and that person pays to have the high-quality support she needs to support her productivity. Some of the most productive teams I have ever worked with are organized in this fashion. This structure allows great talent to flourish by enabling the superstar to spend all her time doing what she does best without being distracted by the daily operational, administrative, or money-management aspects of the business.

Junior and Senior

The junior and senior team structure is essentially a succession-plan structure: The senior advisor wants to ensure that when he retires, the practice will remain intact and the clients will be managed by the junior partner. These partnerships can go on for years, with the junior partner apprenticing, in effect, to eventually take over the business. Often the junior partner's split eventually increases to 50–50, and in some cases it grows to majority ownership. This team structure can provide high levels of commitment for two reasons: First, since the senior partner typically selects the junior partner, the senior partner has a real commitment to the junior partner's success; and second, the junior partner is committed to the partnership long-term because of the big payoff that comes when the senior partner retires. The clients appreciate the orderly succession plan, and the senior partner can stay in practice longer because she can spend less time at it while the clients are being well serviced by her successor. In many cases this junior and senior partnership involves family members, with the senior advisor bringing in one of his or her children to eventually take over the practice. (A senior advisor looking for a junior advisor to help her bring in new assets or generate more business from her smaller accounts should, in most cases, look for a new advisor with proven marketing and business skills, not an unproven advisor who might look good on paper but does not have the results or the experience.)

BLENDS

The four categories of teams are not always pure, and in some cases there are combinations and blends of more than one category within one team. The purpose of outlining these four is to give you examples of how successful teams can be structured and to encourage you to think through which arrangement will suit you best.

FORMING AND STRENGTHENING A SUCCESSFUL TEAM

There are two parts to the life of a team: forming it and strengthening it after it has been formed. When you form a team (or explore joining one), you need to:

+ Assess your weaknesses and strengths.
+ Ensure that there is a good fit.
+ Try it out first.
+ Have a plan for dissolution.
+ Be definite about fair compensation.

Strengthening a team that has already been formed requires a different set of activities. You must:

+ Align values.
+ Share a vision.
+ Promote good communication.
+ Build in measurement and accountability.

FORMING A TEAM

Assess Your Weaknesses and Strengths

There are advisors who would like to be part of a team but do not know where to start. The place to start is to do an honest assessment of your strengths and weaknesses. Your strengths are what you can offer a team, and your weaknesses are what you need from a team—often teams form so that one member's strengths fill in another member's weaknesses. An example of this might be two advisors, one who has excellent organizational skills, portfolio management experience, and the ability to generate business, and another who has excellent marketing skills but who might not have the time or interest to manage the assets or to provide the required service once the prospect is brought in.

Ensure That There Is a Good Fit

Fit is more important than which type of team you form or join. The best fit among team members occurs when:

- The advisors' professional values are aligned.
- The advisors' goals are similar.
- There is a high level of commitment of time and energy.
- There is willingness to be accountable.
- There is a high level of professional respect.
- The members' skills complement each other.

This list is not all-inclusive, but it outlines the characteristics of the best teams I have observed. Many teams may have some combination of these elements, and I have not found that any one of them is more responsible for a team's success than the others.

Try It Out First

Joining or forming a team is like a professional marriage and should be taken just as seriously. Start by forming a "situational team." A situational team is one in which the advisors come together to undertake a particular marketing activity and split the business that comes from it. This allows team members to professionally "date" before they form a team to determine whether a permanent team is appropriate. Some examples are:

- Putting on a joint seminar.
- Inviting an advisor with a particular expertise to help close a prospect.
- A junior advisor inviting a senior advisor with strong presentation skills and experience to close a prospect.
- A senior advisor identifying a talented new advisor who may be a potential partner and offering him all her resources, with the understanding that the junior advisor will include the senior advisor in most of his prospecting and split the new business 50–50. The case for this approach is that the new advisor will bring in more business with the senior advisor's help than he could on his own, and the senior advisor will be exposed to more opportunities than she would have on her own.

Have a Plan for Dissolution

A team needs to determine in advance what will happen if the team dissolves. The breakup of a team can be very emotional, and the breakup is not the time to make decisions about who gets what.

Be Definite About Fair Compensation

Team compensation should start with all members receiving what they originally brought to the team. For example, if an $800,000 senior advisor joins with an advisor doing $200,000, the combined business should be split 80–20 as a baseline. All new business above that baseline, however, could be split differently. In this example, whichever advisor brings in the new business should have fees split in his favor. The same is true for the advisor who adds secondary products and services to an existing client of another team member. A variation of these ideas is two advisors who team and split the business initially based on what each brought to the partnership, then split all new business 50–50 no matter who is responsible for it. The idea is that over time, each advisor will get an equal share of the business. I have seen endless variations of compensation splits. I believe the best splits are simple and fair to all team members with generous incentives for team growth.

HOW TO STRENGTHEN A TEAM ONCE IT HAS BEEN FORMED

Once you join or form a team, you need to strengthen it. There have been many books written about building teamwork, but these are basic elements I have seen that make the most difference.

Align Professional Values

Having similar values will strengthen a team. Examples of values include work ethic, shared vision and goals, compensation of support staff, communication, and investment philosophy.

Share a Vision

The best teams develop a vision for the team and work every day toward the achievement of that vision. Most advisors are motivated by more than just compensation, and the achievement of a common vision can be a very powerful motivator. It also puts the team in a proactive rather than a reactive mode. The best teams are those whose members are committed to the growth of the team, with each member being willing to commit a lot of energy to the team's success.

Promote Good Communication

Good communication is essential to a team's success. As in any relationship, good communication overcomes most problems. The team should encourage communication by all team members and provide opportunities for team members to share their opinions on how to make the team better. One of the greatest benefits of a team is the ideas and creativity that can result when the team members are all motivated to improve the team. All team members should have the opportunity to review and give input regarding all aspects of the team's activities.

Build In Measurement and Accountability

Every team member should be held accountable for her responsibilities, and team meetings should be held to review accountability. These meetings motivate all the members to excel so they can proudly share their results at team meetings. The frequency of these team meetings should be weekly. I suggest having an agenda with one of the team members responsible for keeping time and making sure the meeting stays on track. Many teams have short daily meetings (fifteen to thirty minutes) to review the day, assign tasks, and follow up on outstanding items.

Fair Compensation

All members of the team including support staff need to feel they are fairly compensated for their work and loyalty. The best teams are generous with compensation for committed, loyal, and productive team members. The value to a team of a motivated, positive, loyal, and highly competent team member is priceless.

EXAMPLES OF SUCCESSFUL TEAMS

The first example is of a vertical team where the senior advisor was a superstar and built a team that supported him. All the business the team generated went through the senior advisor. He paid team members based on what he perceived their value to the team's business to be. The senior advisor spent 100 percent of his time building new relationships and maintaining relationships with his most affluent clients. He was involved extensively in high-profile community activities and, as a result, was considered one of the "movers and shakers" of the city in which he was based. He had deep relationships with many CEOs of public companies and was an advisor to many of the entrepreneurs in this market. His team was built to support these relationships. The team had a process for investing money and providing very high levels of service to these affluent clients. Responsibility for servicing the most affluent clients was assigned to a team member. The senior advisor seldom discussed specific investments with his clients; he delegated the wealth-management process to his team. His role evolved into being a family office for the most affluent investors in this marketplace. This team generated $10 million-plus in business per year.

The second example is a combination of a junior and senior team and an inside and outside team. The senior advisor had been in business for thirty years and specialized in portfolio management. A second partner was added to the team to help develop relationships that the senior partner did not have time for. The second partner was primarily involved in client relationships and portfolio management. Five years later, the team added two junior advisors who had a proven marketing process and results, with the intention of using their marketing expertise to get the senior advisors in front of new prospects. The senior advisors had the investment expertise but needed someone to market their expertise, which the junior advisors could do effectively. The team also added a new member to oversee and develop the team's smaller accounts. Not only has this team's business grown, but there is a strong succession plan for when the senior advisor retires. This team generated $3 million in business per year.

Another example involves two senior advisors, one of whom specialized in portfolio management and one of whom specialized in marketing. The portfolio manager had the credentials, expertise, and experience to put him among the best in his market. He was a good investment manager and had excellent presentation skills. The marketing advisor spent 100 percent of her time finding opportunities for the other partner to be in front of new affluent prospects worth $5 million or more. The marketing advisor looked for other advisors in the firm who might need the team's expertise, spent a good deal of time working with influencers who could refer business to the team, and marketed the team's world-class wealth-management process to different distribution channels and individuals. This team also had a business manager who was responsible for providing first-class customer service and for handling all administrative and operational aspects of the team. This team generated $3 million in business per year, and since its formation its business has grown at 25 percent per year.

Another example is a team with two senior advisors who had two different skill sets. One had a very conservative practice with a large asset base and a relatively low return rate on his assets (ROA). The other partner had fewer assets but a higher ROA. The partner with the higher ROA was an idea machine, always coming up with new ideas for his clients. The higher ROA advisor found ways that the other advisor had never thought of to do more business with the combined practice. The more conservative advisor provided a level of experience and expertise in lower-risk investments that the other advisor did not have. The result was a velocity increase for the consolidated practice and an overall growth rate of more than 20 percent per year. This team does $2.5 million in business per year.

Still another example involved a senior advisor and a junior advisor. The senior advisor had a mature practice, but he was still highly motivated to grow. He brought in a junior advisor he had known for a long time and in whom he had a great deal of confidence. The junior advisor now spends 80 percent of his time marketing for the team and 20 percent of his time working with the senior advisor's smaller accounts. The senior advisor continues to work with his largest relationships and spends 20 percent of his time supporting the junior advisor's marketing efforts and doing joint marketing activities with him. A third advisor works with the smallest accounts and sets up the presentation and seminar logistics for the team, which is its primary marketing method. Not only has the senior advisor's business grown as a result of adding the two junior advisors, but an excellent succession plan is in place. This team does $1 million in business per year.

The last example involves a senior advisor and a junior advisor. The senior advisor was a good portfolio manager and an excellent marketer. The junior advisor had had some success in marketing, but she enjoyed the analytical and client relationship aspects of the business. The senior advisor trained the junior advisor to run the portfolios and support his marketing efforts. The senior advisor now spends the majority of his time marketing to his target market of $5 million-plus investors. The junior advisor runs the portfolio, looks for money-in-motion leads to give to the senior advisor, and helps the senior advisor prepare for presentations and meetings held with prospects. This team generates more than $1 million in business a year.

Advisors who are part of a good team are more productive than those who are sole practitioners. This observation is validated by the testimony of members of productive teams; these advisors can be zealots in support of the team concept. As productive as a good team can be, however, there are many factors that must come together to make a team successful. It is not an easy process and it requires a high level of ongoing commitment, but the results are well worth the time and effort. Being a member of a productive team with shared goals and values is as good as it gets in financial services.

As I have said all along, at least a third of your one hundred relationships need to be $1 million-plus. These clients are difficult to get because everyone wants them. But you can get them if you understand how they think, which is what I will discuss in the next chapter.

SUMMARY

+ Advisors who are members of a team generally are more productive than those who are sole practitioners.

+ The key to a successful team is having a good fit and shared values among the team members.

+ Situational teaming has many advantages. It allows an inexperienced advisor to leverage the expertise, resources, and experience of a senior advisor. It also gives the potential team the opportunity to work together before formalizing a partnership.

+ Teaming can be beneficial in allowing better penetration of accounts through added expertise, different perspectives, and better development of smaller accounts. This can lead to a higher velocity rate for a mature practice.

+ Fair team compensation is essential for a productive team. All members of the team need to feel that they are fairly compensated for their work and that they have the opportunity to grow as the team grows.

+ In looking for potential team members, an advisor should do an honest assessment of his own strengths and weaknesses and look for other team members who could benefit from his strengths and help with his weaknesses.

+ All team members must be accountable and have a forum for regular communication.

+ The elements that most successful teams share are aligned values, vision, frequent communication, fair and generous compensation, and accountability of all team members.

CHAPTER **18**

What Millionaires Need

BUILDING A BUSINESS WITH CLIENTS who have $1 million or more in investable assets is essential to building a million-dollar practice.

This market segment epitomizes the low-percentage/high-payoff dynamic of financial services marketing. This dynamic means that the advisor does not need to acquire many $1 million-plus client relationships each year to have a successful practice, but it can be very challenging to get these clients. Remember that it takes approximately thirty $1 million-plus client relationships to build a million-dollar practice. You should have million-dollar client relationships, but why are they so hard to get?

This is the most competitive market segment, the target of all financial services companies.

♦ The millionaire is desensitized to traditional marketing techniques.

♦ Almost every $1 million-plus prospective client already has an advisor, and that advisor is going to work hard to keep that client.

♦ What you have to do to win million-dollar clients is beyond what many advisors know how, or may be willing, to do.

As challenging as building a practice with $1 million-plus client relationships can be, there is plenty of opportunity to do so. Every year, approximately 15 percent of $1 million-plus investors make a financial advisor change. If there are 10,000 millionaires in your market, this means that every year 1,500 of them will switch advisors. Remember, you need only three or four of these investors each year. If you want to increase your success in acquiring new million-dollar clients, you have to understand how these clients think.

THE MILLIONAIRE MARKET IS DESENSITIZED TO TRADITIONAL MARKETING

So many companies want the business of millionaires that they are bombarded with every kind of marketing imaginable, and they tune it out. The $1 million-plus market has become desensitized to cold calls at home, seminars, dinner invitations, and mailers. These are successful, busy individuals whose time is too valuable for them to be enticed to a seminar by a free dinner. In most cases, people in this market will not even open the envelope from a mailing. Telemarketing to them at home is also a complete waste of time because the majority of them are on the "do not call" (DNC) list, and those who are not are trying to figure out how to get on it. The only exception to this is the retiree market. You can have some measure of success if you identify retirees who have $1 million or more, particularly in older neighborhoods, who might be called less and are not on the DNC list, and invite them to an age-appropriate seminar. While cold-calling millionaires at home is not effective, contacting them at work can be, as long as you have researched each contact to determine how you can provide value to that individual and have the expertise and experience to help them (niche marketing) You must understand this if you are going to effectively acquire $1 million-plus clients.

REACH THEM THROUGH SOMEONE ELSE

If a millionaire is not satisfied with her current advisor, she has many friends and other advisors she trusts who can introduce her to a proven financial advisor. A millionaire does not need to look at an advisor who is unknown. In many cases, the millionaire client may not actually be dissatisfied with her current advisor but is open to alternatives; in fact, this is likely to be the case.

The most effective way to market to millionaires is through referrals from other clients, networking, personal contacts, or referrals from the millionaire's other advisors (such as CPAs, attorneys, Realtors, and business brokers). The objective is to get the opportunity to meet millionaires through someone else.

To be effective in marketing to millionaires, you should include at least these three marketing ideas:

1. An organized, proactive referral process from existing clients (see Chapter 12)

2. Access through influencers—the client's advisors, such as CPAs and attorneys (see Chapter 12)
3. Exposure to millionaires through their outside interests—organizations, social events, or outside activities (see Chapter 14)

Thomas Stanley says in *The Millionaire Mind* that the majority of America's millionaires are business owners (32 percent), corporate executives (16 percent), attorneys (10 percent), and professionals (medical, legal, and sales) (9 percent). These are the niche markets you should focus on. These strategies are not the only way to get in front of the millionaire market, but in most cases they are the most effective.

PROVE YOU ARE BETTER

Once you meet with the millionaire investor and go through the fact-finding process, you must be able to prove that the investor would be better off with you. You must be able to demonstrate that you will serve his needs better; you must prove yourself through your actions, not your words. It takes patience and time, but the reward is worth it; remember that it takes only thirty $1 million-plus client relationships to build a million-dollar practice.

Most, if not all, of the things you must do to prove yourself to a millionaire prospect and make her a client are also things you must continue to do to keep her as a client. In other words, master the methods for acquiring $1 million-plus clients, and you will have mastered the things that will retain them. These are:

♦ Demonstrated professionalism, expertise, and confidence.
♦ Very high levels of service.
♦ A well-thought-out wealth-management process you can clearly articulate and execute.

Demonstrated Professionalism, Expertise, and Confidence

Professionalism and expertise are among the qualities that millionaires want most. This expertise can be shown by an industry-accepted professional designation like CFP or CIMA. This distinguishes you as an advisor from most others and is a concrete example to the affluent investor of your commit-

ment to your professionalism and expertise. These designations and credentials are not required, but they add to your credibility.

One of the most compelling marketing statements you can make to a
prospective million-dollar client regarding your expertise is:

> "Mr./Ms. Client, I have made a real commitment to my professional-
> ism and expertise by studying for and passing my Certified Financial
> Planning Examination. In making a comparison between me and
> your current advisor, I would ask you to ask him or her if he or she
> has made the same commitment."

Generally, the more money an investor has, the more sophisticated he is.
The days of "salesmanship" and "product selling" are over. These tactics
have given the financial services industry a black eye, and million-dollar
investors are wary of advisors who appear to be salespeople.
Professionalism and expertise are the most valuable commodities today.
Million-dollar clients are attracted to advisors who take the time to understand their situation and what is important to them and who have the
expertise to provide solutions to meet their goals.

Very High Levels of Service

If you want to attract millionaire clients and keep them, you need to provide
consistently superior service. Millionaires are "spoiled" in many ways
because they are so sought after. People in this market are used to receiving
excellent service in all aspects of their life. They know the difference between
good service and outstanding service, and they expect the best. The advisor
who wants to build a million-dollar practice must have a very high-level
service process:

+ Work with only a limited number of affluent clients.
+ Contact your clients at least monthly.
+ Resolve client problems quickly through your client associate.
+ Make sure each client is satisfied by having your client associate provide
  "high touch" and proactive service.

Newer advisors with scant client associate coverage may need to take on
these tasks themselves, staying close to their million-dollar clients and
ensuring that their needs are being taken care of.

Millionaire clients expect to develop a relationship with their advisor.

The advisor needs to look at these clients as more than just clients and must be willing to commit time to developing these relationships. Being attuned to the client's personal life can be just as important as understanding her investments.

The best advisors commit to building personal relationships with their clients by spending time on outside activities in which the advisor and the client may have a mutual interest (golf, fly fishing, hunting, or cooking, for example); by meeting the client's children; by attending important life events like marriages, funerals, and visits to the hospital; and by going to dinner.

The most successful advisors I have worked with provide a "family office" to their very best clients. These advisors are trusted counselors in every area of the client's life, not just financial matters. They have proven providers of almost every kind they can refer their clients to. This offers wonderful networking opportunities as well. The advisor who is committed to working with millionaire clients must understand that the relationship is as important as the investments.

A WELL-THOUGHT-OUT WEALTH-MANAGEMENT PROCESS

Having a proven, well-thought-out wealth-management process that is tailored to the individual's financial needs and goals is a valued commodity to most millionaire clients. To attract and keep the millionaire market, however, not only must you have a well-thought-out wealth-management process, but you must be able to explain it articulately and clearly.

Millionaire investors expect leadership from you. They expect you to have so much experience and expertise in this process that you exude confidence. By nature, investing has an uncertain outcome, but the successful advisor who has built a process that minimizes risk while providing competitive returns is very appealing to this market. The more convinced you are that your process of investing money is the right one, the more attractive you will be to the millionaire prospect. The most successful advisors I have worked with are those who were most confident about their wealth-management process.

Millionaire investors are interested in five key financial areas. If your wealth-management process meets their goals in these areas, you are likely to attract and keep millionaire clients. The areas are:

1. Preservation of assets and reasonable returns
2. Competitive and transparent fees
3. A long-term financial plan
4. Performance monitoring
5. A simplified financial life

Preservation of Assets and Reasonable Returns

If you want to attract and retain clients in this market segment, you need to have a wealth-management process built around these clients' conservative investing style. The majority of millionaires have made their money already and their highest priority is to preserve it while having reasonable growth. Many millionaires are in their late fifties and sixties and do not have time to rebuild their portfolios; they want to keep what they have and stay ahead of inflation.

Their portfolios need to have the correct asset allocation for their level of risk tolerance and must be well diversified and conservative. You must meet with these clients regularly (at least quarterly) to review the performance of their portfolio, to remind them of their investment objectives, and to remind them of what a reasonable return is given their risk tolerance.

It is appropriate to allocate a small percentage of the portfolio to a more aggressive position. Examples of this may include private equity, hedge funds, and managed futures. Generally, these investments are well-diversified and can add growth to the portfolio by being noncorrelated assets. The key concept in making this work is allocating only a small percentage of the portfolio to these more aggressive investments.

Competitive Management Fees

The $1 million-plus market is very competitive, and while the lowest-cost provider will not always win, the millionaire client needs to feel that she is getting a good value.

Since the measure of a portfolio's performance takes into account the fees to manage it, management fees can affect performance. It is hard to consistently generate double-digit returns if you are managing a large portfolio conservatively. Keeping this in mind, every 25 basis points makes a difference, and to achieve acceptable performance, you have to price the management of the investments competitively. In today's environment, it would be hard to justify charging a $1 million-plus relationship more than 1.5 percent for a blended portfolio; 1 percent or less would be more in line, depending on how many total assets they have with you. Just as important as the fee is the transparency of pricing ensuring that your clients know exactly how much they are paying for your advice.

The key to generating more business from these relationships is to expand wallet share through appropriate products and services. By broadening the relationship through liability products, insurance products, estate planning, and trust services, you can increase the business these relationships generate without adding to the cost of the portfolio management. These are all areas of the millionaire's financial life that must be addressed. The advisor who recognizes the importance of these needs, develops an expertise in these areas, and incorporates that expertise into his practice will be going a long way toward attracting and retaining the $1 million-plus market segment.

Planning and Wealth Management

The planning and wealth-management process is also an important priority for the $1 million-plus client. Relating an investment strategy to an overall plan is especially important to this segment. It is essential that you take the time to really understand your clients' objectives and emotions as they relate to their investments.

Issues like retirement objectives, real estate purchases, estate planning, risk tolerance, insurance, lending needs, and charitable inclinations are all key factors in developing the kind of business relationship that is required for this segment. The more time you spend on these areas, the better. Studies show that for many millionaires, how the liability side of the balance sheet is managed can be more important than the asset side, and estate planning and insurance are also important to this affluent segment; tax minimization and transfer of assets can be achieved with good estate and insurance planning.

You can differentiate yourself by addressing these areas through the financial plan. Most advisors do not spend enough time up front in the long-term planning process; advisors who do will differentiate themselves in a positive way.

Performance Monitoring

In addition to the plan, you should make monitoring performance periodically (at least quarterly) a high priority. In most cases, the client's satisfaction is related more to being on track with the long-term plan than to absolute return. Periodically reminding clients of performance as it relates to risk and the long-term plan will have a positive impact on satisfaction and retention.

A Simplified Financial Life

Another reason to use a thorough planning process is the millionaire's need to simplify her life. If a millionaire client trusts that you have all the products and services she needs, she will be inclined to simplify her life by working with you as her only advisor. The key to making this happen is to work with the millionaire to develop a detailed plan for reaching her financial and related objectives. The advisor who "owns" the plan will "own" the client. Millionaires tend to be very busy with their professions and their outside interests, and if they can consolidate their mortgage, insurance, banking, and estate planning needs with one trusted advisor who has incorporated all these needs into a long-term plan, why wouldn't they? Having multiple providers all working independently of one another does not make sense. By providing a long-term plan and being the single provider, not only is the advisor building a practice that will attract the millionaire market, he is also building in incremental revenues through a holistic and expansive approach, beyond the fees charged for investment management.

THE OVER $10 MILLION MARKET

Clients and prospects who have more than $10 million in assets require a specialization that the advisor must commit to if he wants to attract these clients and prospects. While the millionaire client requires a high level of service, the decamillionaire requires extraordinary service. Most advisors who specialize in this market must limit their total number of relationships to between twenty-five and fifty. A "high touch" is required, with frequent contact and exceptional administrative and operational service.

You must offer very competitive pricing. This does not mean giving away the business, but the pricing must be competitive for the value received. This market recognizes and appreciates the value of performance and service and is willing to pay for it as long as the price is in a competitive range. You need to have a high level of expertise in trust and estate planning, concentrated stock strategies, and alternative investments. A professional designation, while not required, especially appeals to this group. These people want to work with the very best in the industry.

The bottom line with this market is that it requires specialization and experience with its needs. This cannot be done part time; if you cannot commit to building your business around the decamillionaire, you are better off partnering with another advisor who can. You may have the contact and the relationship, but not the specialization. In that case, you should situationally team with someone who is committed exclusively to this market (this is a form of subcontracting). Properly managed, the amount of business a decamillionaire can generate is enough to split and still be very profitable.

In my experience, if an advisor who doesn't specialize in decamillionaires acquires one, in many cases the relationship will eventually be lost. This is the most competitive market in financial services, and if the advisor does not have this specialization, it will be only a matter of time before someone who does will make inroads into the relationship and lure the account away. This is a highly specialized market with very specific requirements. Do not try to beat the specialists if you are not one yourself; rather, join them through situational partnering. The $10 million-plus market is lucrative and is a competitive market segment, but if the advisor understands what appeals to this market and builds his practice around these needs, he will be able to attract and retain the $10 million-plus market. This market requires extra work and a longer lead time, but the advisor needs to add only one or two new $10 million-plus relationships a year to build a million-dollar practice over a reasonable time.

If you follow these strategies and have at least thirty $1 million-plus relationships, you will eventually reach the goal of a million-dollar practice. But that is not the end of the road. What comes after that? Read Chapter 19 to find out.

SUMMARY

+ This market is desensitized to the traditional marketing techniques of mailings, cold calls at home, and seminars.
+ Referrals are the most effective marketing approach with millionaires. Referrals from existing clients or influencers (CPAs and attorneys), network sources, personal relationships, and outside activities are the best way to acquire new $1 million-plus clients.

- Service rules. The expectation of service is very high with this group. You must be committed to outstanding service to attract and retain this group.

- The planning and wealth-management process has high appeal to the $1 million-plus segment.

- Professional credentials are important to this segment.

- A conservative investment approach is better than an aggressive approach with this segment.

- Performance and fees are important because of the competition that exists for this segment.

- Insurance, estate planning, alternative investments, and lending are important priorities for this market and provide opportunities for add-on business.

- The advisor must provide strong leadership to the millionaire market. This leadership should be the result of expertise and experience and a well-thought-out wealth-management process.

- Investing in personal relationships should be a high priority for advisors who have $1 million-plus clients.

- Specialization is the key to building a practice that will attract and retain decamillionaires.

CHAPTER 19

Beyond a Million-Dollar Practice

ACHIEVING A MILLION-DOLLAR PRACTICE IN FINANCIAL SERVICES is the standard of success that most advisors measure themselves against. Less than 1 percent of all registered representatives ever build a million-dollar practice. Once you have reached the million-dollar level and have taken the appropriate amount of time to celebrate, however, the obvious question is: What's next? The answer should be another question: What does it take to become a multimillion-dollar producer?

In my experience as a manager and professional coach, I have worked with dozens of advisors who built a multimillion-dollar practice. Of the multimillion-dollar producers, there are a number of them who stood out as best practitioners. A number of these advisors produced more than $3 million in business and managed an average of more than $1 billion in assets, with an average length of service of twenty years. This translates into at least $50 million in new assets per year. One of these top advisors stood out in particular as being extraordinary in his practice management and subsequently his results. This advisor produced more than $10 million in business in each of the four years that I worked with him; in his biggest year, he did $15 million in business.

As challenging as this may appear, these concepts and processes will result in a multimillion-dollar practice no matter where you are located. These advisors' approach and style in building a multimillion-dollar practice varied, but there were also many traits and characteristics that all of them had in common. This chapter is about those common traits and characteristics.

For most advisors, building a multimillion-dollar business is uncharted territory, as there are so few people in the industry who ever achieve this level. Those who do are generally too busy and too competitive to share their practices. I believe that the common traits and practices of these advisors can serve as a roadmap for those who aspire to build a multimillion-dollar practice. I will cover two areas:

1. Business practices of the multimillion-dollar advisor
2. Personal traits of the multimillion-dollar advisor

BUSINESS PRACTICES OF THE MULTIMILLION-DOLLAR ADVISOR

If I had to summarize what it takes to build a multimillion-dollar practice, I would say that it takes everything that is required to build a million-dollar practice, but more of it and done better. All the principles I have already covered in this book apply, except that the energy and execution need to be at a higher level. This deeper commitment is manifested in six areas:

1. Bigger relationships
2. Extraordinary service
3. Stronger relationship focus
4. A team business structure
5. Willingness to invest in one's own practice
6. Stronger marketing focus

Bigger Relationships

What separates multimillion-dollar advisors from million-dollar advisors is primarily the size of the relationships that multimillion-dollar advisors work with: They work with wealthier individuals. A multimillion-dollar advisor should have between fifty and one hundred relationships, with each of these relationships having a minimum of $1 million invested with the advisor. The leverage in a financial services practice is the size of the relationships that the financial advisor works with. It doesn't take any more time to invest $1 million for a client as it does $100,000, but the advisor gets paid ten times as much. Multimillion-dollar advisors realize they can't double their hours to double their business, but they can double the size of their average client. These top advisors don't work with more clients, but they work with more affluent clients than advisors who aren't as successful.

In order to reach the multimillion-dollar level, your goal should be to add at least $25 million in assets each year. You can reach a multimillion-dollar practice and not add assets at this rate, but the $25 million per year is the pace you should strive to reach.

Extraordinary Service

When the majority of your client relationships are $1 million-plus, there is little room for error. The bigger the client, the higher the expectations. These clients are the target of every financial services firm and are prospected constantly. Outstanding marketing brings these clients in, and outstanding service keeps them. Superb service is a prerequisite for adding a net $25 million in assets per year; it is so much easier to grow your assets if you are not losing clients.

Extraordinary service takes outstanding service to the next level. Both you and your client associate must take the time and make the commitment to provide this level of service. Multimillion-dollar clients are the most sought-after segment of the financial services market; the competition for these clients is fierce, and they are being recruited every day. They must receive high-touch, extraordinary service, or they will move to competitors who will provide it.

In many ways, service becomes the differentiating point among advisors. In most cases, performance is a commodity; in a well-diversified, properly allocated portfolio, the differences in returns are not significant. The bottom line is how the client feels about his financial services experience. All the principles I covered in Chapter 15 apply; the difference is that both the advisor and the client associate must take the time and make the commitment to contact clients more frequently, be more proactive with service calls, and have a flawless problem-resolution process. This requires more time and, as a result, fewer relationships.

Having fewer relationships will not hinder you if the relationships you have are all more than $1 million. An example is an advisor who does $4 million in business with thirty total relationships, none of which has less than $10 million in assets. Another example is an advisor who consistently did more than $10 million in annual business who worked only with clients with more than $100 million in assets—he had only fifteen relationships he worked with directly. Having a small number of relationships does not mean that you will do a multimillion-dollar business, but having a small number of very wealthy relationships does.

Every market in the United States has enough million-dollar households that you will never run out of million-dollar prospects to contact.

Good advisors will always get more than their fair share of these prospects if they put themselves in front of them. The number of million-dollar households in the United States is growing so quickly that the number you acquire this year will be replaced by at least that many new ones next year. Besides, more than 15 percent of million-dollar investors make an advisor change every year.

Stronger Relationship Focus

Multimillion-dollar advisors recognize that relationships with affluent clients and prospects are their number one priority. They realize that relationship building is one of the most important factors in attracting and retaining million-dollar clients, and this shows in how they allocate their time—they do the things that their best clients and prospects do. They even build their personal lives around their clients' interests; that is often how they meet their clients. Some examples:

+ One advisor acquired a billion-dollar relationship through Ducks Unlimited and a common interest in duck hunting.

+ Another advisor developed the majority of his relationships through a prestigious country club he belongs to—he played golf every Friday with a rotating, regular group of four foursomes consisting of some of the wealthiest investors in his market (they all eventually did business with him, although it took time).

+ Another advisor plays chess with his largest relationship every week. The advisor had never played chess before he met this client, but he has become very good at it.

+ Another advisor had a number of clients and prospects who had their own airplanes. In order to be in the same circle, he bought a plane before he had a pilot's license, and it wasn't long before he had his license and was inviting clients and prospects to fly with him, instead of his prospects and clients inviting him to fly with them.

+ One advisor hosts intimate, first-class dinners at his home every month and sometimes every week, with fine food and wine; there are typically eight or fewer guests, usually two client couples and two prospective client couples, along with his wife and himself.

These shared interests draw clients, prospects, and advisors together in ways that allow them to simply enjoy spending time with each other. These advisors enjoy spending time with clients and prospects; they do not consider this work, they consider it fun. They have developed excellent interpersonal skills, are good listeners, and focus on the needs of their clients and prospects rather than on their own.

Multimillion-dollar advisors are with their clients and prospects all the time; they delegate everything else to their team. These advisors are aware of the outstanding-service issues and have built a wealth-management process that enables them to have the time to dedicate to their highly affluent clients. They delegate these tasks to high-quality, well-trained members of their team so that they can spend the majority of their time with clients and developing relationships with new ones.

A Team Business Structure

The multimillion-dollar advisor's team plays a critical role in her success. Every multimillion-dollar advisor I have worked with has had a strong team behind her to support her business. Most of these multimillion-dollar teams are vertically organized behind the multimillion-dollar advisor: The multimillion-dollar advisor is the "superstar," and the role of the team is to support her efforts. These advisors build their teams around themselves vertically to support their talent.

The multimillion-dollar advisor is primarily responsible for setting up the wealth-management process, but once it is set up, she spends the majority of her time on the marketing and relationship side of the business. The team handles all the administrative elements, the client service, and the mechanics of investments. This enables the top advisor to spend her time doing what she does best, finding new affluent prospects and building stronger relationships with existing clients.

The majority of these multimillion-dollar teams have loyal, long-term team members. The advisor recognizes the value of effective team members and provides a high level of recognition and compensation. One advisor I know of pays his senior team member (who does not have an advisor number) $1 million each year (the advisor makes more than $5 million). It is not uncommon for these multimillion-dollar advisors to have the same team members for ten years or more.

Sometimes these advisors have junior advisors who have a smaller percentage of the practice. In most cases, this is a succession-planning team blended with the superstar structure—the multimillion-dollar advisor is grooming a younger advisor to eventually take over the practice when the senior advisor retires.

Willingness to Invest in One's Own Practice

These advisors never wait for the firm to give them money. They do what they need to do to make their plan work. If they need another team member, they pay for it themselves. If they need an airplane, they buy one and pay for the fuel themselves. Their client events are always first-class and cost a lot of money, but they pay for the events whether or not the firm reimburses them. They belong to the most prestigious nonprofit boards in their communities and are willing to make the donations required to secure a board position. They often belong to the best country clubs and then become leaders within their clubs. They look at this as reinvesting retained earnings in their practice.

Stronger Marketing Focus

The multimillion-dollar advisors I have worked with market all the time. They market and think about marketing more than advisors who don't do their level of business. They have learned that consistent marketing is the key to consistent growth, and they have developed marketing activities and processes that work for them. These marketing activities do not generally involve the traditional marketing techniques of cold calling, seminars, and mailings. The majority of the marketing activities used by multimillion-dollar advisors are of the following seven types:

1. Influencers and client referrals
2. Internal marketing (situational partnering)
3. Client and prospect entertaining
4. Membership marketing
5. Philanthropic marketing
6. Pathing
7. Rolodex marketing

Influencers and Client Referrals

Multimillion-dollar advisors all have a network of influencers (CPAs and attorneys) who refer clients to them and have a systematic process for getting referrals from clients. This is a necessity, since the majority of $1 million-plus investors get their financial advisors either through another advisor or an influencer, or from their friends (who are also $1 million-plus investors).

Multimillion-dollar advisors are especially good at getting referrals from clients and influencers.

To reach the multimillion-dollar level, you must have outstanding service, good relationship skills, and a successful wealth-management process. All these elements together produce a favorable experience for most clients, which means that they are willing, almost eager, to give you referrals. Also, multimillion-dollar advisors are leaders and are confident of what they offer; they believe that they are the best, and they have no hesitation about asking clients to refer prospective clients to them.

Internal Marketing (Situational Partnering)

Multimillion-dollar advisors have a high level of expertise and experience. They have confidence in themselves, and they market themselves internally within their firm; many advisors have gaps in their own skill set that the multimillion-dollar advisor can fill. This can be especially true of less experienced advisors, who can uncover prospects but lack the ability to close them. Leveraging the contacts and efforts of other advisors can put the multimillion-dollar advisor in front of many more qualified prospects than he could find on his own. This is profitable, even if they split the business. I know multimillion-dollar advisors who have grown their business by as much as 20 percent per year through an organized internal marketing process.

Client and Prospect Entertaining

Client entertaining is something all multimillion-dollar advisors do. The types of entertaining they do can be very different, but what they have in common is that they all do it. In many cases, their clients have become their friends, so this kind of entertaining comes naturally and can be fun. Of course, they encourage their clients' friends to join them. These client entertainment events are small and intimate, so that maximum relationship leverage takes place. Because friends of affluent clients are generally also affluent, it is not necessary to have many prospects present for the marketing to be successful. These events not only provide great introduction opportunities for prospects, but they also serve as excellent retention tools for existing clients. Examples of these events include fine dining at the advisor's home, hunting trips (often out of state or out of the country), golf outings, ski trips, fishing trips, spa trips, and shared vacations.

Membership Marketing

Several of the multimillion-dollar advisors I have worked with use memberships at high-profile country clubs as an effective client acquisition platform. These advisors do not openly prospect at the club but become involved in its leadership. The more involved they become, the more $1 million-plus prospects they meet, and they soon became part of the fabric of the club.

These advisors attend all the major events and in many ways build their social life around the country club. This is a relationship business, and being involved with a country club that has affluent members gives an advisor a perfect opportunity to meet and develop relationships with affluent prospects. Business inevitably follows.

Philanthropic Marketing

The most successful advisor I have ever worked with, a decamillion-dollar advisor, was a leader in the most important high-profile philanthropic organizations in his marketplace. As a board member of these organizations, he had the opportunity to meet and develop relationships with the other board members, who were inevitably $1 million-plus investors. This required a major time commitment on his part, but the quality of the prospects he worked with was high, and over time he acquired a good number of his best clients through his philanthropic involvement. If anyone asked the leaders of this community who was a leader in financial services, his name would inevitably come up. His reputation validated the effectiveness of this strategy.

Pathing

Pathing is a marketing technique I have seen several multimillion-dollar advisors use:

1. The advisor identifies key prospects to do business with.
2. By doing some research, the advisor finds out where his target prospects live and which social, philanthropic, and professional organizations they belong to.
3. The advisor determines what people he knows who belong to one or more of the same organizations.
4. The advisor asks one of these people if she would feel comfortable

introducing the prospect to him through some activity that they would have a common interest in. This might be meeting over lunch, playing golf, having dinner, or going to a sporting event.

5. Once the introduction is made and the advisor and prospect have spent some time together, the advisor takes the next step on his own to further develop the relationship with this prospect, which often means inviting the prospect to another activity or event.

6. As the relationship develops, the subject of investments inevitably comes up and the most successful advisors can use this as an opportunity to begin the transition process from the personal to a business relationship. The objective is to over time have a serious discussion of how the advisor can help the affluent individual with her investments. Most millionaires are willing to get a second opinion or advice from another advisor they know and trust.

Rolodex Marketing

For the multimillion-dollar advisor, Rolodex marketing is a combination of many of the other marketing techniques. Being involved in a high-profile country club, taking a leadership role in philanthropic organizations, being involved in social networks, developing a network with influencers—these all lead to meeting affluent investors.

Many of these relationships are interconnected, and that is when it all comes together. Many times the people who are board members of philanthropic organizations also are business leaders, are members of the same country club, and run in the same social circles. These individuals become the core of the advisor's business; they refer other affluent prospects to the advisor, and the circle continues to widen. Those referred know the advisor by reputation and are drawn to him. These interconnections lead to deeper relationships because of common interests and involvement.

The multimillion-dollar advisor becomes part of this group and emerges as one of the community leaders. It takes years to develop this kind of reputation and build these relationships, but once all the pieces come together, a multimillion-dollar practice will result.

PERSONAL TRAITS OF THE MULTIMILLION-DOLLAR ADVISOR

All the multimillion-dollar advisors I work with share certain qualities.

Deep Motivation

These advisors are all high achievers and are goal-oriented. The word *over-achiever* fits every one of them. They are driven to achieve beyond the money they make. Once they have reached a certain level of income, it is all about the achievement; each one of these advisors can tell you where he ranks nationally within his firm or their Barron's ranking in their state and nationally. They have as much passion for their achievement as they do for financial rewards. They value being part of the inner circle of top advisors, and they value being recognized by their senior management, and just as important, by their peers.

This high level of motivation is what fuels them to continue to market no matter how successful they become or how many years they have been in the business.

Process-Oriented

These multimillion-dollar advisors are also very organized; they have developed a process for every aspect of their business. They have a process for wealth management, for client meetings, for presentations. They set up these processes, and their team implements them; the team can generate high-quality marketing presentations literally in minutes. The advisor develops the processes and the business, and the team does the rest.

Client Leadership

These advisors all provide strong leadership to their clients. They are confident of their ability to serve their clients and make them money. They believe strongly that their process for investing money is the best, and that conviction comes across to their clients and prospects. Affluent clients and prospects expect their advisor to know what she is doing, and these multimillion-dollar advisors never hesitate and are always convinced that they can do a better job than anyone else anywhere.

Clear Personal Goals and a Vision for Their Practice

Every multimillion-dollar advisor I have worked with has a clear vision of what his long-term goals are and how he is going to reach them. They break these goals down to annual, monthly, and daily targets and hold themselves accountable to these goals. They also set goals for their activities because they realize that the right activities lead to the right results. These advisors may fine-tune this vision or even change it, but they always have a vision and a plan. They can clearly articulate their market strategy, their business plan, their goals, their service model, their team strategy, and what support they need from management. The visions may vary from advisor to advisor, but they all have a vision, and it is crystal clear.

THE NUMBERS FOR A MULTIMILLION-DOLLAR PRACTICE

Only 5 percent of advisors who are in the business three years or more ever achieve a million-dollar practice, and less than 1 percent ever achieve a multimillion-dollar practice. It takes relentless marketing; a highly organized, process-based business; a strong team; outstanding relationship-building skills; and a high drive to achieve. For the advisor who is committed to achieving a multimillion-dollar practice, there is a high price to pay, but the rewards in terms of recognition and compensation are more than worth the effort for the select few who reach this level of business.

In order to reach the multimillion-dollar level, you should strive to bring in at least $25 million in new assets each year. This means bringing in ten new $1 million-plus relationships each year (includes upgrades).

In order to bring in this $25 million, you should realize that you can reach approximately 50 percent of that goal by bringing in new assets from existing clients. These are the easiest assets to bring in because you already have a trusting relationship with your clients.

Client surveys have consistently shown that most clients have between 50 and 99 percent of their total assets held somewhere other than the institution with which they have their primary relationship. If you have $100 million in assets under management, then your clients probably have at least another $50 million held outside your firm. If you can bring in 25 percent of the assets held elsewhere in a year, you will acquire $12 million in new assets from your existing clients. This is 50 percent of your goal of $25 million per year. You can bring in another 50 percent ($12 million) through the marketing methods that the multimillion-dollar advisors use, described earlier.

To reach the multimillion-dollar level, remember above all that it is the size of your relationships that matters, not the number of them. All the techniques and strategies we have already covered apply to the advisor who wants to reach this level; he just needs to take these techniques and strategies to a higher level, and draw on an even deeper level of motivation.

We have now covered all the elements of building the foundation for a million-dollar practice, what to do with that foundation to actually build that practice, and what to do to go beyond a million-dollar practice. In Part 3, I'll present some of the market action plans you can use to build your million- and multimillion-dollar practice.

SUMMARY

♦ The principles for building a multimillion-dollar practice are the same as those for building a million-dollar practice; they just have to be executed more often and better.

♦ The key in financial services is the size of each relationship. The more affluent your client relationships are, the more business you generate.

♦ High-quality service is essential. You must have or build a strong service model.

♦ The highest priority of multimillion-dollar advisors is building relationships.

♦ A multimillion-dollar practice entails relentless marketing.

♦ All multimillion-dollar advisors I have worked with have a team. These teams are structured vertically, and members of the team are extremely loyal.

♦ The personal characteristics that multimillion-dollar advisors have in common are an achievement orientation, a highly organized and processed-based practice, strong leadership, deep motivation, and a clear vision for their business.

♦ Multimillion-dollar advisors are willing to invest in their own business. They do what they need to do to make their plan work. They look at this as retained earnings to grow their practice.

♦ The majority of the marketing activities used by multimillion-dollar advisors are of the following seven types: influencers and client referrals, internal marketing (situational partnering), client and prospect entertaining, membership marketing, philanthropic marketing, pathing, and Rolodex marketing.

♦ If you have a goal of increasing your assets by $25 million per year, you can meet this goal by bringing in assets your clients hold at other institutions and by implementing the marketing methods described in this chapter. You need to have between sixty and one hundred $1 million-plus clients for a multimillion-dollar practice. You should continue to upgrade these clients, and you should not have more than one hundred relationships in total.

MARKET ACTION PLANS

CHAPTER 20

Seminars

MANY ORGANIZATIONS AND INDIVIDUALS WANT AN EXPERT to explain and interpret the opportunities available in today's market. You can position yourself as that expert if you are proactive in contacting these organizations and groups. Seminars may be one of the most effective market action plan techniques you can use because, done properly, they set you up as being a teacher and authority rather than a salesperson, and this means you will get follow-up appointments more easily than with almost any other marketing technique.

KEY SUCCESS FACTORS

In order to make any seminar work, you must address all three of the following key success factors:

1. **Be knowledgeable and select an appropriate topic.** The topic you select can vary—the subject is not as important as your being knowledgeable and getting in front of the right audience. To come across as an authority, you must know your subject well, which means you need to put in enough time up front to learn your subject.

2. **Prepare.** Prepare not only your talk or class or presentation, but also your target market for that seminar, your contact list, and your contact process. See the individual seminar approaches later in the chapter for specifics.

3. **Follow up.** Your follow-up will determine the ultimate success of your efforts: From the beginning of the seminar, prepare the follow-up. Explain to the people in your audience that rather than giving them infor-

mation they may not be interested in, you would like them to indicate after the seminar what follow-up information they would like from you. Pass out response cards in advance and collect them after the seminar. The same applies to the classes you give. An example of a response card is provided later in this chapter.

Always call the prospect and offer to personally deliver the material she requested, by appointment.

FOUR MARKETS FOR SEMINARS

Here are four groups or markets that you can target with seminars:

1. Ready-made audiences
2. Business owners
3. Companies
4. Retirees

Ready-Made Audiences

As I mentioned, one of the three keys to successful seminars is getting the right audience. The easiest way to get in front of an audience of affluent investors is to approach ready-made audiences. Ready-made audiences are groups of people who already belong to an organization that has regular meetings. Examples of these organizations are business clubs and non-profit organizations, service groups, churches and synagogues, YMCAs/YWCAs, and retirement communities.

Topics for these ready-made audiences could include:

1. The wealth-management process—how to do it right
2. XYZ Financial's view on the current investment environment
3. Behavioral finance—how emotions can adversely effect investors' decisions
4. The pitfalls of investing and how to avoid them
5. Investment basics—the importance of the fundamentals
6. The big three: taxes, inflation, fees, and how to reduce their impact

The following are particularly good ready-made audiences.

Business Clubs and Service and Nonprofit Organizations

Go to the local chamber of commerce and get a list of all the organizations that are in that chamber's region, such as Rotary, Kiwanis, business clubs, garden clubs, and other such organizations. Be sure to get the name of the contact person for each organization (it should be listed with the organization). Call the contact person and offer to do a seminar for his organization at a time convenient to him. Give the contact person a list of topics you could present, but also be open to any investment topics the contact person might want to suggest. Generally, clubs that meet regularly are always looking for interesting speakers at their meetings, and they should be receptive to your offer if you are flexible on your topic.

Churches and Synagogues in Affluent Areas

Most of these churches or synagogues have men's or women's clubs that meet regularly, and these also need interesting programs. Contact the church or synagogue office and find out the contact person for the organizations within the church.

Your Best Prospects' and Clients' Organizations

Ask your best prospects and clients which organizations they belong to and call these organizations with an offer to speak. This is especially effective in the adopt-a-town market action plan (see Chapter 25); being endorsed or invited by an existing member gives you instant credibility. It's also an excellent way to raise community awareness of your presence.

YMCA/YWCA Classes

Contact the local YMCAs or YWCAs in the affluent communities in your market and offer to do a series of classes (usually not more than four) on the basics of investing. The YMCAs/YWCAs offer many classes and are always looking for interesting topics for their members. Conducting one-hour classes is a small time commitment that will get you in front of a group of interested, and often affluent, investors. The same technique can be applied to community colleges offering adult education programs.

Local Businesses

Contact the HR directors at larger companies in your market and offer to do pre-retirement seminars. This should be positioned as a "free benefit" that the company can offer its employees who are retiring within the next five years. Assure the HR contact that your presentations will be generic and not product-specific, and offer to provide her with a preview of your seminar. In the seminar, be sure to cover the importance of developing a long-term plan, the basics of successful investing, how to determine the amount needed to retire, and how investment needs change after retirement.

Business Owners

One of the most successful seminars for business owners I have ever attended was one titled "Maximizing the Value of your Business." In Chapter 26 I have provided the details of how to set this seminar up.

Companies

This approach involves making a strong connection with a Fortune 1000 company located in your market and providing seminars regularly to its employees. Because you are focusing on a single company, it is important to develop an expertise in the company's benefits and retirement plans. These seminars are not connected with the HR department and are held off-site.

The keys to success here are maintaining the consistency of the seminars, setting the dates in advance, and ensuring good attendance at each seminar. Your objective with these seminars is to show that you are an expert. Educate, don't sell.

To begin, you need at least one personal contact within the company, and ideally several (although if you follow the approach I outline here, you will eventually get them). These contacts can be clients, prospects, friends, or individuals you know through them. From your contacts, find out the names of employees who have received awards, have relocated to the area, or have retired. Invite these prospects to the seminar. The ideal prospects for these seminars are those who have at least $250,000 to invest. Ideally, the seminar will attract prospects who work for the same company, who are retiring at about the same time, and who are in the same geographic area.

I recommend that your seminar cover such topics as "Life After ABC Company," "Net Unrealized Appreciation," or "Pros and Cons of Existing Retirement Plans—What They Could Mean to You" or "What Are Your Cash Flow Needs in Retirement and How Much Do You Need to Fund Those Needs." Focus most of the seminar topics on retirement plans. You might also include outside experts to discuss stock options or estate planning.

To have the most impact, these seminars should be presented every two months over a one- to two-year period. Invite all the contacts you have in that company, as well as current clients and prospects and past seminar attendees. E-mailing the invitation to prospective attendees generally produces good results—e-mailing is a quick, fast-response, low-cost way to invite people. Each seminar you give will provide you with more names for your mailing list, and once you have given a number of seminars, you will have built a critical mass of prospects: For larger companies, you could have an e-mail list of hundreds of people to whom you can send invitations. The key to good attendance is building the e-mail list, constantly adding to the list with the objective of building it to over a hundred names. The people on the list will get used to hearing from you, and eventually awareness of you will spread by word of mouth through the company, and it will become easier to add to the list. Constantly upgrade your e-mail invitation list.

Limit the total cost of the seminar to under $500 by offering it at a nice, but not extravagant, hotel. It is sufficient to provide soft drinks (no alcohol) and cheese trays. Arrive an hour in advance of the seminar to prepare and to meet and greet guests. Also plan to stay after the seminar, which is when you are likely to make the best connections.

As the RSVPs begin to arrive, do some research up front to find out as much as you can about each attendee's situation, especially the date she plans to retire, if you can. It is important to confirm positive RSVPs the day before the seminar.

This process should generate an average of fifteen attendees for each seminar. At the beginning of the seminar, hand out a package about your team and include a questionnaire that asks the following:

- The date the attendee is likely to retire
- The names of other colleagues and friends he thinks might be interested in your seminars
- Topics he would be interested in for future seminars

The questionnaire should also:

- Offer a complimentary retirement analysis and consultation
- Include a calendar of future seminars
- Ask for feedback on the seminar (an evaluation form)

Set up the follow-up by having a call to action at the end of the seminar. Position yourself as a resource who can educate. Offer a free retirement analysis. Encourage attendees to agree to a follow-up meeting; it is okay to mention that the price of admission to the seminar is accepting a follow-up call. Another way to set up follow-up contact is to mention that a large-group question-and-answer session on these topics can be uncomfortable, and as a result you will follow up individually to get feedback and answer questions.

The follow-up is the most important part of this process. Many of the attendees will agree to a follow-up meeting. If an attendee did not answer all the questions on the questionnaire, call him to get the missing information. If he does not want a meeting, you should still make the follow-up call to get feedback on the seminar with the idea of making a connection (this should be done very softly). Try to follow up with every attendee, if you can.

Over time, approximately 25 percent of attendees will agree to a follow-up appointment within twelve months of a seminar. If you have an average of fifteen attendees and you hold six seminars a year, you should have about seventy-five attendees a year; if 25 percent of them agree to appointments and 25 percent of these appointments lead to clients, then this process should help you acquire approximately five affluent new clients per year.

Retirees

Generally, retirees have the time to attend seminars and are very interested in investment topics, but they prefer to know the advisor before having an appointment with her. Seminars meet all these needs and are effective with this group. One of the most effective prospecting calls you can make is to call retirees and personally invite them to a seminar tailored to their interests, with a free meal included. In order to stimulate interest, it is key that you make obvious the value that the seminar will have for them. Follow up the call with a written invitation and then a reminder the day before the seminar. Another effective technique with retirees is to contact the recreational directors of retirement communities and assisted living communities (not nursing homes) and offer to provide seminars or a series of classes on investment topics that would be of interest to their residents. (Refer to Chapter 32 for more ideas and information.)

Example: Information Request Response Card.

(front)

☐ Please send me XYZ Financial's most recent economic update research report.

☐ Please send me XYZ Financial's research on the following companies:
_____, _____, _____, _____, _____

☐ Please send me XYZ Financial's report on fixed income opportunities.

☐ Please send me XYZ Financial's report on tax law changes and how they affect investments.

☐ I would like to discuss a cost-free financial plan that XYZ Financial offers.

☐ I would be interested in a complimentary follow-up appointment to review my current investment situation.

(back)

Name _____

Work Address _____

Work Phone Number _____

Home Address _____

Home Phone Number _____

E-mail Address _____

SCRIPTS

Seminars for Clubs or Similar Organizations

"Mr./Ms. Prospect, my name is Joe Advisor, and the reason for my call is that XYZ Financial encourages us to serve the community by providing timely informational talks, and I thought you might be interested in having me give one of these talks at one of your club's meetings. Examples of these talks include [give details], and they generally take twenty to thirty minutes. I can also tailor a talk to your group's needs if you would prefer a different subject. Is this something you would be interested in?"

Seminars for YMCA/YWCA/Adult Education

"Mr./Ms. Program Director, my name is Joe Advisor, and I'm a financial advisor at XYZ Financial. The reason for my call is that I want to offer to do a series of four classes that covers the basics of investments. We have had good feedback from our past classes, and we wondered if you would have an interest in reviewing our course outline and considering us for your program."

Seminar Follow-Up

"Mr./Ms. Prospect, this is Joe Advisor from XYZ Financial. I enjoyed meeting you and talking to your group about investments last week. I am following up on your response card, and I want you to know I have prepared all the information that you requested. I also want to offer to bring it to you personally, as I will be in your area next Thursday. I thought that if I could get a chance to talk with you about your specific situation, I could provide some valuable free advice that could help you, given the volatile investment environment we are in. Would you be available next Thursday for me to spend a few minutes and bring by the information you requested?"

CHAPTER 21

Event Marketing

IN THIS MARKET ACTION PLAN, I cover some of the most fun and effective marketing activities you can carry out: prospect events. Here are the four types that we will talk about:

1. Client appreciation event
2. Client advisory board
3. Lunch roundtable
4. Unique events

Almost all these events depend on your having some clients (and even some prospects and influencers) who are "raving fans" of yours, clients who are especially appreciative of your hard work, expertise, and skill.

CLIENT APPRECIATION EVENT

A client appreciation event is a fun event that is focused on the interests of your best clients; these events should be held monthly. Golfing is a natural venue for the event, but it could also involve fly fishing, wine tasting, or cooking. Invite your best clients and influencers and ask each of them to bring a friend, neighbor, or business associate who would enjoy the event. An excellent source of names is a client who is receptive to providing referrals.

In the case of a golf event, start with registration and follow with a one-hour lesson with the local professionals on chipping, sand shots, putting, and so on. After the lesson, have lunch and give a presentation on a general subject that would have a wide appeal to attendees, with the speaker being the sponsor of the event. The presentation should take no more than thirty minutes and should be followed by five or six five-minute presentations on your approach to the business or some other relevant business topic; you can do these yourself or you can have members of your team do them. End the meeting by thanking the attendees and by telling them that one of the purposes of the event is to grow your clientele, and mention that you could bring value and good performance to new relationships and would appreciate their referrals. Follow the presentation with golf and an awards ceremony.

CLIENT ADVISORY BOARD

This board makes your best clients and centers of influence a part of your acquisition process. Identify your top clients who are also potential centers of influence. Typically you should identify eight to ten clients, but it is also okay to include referral sources that are not clients—limit these to two or three. Send these clients and other referral sources an invitation to become a member of your client advisory board, and invite them to dinner. Send the invitation two to three weeks in advance of the event, and hold these events twice a year. Have someone on your team make a follow-up call within four days of sending the invitation. Make a second follow-up call several days before the dinner as a final reminder.

Hold the dinner in a private room, with a small bar set up in advance for cocktails before dinner. Have cocktails for approximately thirty minutes. Before dinner starts, thank the clients for attending and for agreeing to be part of your advisory board, and introduce your branch manager. The branch manager should make a short presentation endorsing you and setting up the referral process. The sponsor of the dinner (a strategic partner) should also welcome the clients, mention that she is a strategic partner of yours, and endorse you. Having the branch manager attend is not a necessity, but it is a nice addition if you have a manager who is willing; a positive endorsement gives you credibility. After these introductory remarks, begin the process of asking for feedback from the clients. Stimulate the conversation by doing the following:

- Ask what we are doing well.
- Ask what we could do better.
- Ask how we can improve our service.
- Share marketing material and get feedback on it.
- Share marketing ideas and get suggestions for growing the business.

This should end up being an open discussion, with the clients doing most of the talking. It should be informal, not a presentation.

During the course of the dinner meeting, pass out a questionnaire and explain that you will follow up with each client within a week to discuss the questions in more detail. Within a week of the dinner, call each client (or, even better, meet with him) to review the questionnaire, solicit referral names, and discuss next steps. This will result in referrals, excellent feedback, and stronger relationships. The day after the event, send a personal hand-written thank-you to each participant.

I recommend that you invite this same group to at least two of these advisory group dinners per year. It is not necessary to have your branch manager involved after the initial meeting of each group.

Script for Following Up on the Invitation

"Hi, this is [name] calling from [team/office name] at XYZ Financial. I just wanted to call and follow up on the invitation we sent you last week regarding our client advisory board and see if you can come."
If the answer is yes, then:
"As I mentioned in the invitation, our team is putting together a group of a few of our best clients, whose opinions we respect, to use as a sounding board. As we continue to improve our wealth-management process, we plan to use the group to help us understand how to market our practice more effectively and how to deliver additional client services. In addition, we would like your input on ideas for finding and developing prospects."

Client Advisory Board Questionnaire

Put this questionnaire in a folder with marketing material personalized for each participant at the dinner.

1. When you think of our team, what words come into your mind?
2. When you think of XYZ Financial, what words come to mind?
3. Why do you do business with us, and what do you value the most in your relationship with us?
4. What are some suggestions you have for how to improve our marketing of ourselves?
5. How could this relationship be improved for you?

6. Are there individuals, groups, or associations that you feel we should be meeting with?

7. We have enclosed our most recent marketing brochure, and we would appreciate any comments or feedback as to its impact.

8. Please share with us anything else you would like to provide.

Follow-Up Agenda After Client Advisory Dinner

Your objective is to obtain one-on-one follow-up meetings with all participants; contact them within a week to set up these meetings.

Script for Follow-Up Face-to-Face Meeting

"First, I want to thank you again for meeting with me and serving on my board of directors. I want to let you know how much respect I have for you, and I/we really value your opinion. As we discussed during the meeting, I am at a point in my career where I am ready to take my business to the next level."

Then ask open-ended questions like the following:

♦ Did you have a chance to review the questionnaire and marketing piece I sent with you when you left our meeting? (This refers to the client advisory board questionnaire.)

♦ How do you think this marketing piece positions my team/me?

♦ Would you make adjustments?

♦ Are there any additional services that you think are missing?

♦ Are there services I offer that you were not aware of but might need?

♦ What suggestions do you have for me for using this piece?

♦ Are there groups, associations, or individuals you know that I should be speaking to or targeting?

♦ If you were putting together a board of directors of five successful business owners who were colleagues of yours, who would you choose? Are those people I should be talking to? How would you recommend that I get in touch with them?

Remember to let the client talk; you are only facilitating the discussion. You should be talking 5 percent of the time and listening 95 percent of the time.

LUNCH ROUNDTABLE

Invite six clients to a lunch roundtable seminar. Tailor the topic to the interests of this particular client group or choose a topic of general interest, such as your firm's view of the current market. Ask each client to bring a nonclient guest who would also be interested in the seminar. Typically, six clients and two or three prospects will attend.

I recommend that you put on the same seminar every month. This gives you the opportunity to invite new prospects every month to a seminar that has already been organized. Alternatively, you can send out a schedule of three or four lunch roundtables to selected clients, allowing them to choose which ones they want to attend. This is a nonthreatening way for clients to introduce you to people they think you should know. It also gives you the chance to get referrals without directly asking for them. Many clients and prospects prefer lunch seminars because they take less time and avoid conflicts with family commitments. Schedule these lunch roundtables from 11:30 A.M. to 1:00 P.M.

Lunch roundtables are an inexpensive way to educate clients, increase the opportunity to do more business with them, and add value to the existing relationship. It also provides an excellent opportunity to meet new prospects that clients bring and to advance the prospecting process with current prospects by inviting them to a seminar on a topic they are interested in.

UNIQUE EVENTS

This idea emphasizes creative follow-through to get an individual appointment with the prospect. You should plan to have these events once a quarter. The event itself is unique and has the objective of providing a different and memorable experience. One of your most successful events could be a group discussion with a local author that will appeal to your prospective clients. Developing such an event can be as simple as contacting a local bookstore and getting a list of local authors from the bookstore staff, then contacting one of these authors and asking her to do a talk on her book. This makes for a unique event that has a high level of appeal and good prospect attendance. Other examples of unique events are art shows (local artists), wine tastings (with wine experts), and beer tastings. Be creative!

During these events, set up the follow-through by finding out as much as you can about the prospect. If you are hosting a wine event and can find out what wine the prospect likes best, you should call and offer to person-ally deliver it to the prospect. Similarly, you could offer to bring a signed copy of a book if an author has spoken at one of these events. The objective of the follow-up is to get an appointment with the prospect so that you can show how you are different and show your unique wealth-management process.

Invite your clients and encourage them to bring a guest they enjoy spending time with. This is also an excellent venue to develop stronger relationships with the prospects in your pipeline. You can also deepen your personal relationships with your influencers (CPAs and attorneys) by inviting them as well. Mixing and mingling with your clients and prospects gives them a different perspective on you as a professional as well as a friend.

A Script for Follow-Up to a Unique Event

"Mr./Ms. Prospect, this is Joe Advisor at XYZ Financial. I enjoyed meeting you at [describe recent event], and I hope you enjoyed it too. At the event, I briefly mentioned our wealth-management process. I want to follow up and share our process in more detail. I also want to give you a memento from our seminar. May I schedule an appointment to deliver the memento and discuss our approach to wealth management?"

CHAPTER 22

Marketing Through Social Media

THE FUNDAMENTALS OF MARKETING in the financial services business are the same as they have been for the thirty-two years I've been in the business, and I predict they will still be the same thirty-two years from now. Financial advisors must put themselves in front of new affluent individuals and build trusting relationships with them, and those financial advisors who are always doing this are the ones who reach a million-dollar and beyond financial services practice.

But while the fundamentals haven't changed, the methods to execute those fundamentals have changed. What has changed over the years are the ways financial advisors can market themselves. The marketing methods I used when I first started my career were mail campaigns, seminars, and cold calling, and while to some degree when done right those methods still work today, they are not as effective as they used to be.

Technology has changed all industries, and financial services is no exception. If building relationships with affluent individuals is the marketing objective, then use of social media is one unique aspect of technology that directly enhances the financial advisor's ability to achieve that in a much more efficient and effective way. Social media includes web- and mobile-based technologies that are used to turn communication into interactive dialogue among organizations, communities, and individuals. The best-known vehicles for social media are LinkedIn, Facebook, and Twitter, but the list grows exponentially every day. In short, social media is providing the financial advisor the technology to increase his reach in a dramatic way.

Social media ties in with the old concept of six degrees of separation. This concept is grounded in the idea that any one person in the world is linked with any other person with no more than six people in between: you can meet anyone in the world through other people if you are strategic and purposeful. Successful financial advisors have used this concept for years, but social media has made this concept infinitely easier and more practical.

For example, I am a frequent user of the social media Internet tool LinkedIn. I currently have 363 people that I am directly connected to. Through those 363 people I have access to all their connections, which is 100,000 individuals. In other words, within two degrees of separation I have access to 100,000 people, each of whom may be considered a prospect. The amazing thing is not only the volume of those connections but also how easy it is to gain access to them.

Imagine going to one of your clients' homes and asking if you could spend time alone in her office to review her Rolodex or computer, or even her address book, and then ask her questions about people you would like to know more about. In the past this was simply not possible, nor was it socially acceptable. Through social media giants like Facebook and LinkedIn, though, all this information is available and easy to access.

While there are definite potential uses for both Facebook and Twitter, these social media outlets are beyond the scope of this chapter. Instead, I will focus on LinkedIn, which in my view is the most powerful social media tool for establishing business connections and marketing. Brandon Gadoci, in his book *The Magic List*, succinctly states, "Properly using LinkedIn is about increasing the number of people you know so that you gain access to the people you don't."

My objective is not that this chapter be an all-inclusive technical guide on this medium but rather to focus on seven strategies that, if employed, will enable financial advisors to enhance the execution of their own marketing fundamentals. These seven primary strategies are:

1. How to build and increase your connections
2. Generating Referrals—Development of affluent individual leads
3. Location—Identification of and introductions to new affluent individuals by location
4. Industry—Identification of and introductions to new affluent individuals by industry
5. Company—Identification of and introductions to new affluent individuals by company
6. Recommendations—How to increase referrals and develop stronger client and prospect relationships

7. Updates—How to use weekly updates to build deeper relationships and find money-in-motion opportunities through new connections

Throughout this book I have introduced many strategies and tactics on how to acquire new clients and assets. I believe that LinkedIn and other social media outlets will enhance many of these strategies to include:

1. Increased referrals
2. Rolodex marketing and past background
3. Prospect pipeline follow-up to convert prospects to clients
4. Research of prospects for qualification, sincere compliment, and turning a cold call into a warm marketing contact

GETTING STARTED: BUILDING AND INCREASING YOUR CONNECTIONS THROUGH LINKEDIN

To maximize the potential of LinkedIn to execute the marketing fundamentals, you must commit to getting connected to and having access to as many connections as possible. By establishing and increasing your connections you are extending your reach and potential to meet new affluent individuals.

The first step is to open a LinkedIn account through the website www.linkedin.com and get set up. Take the time to set up your profile and include a photo; it brings you to life for potential prospects. Also be sure to include your educational background and current and all past employers, all of which will come into play later in the chapter.

Once you are set up on LinkedIn the next step is to connect this account to your current e-mail address book. This is how you will "Add Connections." LinkedIn will automatically generate a short e-mail from you asking those in your address book who are also on LinkedIn to connect with you. The likelihood that your invitation will be accepted by someone you know is extremely high. In my experience every invitation I have made to someone I know to be connected has been accepted.

You can also become connected to someone you would like to meet by entering his name and seeing if he is on LinkedIn. If so, you can request to be connected to him. If he is on LinkedIn you will see his name. Click on it and you will be taken to his profile. Once on his profile you will have access to all the information he has posted on his LinkedIn site and you have the opportunity to click on his "connection" tab. The connection tab takes you to an invitation you can send inviting him to be connected to you. He will receive your invitation through his e-mail and will have the opportunity to accept your invitation as a connection.

By using these two primary methods, you can easily build your LinkedIn connections to two hundred, which provides the critical mass to really take advantage of this social media resource (providing you with approximately 30,000 connections through two degrees of separation). You can also enter every significant client, strong prospect, affluent personal connection, and family member. The objective is to build up your connections to as many people as you can. Once you are connected, you will also have access to their connections, including their:

1. Current position
2. Past experience
3. Education
4. Company website
5. Outside interests
6. Recommendations
7. Age (determined by when they graduated from college)

GENERATING REFERRALS

You can now start the process of identifying all the people you would like to meet through your clients, prospects, and other personal connections. While it's impossible to determine a person's net worth of investable assets through LinkedIn, it is easy to qualify individuals through their current position and past experience.

Once you have identified some of the people you would like your primary connection to introduce you to, you can approach that person and request an introduction. Providing referrals through social media is more like an act of reciprocity than an intrusion: If a client has a high opinion of her financial advisor she will be happy to introduce him to someone she is connected to. I would strongly suggest, however, that you make the initial request personally, and not through the computer. Use the following script:

> "Mr./Ms. Client, Joe Smith is on my marketing list and I am interested in meeting Joe. I noticed when I was browsing on LinkedIn that Joe was one of your connections. I wanted to ask you if you would

be comfortable providing me with a favorable introduction to Joe/putting in a good word for me before I call/sending him an e-mail introducing him to me/allowing me to use you as a positive reference/inviting him to lunch with both of us so I can get to know him."

Through this process you have handed your client a name of someone you have researched that your client is connected to, and you have asked your client's help in providing a referral. If your client is pleased with the work that you have done for him he will probably help you.

CONTACTS BY LOCATION

Another way to sort through the thousands of connections you now have access to is by their geographic location. The first step is to go to your LinkedIn home page and use the search feature and enter "locations," which will take you to the locations where you have the most connections. The next step is to identify all your connections in a particular location, which will be sorted by degrees of separation from you.

The value of sorting contacts on LinkedIn by location is the ability to connect with people you may not know who are already in your market area. It is also useful for when you are traveling outside your market area. Many financial advisors have affluent clients and prospects outside the market that they reside in. When visiting those clients to do a performance review or other type of meeting, I suggest that you use LinkedIn as an opportunity to discover connections they have in that location whom you would like to meet during your visit. You can research those connections and develop a plan to get introduced to those selected prospects by the people you know in that location.

The following are some examples of how you might get introductions:

"Mr./Ms. Client, as you know I am planning to visit you in [out of town location and date] to do our annual review. I am looking forward to seeing you and [spouse's name] again during my visit. I also wanted to mention to you that I'm always looking for opportunities to meet new people who could become new potential clients. I noticed when perusing LinkedIn that one of your connections is Fred Smith, whose profile shows that he just changed jobs last month. Perhaps my experience in dealing with 401(k) accounts could help him. Would you feel comfortable introducing me to Fred, say over lunch when I'm in town?"

"Mr./Ms. Client, I am looking forward to my trip to [location and date] to visit with you and provide a review of your investments. In preparing for our visit I was reviewing my other LinkedIn connections that are in your location and noticed that Jim Jones was someone you were connected to who has recently retired. You may remember that the transition from the accumulation of wealth to distribution of wealth is something I specialize in, and I believe I could provide some value to Jim as he transitions into retirement. I also noticed that Jim enjoys golf, and I wanted to ask you if you would feel it appropriate to invite him to join us on the golf outing that we had set up during my visit."

"Mr./Ms. Client, I am looking forward to my trip to [location and date] to visit with you about your investments. In preparing for my trip I was reviewing LinkedIn connections that are in your location and noticed that Susan Simms was someone you were connected to and is an executive in your company. Since we were planning to meet at your office I wanted to ask if you would be open to introducing me to Susan after our meeting if she was available?"

CONTACTS BY INDUSTRY

You can also combine your expertise in niche marketing and sort contacts and connections by industry. The first step is to go to your LinkedIn home page and use the search feature to find the industries that you have the most connections in. Simply enter "industry" in the search field. By going to your industries with your connections you can segment your connections by the "niche market" that they are in.

By being able to view all your connections (first, second, and third degrees of contact) in that industry, you can identify individuals in your niche market that you would like to meet. As you are developing and expanding your list of potential prospects in your niche market, LinkedIn can be an excellent source of names. As a niche marketer you will always have a higher level of receptivity with your prospects because of your expertise and experience with their particular industry/occupation and because you are an insider. You can ask to be introduced by one of your first connections to your target niche market prospect that you uncover through LinkedIn, or you can contact the person directly through a warm market contact.

The following are some examples of how you might approach your target niche market prospects.

"Mr./Ms. Client, as we have discussed before, I have developed both experience and expertise in working with people in the law profession. In reviewing connections within the law profession I discovered that you were connected to Jim Smith, and Jim is someone I have been trying to meet. I wanted to ask if you would be open to introducing me to Jim over lunch or before I call Jim next week if you would share with him that I have experience in working with the unique investment issues that apply to lawyers."

"Mr./Ms. Prospect, this is Don Jones with XYZ Financial and the reason I am calling you is that I have both experience and expertise in working with the unique investment issues that successful attorneys like you face. I understand that you recently made partner in your firm. Congratulations. I also wanted to mention that I work with Jim Smith at your firm and he told me he would be glad to provide a reference for me when I contacted you. I wanted to ask if you would be open to meeting with me and allowing me to share my investment experience with you to see if I could add value to your current situation."

CONTACTS BY COMPANY

Within your niche, you can further "drill down" to locate people in specific companies. The first step is to go to your LinkedIn home page and then locate the search box toward the upper right and find Advanced Search and click. (There is also a companies tab you can click on the home page.) The next step is to find the company field and enter a company where you have a concentration of clients and/or people you know. From there, you can search and browse.

When entering a company name you are presented with a list of contacts sorted by their degree of separation from you. If you can identify potential prospects that your primary contact/client is connected with, they can provide you with an introduction to your targeted prospect in your targeted company.

Financial advisors have struggled with getting corporate directories and generating leads within companies for as long as I've been in this business. Short of grabbing flyers off the company bulletin board or convincing your client to send you a copy of the company directory, there has in the past been no great way of exploring a company for targeted prospects—until now through LinkedIn. The opportunities are endless with a company search. You can see if your prospect has received a promotion within the company, which offers an opportunity to congratulate her when you contact her. You can also become familiar with the company's benefit/retirement plan and conduct an offsite retirement planning seminar.

Along with searching for a specific company you can add other criteria like location and school. For example, if you are a financial advisor based in Cincinnati and you are also an Ohio State graduate, you could enter in the advanced LinkedIn search "Procter Gamble, Ohio State, and Cincinnati" and all your connections and their connections who meet that criteria would be listed. By having this information you could warm up a prospect contact by referencing that you both went to the same college. Or if your primary connection also went to the same college as you and your targeted prospect, you could use that as way for her to introduce you to your targeted prospect.

The following are some examples of how you might approach your target company prospects:

"Mr./Ms. Client or Primary Contact, as you know I have both experience and interest in working with individuals as they plan their retirement strategies. I noticed that Jim Jones is on my marketing list and is approaching retirement age, and that he not only works at your company but that you are also connected to him on LinkedIn. I wanted to ask if the next time we meet at your office if you would feel comfortable introducing me to Jim."

"Mr./Ms. Client or Primary Contact, the most important time in an investor's life is the five years before his retirement. I enjoy educating individuals about retirement planning and wanted to contact the right person at your company about providing complimentary education seminars on retirement planning. I noticed that you were connected with Jan Jones, the HR director at your firm, I wanted to ask if you would feel comfortable introducing me to Jan so I could offer to provide interested employees with this complimentary retirement planning seminar."

"Mr./Ms. Client or Primary Contact, I was planning on hosting a retirement planning seminar for employees of your company who are within five years of retirement. There were several people in your company who I noticed were approaching retirement age and who you were connected to you on LinkedIn. Do you think those individuals would be good prospects for me to invite to the seminar and get to know as potential clients? When I invite them to the seminar could I use you as reference as someone that I work with and have helped in developing retirement plan strategies?"

CONTACTS BY ALUMNI

There are two ways to use LinkedIn to connect with fellow alumni. The first way is to go to your LinkedIn home page and find the Advanced Search and click. You can then enter your college and do a search of all the people with whom you have some connection. You can also add additional criteria such as location and specific companies and LinkedIn will search for all of your alumni connections who meet those criteria.

Another way to use this tool is by completing your own profile to include where you went to school. Go to your contacts tab and click, and the drop-down bar will appear with your college. When you click on the college it will show you how many of your alumni you are either connected to or are on LinkedIn. For example, I have access to 1,900 University of Georgia Business School alumni. LinkedIn can then sort my fellow alumni by "Where they work" and "Where they live." If I lived in Atlanta there would be more than a thousand University of Georgia Business School alumni I could connect to and have access to their profiles. But since I live in Denver there are only twelve University of Georgia alumni I could connect with. While the number of Denver alumni is much lower, the potential connection would be much stronger since we live many miles away from our alma mater.

Another tool LinkedIn provides is for "degrees of contact," which shows on the side of each profile how you are connected. You can use this information by searching through your fellow alumni profiles to identify potential prospects. Once you have identified the prospects, you can see who your common connections are and then you can approach the primary contact and ask for a favorable introduction. Some examples of how you might use contacts by alumni are as follows:

"Mr. /Ms. Fellow Alumni, my name is Jim Miller and I am a financial advisor at XYZ Financial. The reason I am calling you is that I have both experience and expertise in working with successful executives like yourself. I wanted to congratulate you on your success as senior vice president [or recent promotion] of your company and also mention to you that we have a few things in common. Like you, I am a University of Georgia alumni and I believe we both know Jim Smith [expand on this connection if applicable]. At this point in your life and career you deserve to have an advisor who understands the complex and unique financial issues that a senior executive like you has, and that would be me. I would like to have the opportunity to meet with you personally and share my experience and expertise with you as it relates to your investments."

"Mr./Ms. Client or Personal Contact, I noticed that Jim Smith is an executive vice president of your company and also a fellow University of Georgia alumni. I also noticed that you were connected to Jim on LinkedIn. I wanted to see if you would be open to introducing me to Jim over lunch some time, or if I could get tickets for the next basketball game if I could invite you and you could ask Jim to join us."

"Mr./Ms. Client or Personal Contact, I wanted to mention to you that I have been trying to meet Ann Smith for a while, and in reviewing my LinkedIn connections noticed that you and Ann were connected. Ann and I are both University of Georgia alumni and we graduated about the same time, and I'm sure we have a lot in common. I wanted to ask you if you would be open to sending Ann an introductory e-mail for me [or inviting Ann to lunch] as an opportunity for me to get to know her and start to build a relationship."

RECOMMEND YOUR CLIENTS AND PROSPECTS

It's hard to describe the amount of goodwill that is generated when one of your connections is notified that you have written a LinkedIn recommendation for them. This recommendation accomplishes many things: It develops your relationship at a deeper level with both clients and prospects, and it sets up the potential for reciprocity. Reciprocity can come in many forms, which can include more assets, more referrals, and more business from existing clients. For existing clients that you write a recommendation for, it becomes an easier conversation in the future to ask for a LinkedIn introduction to one of their connections whom you would like to meet.

The first step is to go to your LinkedIn home page and in the profile section click on recommendations and scroll to the bottom of the recommendations page where there is a section to make recommendations to your connections. Enter the name and then write a brief recommendation for your connection (prospect or client). Afterwards, your contact will be notified directly from LinkedIn.

WEEKLY UPDATES

Weekly update e-mails provided by LinkedIn give you the opportunity to further develop relationships with your contacts and identify money-in-motion opportunities. Every week LinkedIn lets you know which of your connections have posted updates to their profile. These updates can include a job change, profile change, title change, adding a skill, adding a connection, and posts to the various groups they belong to. And each one of these updates provides you with an opportunity to create a new client:

♦ **New job change.** Congratulating your connection on a new job gives you the opportunity to develop the relationship further. It can also give you an opportunity to discuss a potential IRA rollover and how your expertise could help them with these assets. Additionally, at the end of each year LinkedIn sends you a summary of all of your connections who have changed jobs.

♦ **Profile change.** A change in a profile provides you with the opportunity to stay connected and congratulate the person if appropriate. A change of circumstance could provide an opportunity to offer to help with any investment needs the person might have.

♦ **Title change.** Congratulating your connection gives you the opportunity to develop your relationship further. It also helps you to prequalify a potential prospect based on the position he holds with his organization; typically a posted title change means a promotion.

♦ **Add a skill.** Congratulating your connection gives you the opportunity to develop your relationship further.

♦ **Honors and awards.** Congratulating your connection gives you the opportunity to develop your relationship further.

♦ **Posts.** Any posts that your connections make give you an opportunity to communicate, connect, and further develop your relationship with these connections.

NEW ADVISORS

Much of this chapter was written for experienced advisors who have existing clients they can use as connecting points for targeted LinkedIn
prospects. New advisors, however, can apply the same techniques with their
personal contacts, past work associates, and prospects. The key for new
advisors is to build up their LinkedIn network as fast as they can while they
are building the foundation stage of their career. Most new advisors should
be able to enter at least two hundred different prospects, personal contacts,
and past work associates they know. If you enter those two hundred initial
connections, that should give you access to approximately 30,000 connections. Each of those 30,000 connections has the potential to be a warm
rather than a cold lead.

This is a networking resource that every new advisor should become familiar with and use from day one of her financial services career. A warm introduction is always much more effective than a cold call, and LinkedIn provides
the vehicle for any new advisor to make many more warm contacts through
introductions than ever before using the tactics described in this chapter.

SUMMARY

- Like any other prospecting method, LinkedIn requires work. Spend
  time getting familiar with the website before you post your home page.
- LinkedIn is not a substitute for getting in front of new affluent
  prospects, but it can be an invaluable resource in facilitating appointments and referrals.
- Social media provide one of the clearest ways to market through your
  clients and prospects to generate referrals.
- Use LinkedIn to reconnect with former colleagues, college alumni,
  clients, and prospects
- Use LinkedIn to drill down to specific companies and industries that
  you can connect with via your own niche marketing.
- Writing recommendations is an effective way to build goodwill between
  existing clients and prospects.
- For new advisors: By building up your connections, you will have the
  ability to make thousands of "warm" contacts rather than "cold contacts."
- The objective is to build your connections to at least 200, which provides
  the critical mass to take advantage of LinkedIn as a marketing tool.

CHAPTER 23

Networking

THE MOST IMPORTANT INGREDIENT FOR SUCCESS in networking, no matter how you do it, is the right mindset: Your highest priority should be to help other professionals get business. If you find business for others, they will find business for you. There are six ways you can participate in networks to grow your business:

1. Join a networking club.
2. Network within an occupation.
3. Use prospect pathing.
4. Join special-interest or charitable organizations.
5. Build your own networking group.
6. Network with new acquaintances.

JOIN A NETWORKING CLUB

One way to build or expand your core networking group is to join a networking club. These clubs can generally be found in the business section of the newspaper where the calendar of weekly business events is posted. Joining a networking club is only the beginning—you should assume a leadership position immediately. As a leader, you will be respected by the group, and you will have the opportunity to move the group in the right direction. The best networking groups generally are smaller but are made up of high-quality people who are committed to helping one another. Ideally the group should meet weekly, and members should ask one another for a profile of the clients they would like. Examples of this are:

"I'm looking for individuals who are retiring or changing jobs."
"I'm looking for women who were recently divorced, are in the process of getting a divorce, or were recently widowed."

Don't assume that your fellow networkers know what you are looking for. The more specific you are, the more likely you are to get referrals.

As a leader of this group, you should lead by example and be relentless in your search for potential business for your fellow networkers. Examples of finding business for fellow networkers are:

♦ Listening for people who have aches and pains (chiropractor).
♦ Asking your boss to do printing with a fellow networker (printer).
♦ Asking clients and friends their summer plans (travel agent).
♦ Asking clients and friends if they are happy with their CPA (CPA).
♦ Asking clients and friends if they have a will and a trust (trust attorney).
♦ Asking your boss if he needs an event planner or caterer for a company event.

The key is that you be capable of and committed to providing network opportunities for the members of your group.

NETWORK WITHIN AN OCCUPATION

To network within an occupation, identify an individual in a targeted occupation and approach that person. An example of this would be a divorce attorney (she can provide you with money-in-motion opportunities). Call a divorce attorney and mention your need for someone like her to help your clients and prospective clients, and then invite her to lunch or breakfast to get acquainted. The key to being a good networker is being a great listener: Ask about how this person does business, her philosophy, and which CPAs she uses (another potential client source).

At the same time, you must come across as a confident, intelligent professional. This is best accomplished by asking intelligent questions. After you've spent the first part of the meeting asking about the other person, she will ask about you, and that gives you an opportunity to showcase your practice and how you could add value for her clients. The follow-up to these meetings is critical: Stay in touch. Provide timely information, keeping your name in front of this person.

USE PROSPECT PATHING

Prospect pathing uses the six degrees of separation rule. This rule states that you can meet anyone in the world you want to through no more than six people. Identify your best potential prospects, finding out all you can about them and finding common links with people you know who can help you meet them. This marketing technique is prospect pathing.

The more organized you are in this process, the more success you will have. Start with the target prospect, then research where he lives and which social and philanthropic organizations he belongs to. Identify someone you know who has a common link with the prospect that would help you. Explain the common link that this person has with your target prospect, and ask her help in getting an introduction.

JOIN SPECIAL-INTEREST OR CHARITABLE ORGANIZATIONS

The first step in this marketing plan is to identify what organizations to join. Identify the prospects you would like to do business with and determine what organizations they belong to, or ask your prospects what organizations they belong to. Decide what charitable causes or special-interest organizations you are interested in. As an example, if you have an interest in flying, you could look at the local private airport's website for information; you would probably find clubs or organizations that meet at that airport. By joining one of these organizations, you will become an "insider" and a contributor to that organization. As other members come to know your background, you will find business opportunities.

The same principle applies to charities that you have a personal interest in. By joining these organizations and offering your services, you will find others with similar commitments. As you contribute your time and expertise to these organizations, you will gain members' respect, and as they come to know what you do, they could become future clients. Remember, the majority of affluent investors get their advisors through referrals. Networking proactively creates referrals.

Be sure you are passionate about whatever organizations you join. If you do not give enough time and energy to make an impact, you will not build the kind of relationships that can ultimately lead to new clients. You should expect that it will take at least six months to a year after you become actively involved in an organization before any new clients are generated.

Once you decide what organizations you want to belong to, volunteer to help those organizations. Volunteer for everything you can in every organization you belong to, and work hard at everything you do for these organizations. Developing a reputation as a hard worker is key to this marketing strategy. If you are willing to work hard, you will quickly be asked to assume more responsibilities and will be given leadership positions quickly. This kind of marketing takes a great deal of time, and in the beginning it may require working nights and weekends.

As you gain more responsibility and move into leadership positions, you will begin to get to know other leaders within the organizations. In most cases, these people are your prospects. The key is to build relationships with these prospects without asking for their business. You want to avoid, at all costs, getting a reputation for using the organization to solicit business. You will earn your business by working with your prospects on a cause that both of you have a passion for. The prospect will give you a reason to move into a business conversation as you get to know him. He might mention a mortgage or an educational or investment issue, and that will give you an opportunity to provide advice. The key to this technique is to listen and understand your prospect's business and professional life.

As your reputation builds within the organization you belong to, it will also build outside the organization. With a good reputation, you will be invited to other organizations within your community; this, in turn, will lead to more opportunities to meet new prospects as you emerge as a leader in those organizations.

Belonging to several organizations is important to get the critical mass to make this market action plan work. If you are committed to networking as a market action plan, then your goal should be to belong to two to three different organizations. This should translate into at least one event or meeting per week.

BUILD YOUR OWN NETWORKING GROUP

The first step in this market action plan is to write out a list of occupations that you believe can potentially give you business. Next to that list, write another list of those occupations that you believe you could give business to. There should be an overlap between the two lists; this overlap is the basis for your networking group. Examples of this overlap could be CPAs, Realtors (specialists in corporate relocations), business brokers, mortgage brokers, commercial Realtors, estate attorneys, divorce attorneys, and insurance agents.

Once you have determined the occupations that should form your networking group, you need to determine the names of the people you will use in each occupation. You want high-quality professionals who have a good reputation in their field. Use every contact you have to identify these individuals. Once you have identified the individuals you want to use, contact them and invite them to join your networking group.

The networking group should start small but can grow over time to as many as forty people, with no competitors allowed. This networking group becomes your "super-Rolodex" that can add value to your clients and prospects. The people invited to the networking group must provide goods and services that you know your clients and prospects will need. An example: If a daughter of one of your clients is getting married, you could refer a florist and a caterer. Another possibility is to focus on the needs of business owners; owners could be served by commercial Realtors, telecommunications professionals, temporary agencies, attorneys, and other such professionals.

Individual members should represent diverse businesses. Aim for a diverse membership with regard to gender, race, age, and background. Aim for clusters of people who can take referrals as a single group, such as a caterer, a florist, a photographer, and a travel agent—they can all take a referral for a wedding. Invite potential new members to come to one of the meetings to see if there is a good fit. Have fun together to keep it interesting. Plan social events on weekends that include spouses and children.

In asking the networking group for what you are looking for, you must be very specific. Examples could include:

- "I'm looking for someone you know who will retire next year."
- "I'm looking for someone who has been with the same company for ten years and who is changing jobs."

Another way to help generate referrals from your group is to tell a story about a specific client you helped, describing how you solved that client's problem, then asking the group members if they know someone who may be in a similar situation. You must teach people what you do and how you help people so that they can send you referrals. This will not happen if you just ask for referrals without being specific about the type of people you are looking for and the circumstances you can help with. It is important before you call the referral that she is expecting your call and that you have identified a specific need you can help with.

The following is an example of the format of a very successful networking group:

- The networking group meets once a week from seven to eight-thirty in the morning. It costs $300 annually to belong, which pays for the cost of breakfasts throughout the year. The meetings are very structured, with a set schedule.
- Each meeting starts with fifteen minutes of social interaction, followed by members dividing into groups of four to each table; everyone chooses a card when she arrives, and that determines which group she sits with.
- During the next fifteen minutes, members tell their tablemates about what they do.
- At each meeting, one member is featured, and that member addresses the entire group and talks about his background, his expertise, and what he is looking for.
- The meeting concludes by announcing the speaker for the following week.

One networking group that was developed by a financial advisor was the most organized I have ever seen. This financial advisor formed an executive committee of five other individuals who she knew were top professionals representing different industries who were interested in developing a strong network group. Each executive committee member named three to five other individuals they knew who fit the criteria of being top professionals in their field and representing different occupations. These individuals were reviewed by the entire executive committee and invitations went out to thirty individuals. Twenty accepted the invitation to join the network group.

The group meets every month at a different location, usually a well-known restaurant at 3:00 P.M. Light appetizers and drinks are served and the meeting starts at 3:15. At this time two members are featured for ten minutes. They each give a profile of their business and the type of client they are looking for. After the featured members finish their presentation, each member of the network group has two minutes to share an example of a recent client he helped, what type of client he is looking for, and a brief update of the state of his business. At 4:30 the meeting is finished and members can mix and mingle. Members are strongly encouraged to bring guests.

They also hold monthly mixers where each member is assigned to two other network members for that month to meet and have a chance to get to know each other better.

The executive committee meets every month and discusses new potential members and logistics of future meetings. This network group has developed a directory that includes all members and their business, biographies of the members, and all their contact information. There is also a calendar of events provided to the members with the date and location of each networking meeting as well as who the two presenters will be for that particular meeting.

Script

> "Mr./Ms. Businessperson, my name is Joe Advisor, and I'm a financial advisor at XYZ Financial. The reason for my call is that I'm the president of a small but very committed networking group in this area. We are looking for a [occupation] to be a part of our group. We have identified you as one of the best [occupation] and wanted to invite you to our next meeting. We are serious about helping one another, and I'm sure we can provide some referrals to you. Would you be interested?"

NETWORK WITH NEW ACQUAINTANCES

The key here is to meet new people, either individually or in a meeting of people you don't know. Some good sources of meetings are:

1. Newspaper listings of large meetings or conventions
2. Professional association meetings
3. Chamber of commerce meetings

Once you are face to face with a new acquaintance, start with an "icebreaker" conversation that is nonthreatening and not business-related. It can be as simple as a conversation about the weather, sports, or current events:

♦ "What a beautiful day. Have you heard how long this great weather is going to last?"
♦ "Boy, the traffic coming downtown today was terrible. Did you run into any of it?"

+ "How about [local sports team]? What do you think their prospects are?"

These are just examples; the possibilities for small talk are endless. The key is to make these general, nonthreatening, icebreaker conversations.

The next step is to ask potential prospects what they do or whom they work for. Examples of this step are:

+ "Where do you work?"
+ "Who do you work for?"
+ "What kind of business are you in?"

This takes the discussion to the person's occupation, which sets up the potential networking opportunity.

Once the potential networker answers that question, then the door is open to get more specific. Questions may include:

+ "How long have you been doing what you are doing?"
+ "How long have you been in the business?"
+ "How is business going? Are you having a good year?"
+ "Are you accepting new clients?"
+ "What kind of clients are you looking for?"

The next step is to briefly describe what you do (they most likely will ask you) and with whom you work, and that you are meeting affluent people every day. Also mention that you are always looking for new people to network with; ask the person if she would be interested in meeting for coffee in the next week to discuss each other's business in more detail. Either offer a potential date and time immediately, or ask for her card and offer to call in the next few days to set up the meeting.

If the potential networker agrees to the follow-up meeting, a simple structure should be followed at the meeting. Ask the potential networker more detailed questions about her business. Topics could include:

+ The person's ideal target client
+ The specifics of her firm, business, and offerings
+ What makes her unique
+ Her background and areas of expertise

- How she feels you could best help her
- How she is handling her own investments
- What information you could provide that would be most helpful
- Whether or not she is familiar with the wealth-management process

Offer to describe your wealth-management process and what makes your process unique. Share briefly your background, and share what kind of prospects you are looking for. Examples are:

- People who are retiring or changing jobs
- People who are facing a change in their life circumstances: divorce, death of a spouse, inheritance
- Prospects who may be unhappy with their current advisor

If you feel that this individual has the potential to be someone you would like to network with, you must continue to stay in touch and build on the relationship. The key to successful networking is to be committed to building relationships with people who are willing and capable of providing you with referrals, and in turn you must be committed to providing referrals to them.

CHAPTER 24

Past Experience and Personal Contacts

"EVERYONE HAS A PAST," GOES THE OLD SAYING, and in our case, your past is a tremendous business opportunity, two of them really. One is the opportunity presented by the people you have come to know over the years, and the other is the opportunity presented by the past experiences and outside interests you have had.

PEOPLE YOU ALREADY KNOW

Everyone brings to this job a Rolodex of personal contacts who could potentially become clients. The number and quality of the people in that Rolodex will determine how much you can use this market action plan. Since everyone has some qualified personal contacts, everyone can use this technique to some degree. The objective is to make sure that your personal contacts are aware of your position as a financial advisor without putting either of you in an awkward position. There are several techniques for accomplishing this.

The first step is to identify the personal contacts you have who are qualified investors. Once you have made a list of those who are likely to be qualified, use one of the five marketing techniques I outline next. Be sure to tailor the technique to fit your relationship and the personality of your personal contact. Feel free to use a combination of these techniques, if appropriate.

No matter which of the five techniques you use, be sure to ask every-one you contact for help in identifying others they know who have money in motion. One successful advisor formalized this technique. She identified one hundred people she had strong connections with and asked each of those individuals to be on the lookout for anyone they knew who was changing jobs, relocating to the area, retiring, or getting divorced. She checked in with the people on her list regularly to remind them of what she was looking for. This technique provided her with an excellent prospect pipeline.

Letters

Send a letter to your contacts announcing your new job as an advisor at XYZ Financial. I do not encourage mailings except to your most qualified personal contacts. This is a nonthreatening way to open the door to making the transition from a personal to a professional relationship. It's important to stress how proud you are to be associated with a firm like XYZ Financial and the quality of the training you've received. Provide a postage-paid attachment or envelope with a list of follow-up actions the contact could ask you to take. This is a low-pressure way to make people aware of your position and gives them control over the professional relationship.

Board of Directors

Call your contacts and ask if you could meet with them to get their advice on your new career as an advisor at XYZ Financial. At the appointment, share how excited you are about the training and resources you have received while working at XYZ Financial. Tell them that you are putting together a "board of directors" of influential people you know and respect, to get their insights on building your business. "What advice would you give me in starting this career?" "What's important to you from your financial advisor?"

Perhaps the most important question should be at the end of the conversation: "Can you think of anyone who may be dissatisfied with their current investment situation and who might want a second opinion? Or someone who is going through a change of life circumstances (who is retiring, changing jobs, or going through a divorce or the loss of a spouse)?" Not only are you asking for a referral, but you are opening the door in a nonthreatening way for your contact to talk with you about his own investment situation. Stay in touch with your most receptive personal contacts and truly make them your "board of directors" for business development. Over time, they will provide you with referrals and, optimally, their own business. An excellent source for these personal contacts is successful alumni of the college you attended or fraternity or sorority you belonged to.

Research

Offer to send your personal contacts your firm's best research reports. Explain that you have been so impressed with XYZ Financial's insights into the markets and that you want to share that information with them. Suggest that if they have any questions or need additional information, you will be glad to provide it at no cost to them. You can also use this technique when you host events for your clients and prospects; inviting a personal contact to a fun or educational event is an excellent way to begin the transition to a professional relationship by an offer of free research or information tailored to their interests.

The Rolodex Technique

Write down all the qualified investors you know from your past work and personal experience. For most people, that is at least two hundred names. Call each one of them, acknowledge the past connection, and tell each person what you are doing now. Offer to visit with them personally to see if you can add value to their current situation or provide a second opinion on their current financial situation, and offer to share with them your unique wealth-management process. Based on the experience of advisors who have used this approach successfully, you will get an appointment for every two people you contact. If your Rolodex is deep enough with qualified prospects, this market action plan alone could be the cornerstone of a new financial advisor's business.

Social Prospecting

There is a fine line that you must not cross in social prospecting, and that is this: Never be obvious about what you are doing. You want to respond to others' requests and never appear to be prospecting them. The technique is the same whether you are at a cocktail party, in a golf game, or on a skiing trip. As you get to know the social prospect, start the process by asking questions that are general and nonthreatening:

+ "What business are you in?"
+ "How is business going?"
+ "Do you have a family?"
+ "What do you like to do?"

The prospect will ask you the same questions, and it's important that you have a one-sentence description of your job. For example, when a prospect asks you, "What business are you in?" you might answer, "I am an advisor at XYZ Financial, and I help people reach their financial goals." The door is now open, and the prospect might ask for your opinion about the market. When she does, give your short answer, but then ask if she would be interested in receiving a timely research report that you feel is particularly good. If she accepts, you can send the report, then follow up a week later and open the door to an investment conversation about the research report.

If the prospect does not give you any door-opening opportunities, it's best not to force it. You don't want to get a reputation that could hurt your standing in the community.

Sample Scripts

"Mr./Ms. Personal Contact, as you may know, I'm working with XYZ Financial. As a good friend/business contact/neighbor, I wanted to offer to send you some of our best research. It's the same information I send my best clients. There is no charge or obligation; I just thought it might be of value to you. I have been impressed with the wealth of information available and the quality of XYZ's research, and hopefully you will be too. Would you be interested?"

"Mr./Ms. Past Contact, this is Joe Advisor, and I wanted to have the opportunity to reconnect with you. I have always respected you professionally and personally. I am currently working with XYZ Financial and specialize in working with successful individuals like you. Specifically, my wealth-management process differentiates me from many other financial advisors. I would like the opportunity to reconnect and find out more about your circumstances and see if I could provide some value. Would you be available to meet for coffee next week?"

Sample Letter

Dear Mr./Ms. Prospect:

I am pleased to announce my new position as a financial advisor at XYZ Financial. I have been very impressed with the extensive training I've received, and I am convinced that XYZ Financial is the best financial services firm in the industry.

I wanted to offer you our best resources and have provided a checklist of free information that might be of interest. I'm sure you will be as impressed as I am with the quality and depth of XYZ Financial's services and research.

Please feel free to call me anytime if I can be of service.

Sincerely,
Jane Advisor

PAST EXPERIENCE

Not only are your acquaintances from your past a place to build your business, but so are your outside interests and past work experiences. The first step is to categorize your background by what you have done and what you are interested in. Every job you have had in the past has given you a level of expertise that you should use to your marketing advantage. As an example, if you worked for a large company or owned your own business, you know how that business operates and how people in that industry think. You should use that background and knowledge for your benefit and develop a market action plan that is focused on it.

In some cases this same principle holds true with your parents' background. For example, if your father was a college professor, you know and understand how college professors think and what marketing approach would most appeal to them.

The same principle applies to your interests. If you enjoy flying, motor-cycling, golfing, gardening, fly fishing, tennis, or some other activity, you can relate to others who have similar interests. It is easy to use your background, interests, and expertise to market to others who are interested in the same activity. You know the clubs these people belong to and the special-interest magazines they read. Use this "inside" information to determine the most affluent individuals and contact them, using your shared interests, background, and hobbies.

Scripts

A Shared Employer:

"Mr./Ms. Prospect Who Works at ABC Company, my name is Joe Advisor, and I'm a financial advisor at XYZ Financial. The reason for my call is that I used to work for ABC Company before I came to XYZ Financial. I understand the company benefits plan, and I can relate to your situation at ABC. The training I've received from XYZ Financial has given me some important insights that would make a difference in your financial situation, and I would like to share these with you. I'm going to be in your area on Thursday and would like the opportunity to meet with you."

A Shared Occupation:

"Mr./Ms. Prospect, my name is Jane Advisor, and I'm a financial advisor at XYZ Financial. The reason for my call is that before I joined XYZ, I owned my own business, like you, and I understand the challenges facing a business owner. At the same time, as the result of my training at XYZ Financial, I've become aware of solutions to some of these challenges. I would like to have the opportunity to share with you some ideas that I know could make a difference. I'm going to be in your area next Thursday and would like to have the opportunity to meet with you."

A Shared Hobby:

"Mr./Ms. Prospect, my name is Joe Advisor, and I'm a financial advisor at XYZ Financial. The reason for my call is that I'm an avid motorcyclist like you, and I saw your name as a member of the local Harley-Davidson chapter. As a fellow motorcycle enthusiast, I know we could relate, and I was hoping to have an opportunity to meet with you personally and offer my services as a resource at XYZ Financial. Is there a day next week that works well for you?"

Parents Had Shared Occupation or Background:

"Mr./Ms. Prospect, my name is Jane Advisor, and I'm a financial advisor at XYZ Financial. The reason for my call is that my father was a professor at [University], and while I was growing up, I was able to gain a good insight into the mindset and financial issues that college professors have. Since coming to XYZ Financial, I am aware of financial solutions that I believe would be of value to you. I would like to schedule an appointment with you during your office hours to share some of these ideas with you. When would be a convenient time?"

CHAPTER 25

Adopt a Town

IN MOST CASES, smaller towns outside a large city are underprospected and provide a good opportunity for a financial advisor who is willing to commit time there.

IDENTIFY AND GATHER DATA

The first step is to identify the town in which you want to make a concentrated prospecting effort. Good criteria to use are that it should be its own entity, not a suburb, and the population should be at least 5,000. You want to focus on a town where there is little competition for what you have to offer.

Once you select the town, visit it and write down the names of the businesses that look successful and the names of the streets in the nicest neighborhoods. Also, visit the chamber of commerce to gather as much information as possible, including lists of businesses, clubs, and organizations. Subscribing to the local newspaper is also important, as it allows you to see who the movers and shakers are and to view money-in-motion events. Look through the business pages and identify all the professionals (CPAs, attorneys, physicians) and business owners.

The objective is to immerse yourself in the targeted town and get face-to-face appointments with qualified prospects. Note that you don't necessarily need an appointment with a prospect that you want to see; you can just tell whoever answers the phone that you will be stopping by on a particular day when you are in town. This can work in a small town because of the lack of formality; you only want the person not to be surprised when you show up.

PENETRATE THE TOWN

Once you have gathered all the intelligence you can, focus your prospecting efforts on penetrating the town on many different fronts. One of your objectives is to get face-to-face appointments with centers of influence and build a trusting relationship with them so that they will refer prospects to you.

There are two excellent channels for reaching centers of influence: civic and social organizations, and bank directors.

Contact the president of each civic and social organization in the town and offer to give a seminar to that group on your firm's current market insights. Organizations typically are looking for new topics and presentations for their programs. This gives community leaders the opportunity to see you in a professional "teaching" role.

Bank directors (board members) are another excellent source for centers of influence. They are not employees of the bank or bank officers, but they are usually the largest depositors of the bank and centers of influence in the community. You can either use the bank's website to identify the directors or call the bank directly and ask who its directors are.

Make a commitment to visit the town at least twice a month for at least a year. Ideally, you should visit once a week. It takes twenty to thirty visits to a new town to build a core of clients and prospects who can then become advocates for you in that town.

You want to reach the centers of influence in each town and have them become cornerstones in building a client base. Once you have identified the centers of influence and built a relationship of trust with them, they will become key referral sources.

Every time you visit, see as many existing prospects as possible (no appointments needed) and drop off information. (For more information on developing prospect relationships, see Chapter 7.) The community needs to feel that you are serious in your commitment to the town, and the more time you spend there, the more credibility you will have. Here are five marketing strategies you can incorporate that work particularly well:

1. Build a network of the influencers—CPAs, attorneys, and others (see Chapter 28).
2. Host client and prospect events, such as golf games, fishing clinics, and educational seminars (see chapters 12 and 21).
3. Give seminars for prospects: target affluent neighborhoods and follow

up with personal calls to your prospects in that town to invite them (see Chapter 20).

4. Subscribe to the local newspaper and look for money-in-motion opportunities. Contact these prospects and set appointments.

5. Make marketing contacts with business owners and professionals with the intent of making a face-to-face appointment when you visit the town.

The smallness of the town will work in your favor if you make the time commitment. In touching these prospects in many ways (i.e., appointments, drop-bys, referrals, and speaking engagements), you will increase your credibility. Word will begin to spread that you are serious about your commitment to the community and that you are a person who can be trusted.

Gradually, you will be able to slow down your adopt-a-town marketing in your adopt a town as you build scale and a reputation and rely more on referrals and following up with referrals, and you will not need to visit the town as frequently—you can cut your visits back to once a month or once a quarter after twelve months of concentrated effort.

Use the same techniques for the smaller towns and communities that are on the way to the target town. It is possible to "adopt a region," which is good time management. Also, you can apply the adopt-a-town market action plan to a larger metropolitan area, but you must first divide the metropolitan area into its separate entities; each of these communities has its own newspapers, and in many cases its own chamber of commerce. You lose the competitive advantage, however, because all these communities have access to all the firms in the larger metropolitan area.

If you immerse yourself in the town for twelve months, you are likely to get good results, since most of your out-of-town competitors will not make the time commitment they would need to counteract your initiative. These towns do not have many, if any, financial services firms, and you will have a real competitive advantage. You will also find that some investors are willing to invest outside their local communities for confidentiality reasons, and when they are given the opportunity to do so with a broader platform and with an individual they trust, they will take it.

Scripts

Introduction to Community Leader:
"Mr./Ms. Prospect, My name is Joe Advisor, and the reason for my

call is that I've been assigned to cover [your town name] by XYZ Financial [or my manager]. Since you are a community leader, I wanted to get your thoughts on how XYZ Financial should best approach your town. I am going to visit on Thursday, and I hoped that you might be available for a short appointment."

General Introduction:

"Mr./Ms. Prospect, my name is Jane Advisor, and I work for XYZ Financial. I have made a commitment to focus on your town, [name of town], and I am hoping that when I am there on Thursday, I could have a short meeting with you to introduce myself and share with you some ways that I could be of value pertaining to your investments. Would you be available?"

or,

"Mr./Ms. Prospect, my name is Joe Advisor, and I work for XYZ Financial. I have made a decision to focus my time and energy on your town, [name of town]. I will be there on Thursday and wanted to offer to drop by and introduce myself and give you some information on some attractive opportunities that we believe exist in the market today. Would you be available?"

Introduction to Associate:

"Mr./Ms. Associate, my name is Jane Advisor, and I work for XYZ Financial. I am going to be in [name of town] on Thursday and will drop by to see Mr. Smith. I would appreciate it if you would let him know I will come by to see him on Thursday. By the way, what is your name? Good, I'll look forward to meeting you when I stop by."

CHAPTER 26

Business Owners

BUSINESS OWNERS ARE AMONG THE MOST ATTRACTIVE TARGET markets for many different reasons. First, you can build your business through them in many different ways; second, they have a decision-making mentality; and third, they include more millionaires than any other group in the United States. A recent survey found that 52 percent of investors with a net worth between $1 million and $10 million are business owners, 67 percent of those with between $10 million and $50 million are business owners, and 85 percent of those with more than $50 million are business owners. The higher the net worth, the higher the percentage of business owners. Lastly, most profitable business owners will have a significant liquidity event when they sell their business.

Not all business owners are successful, so it's important to prescreen owners before you contact them. There are three relatively easy screens to determine qualification:

1. Size of business ($1 million-plus in sales)
2. How long the business has been operating (five years or more)
3. Whether or not the business has been profitable over the past several years

The appointment is critical, as it is essential for building a relationship. Many business owners may object to an initial appointment, but if you can show them that meeting with you will be of value to them, you should secure a ratio of contacts to appointments of about ten to one. To do this, talk to the business owner about what you can do for his business—for most business owners their business is their life, and their personal finances are often a lower priority. Also explain that by meeting the business owner at his place of business, you can not only gather the necessary information but also see firsthand how the business is run.

You need to get the appointment on the basis of helping the business owner be more profitable, but once you have the appointment, you should discover everything you can about the business owner. One of the reasons this group is so attractive is that there are many ways to do business with them: personal business, retirement plan, the potential sale of their business, and lending opportunities. Base your follow-up on all potential needs, not just on the profitability solutions. This is why, if you make a commitment to marketing to business owners, you need to understand the products and services that are available that will add value to their businesses.

I recommend two approaches in reaching out to this market: contacting business owners directly, and building a network of other professionals that can help the business owner add value to her business and develop transition strategies.

DIRECT CONTACT

Contacting business owners directly will work better if you follow the seven steps I outline here:

1. Develop a list of privately owned businesses that have been in existence for five or more years, have sales in excess of $1 million, and are profitable. Have at least one thousand names on this list that meet these criteria. Supplement this list with names you gather from local papers that recognize successful business owners.

2. Use a contact script you are comfortable with that identifies you as a specialist who can help business owners bring more to their bottom line.

3. Develop a level of expertise and specialization in the needs of the small business owner. Become an expert in solving the needs of the business owner.

4. Focus your efforts using a specialized approach. Concentrate on one or two industries and get to know everything you can about those industries. Subscribe to and read the industry trade journals, and join the associations that are part of the industries that you've decided to focus on.

5. Make use of trade journals and associations specific to the industries you have chosen. Trade journals will provide you with invaluable information about the "movers and shakers" in a particular industry and will give you a level of expertise that will impress your prospects. Additionally, joining the associations gives you access to the members of your targeted prospect group.

6. When you have the appointment, ask questions, listen, and offer compliments. This will give you important follow-up information and will build rapport. Business owners get too little recognition, so any time you can find a way to recognize them for their accomplishments in your meeting, do so. Focus on the entire range of opportunities with the business prospect. Ask for a tour of the business; nothing makes a business owner feel better. If the appointment goes well, ask for a referral.

7. One of the best ways to qualify business owners is to talk with them about whether or not they have a retirement plan for themselves and their employees, and offer to do complimentary retirement reviews for them. See Chapter 31 for more details of this approach.

BUILD A NETWORK

Most successful business owners know they will have the opportunity to sell their business and have a significant liquidity event. In many cases this will fund their retirement and will represent their most significant asset. Even though these successful business owners know they will have this opportunity, most don't know how to determine the value of their business or how to find a buyer.

Furthermore, there are many things business owners can do to increase the value of their businesses when they are ready to sell. If you can provide them with the resources on how to increase the value of their businesses and help them understand what their transition options are, you will differentiate yourself from your competition and be in high demand from your business owner clients and prospects.

The first step in this process is to understand the mindset of the successful business owner. I recommend Ned Minor's book *Deciding to Sell Your Business*. It is an excellent resource that provides a number of case studies. The next step is to develop a short list of middle-market investment bankers who specialize in middle-market business owners (value of business between $10 million and $100 million), business brokers (value of businesses less than $10 million), and merger and acquisition attorneys. Then contact these professionals and suggest a meeting to discuss building a mutually beneficial network relationship. The following is an example of this script:

> "My name is Jim Smith and I'm with XYZ Financial. The reason for my call is that I work with a number of successful business owners who might have an interest in the future in selling their businesses. I am assembling a team of experts to help my current and prospective business owner clients and wanted to invite you to a discovery meeting to determine if we could potentially add value to each other's business."

By asking for a meeting in this manner, you are positioning this as an opportunity to "educate" and not to "sell" each other's prospects and clients, with no obligation to do business. Most financial advisors make the mistake of asking these professionals for referrals of their clients who are having liquidity events but don't offer to provide them with potential referrals. The last important step in the process is to share with your new network your wealth-management process and how you are different and the value you provide to your clients. They need to develop a high level of confidence in your ability to make a positive difference with the client experiencing a liquidity event that they will refer to you.

For the investment banker, business broker, and merger and acquisition attorney, you will provide them with potential leads of business owners who will sell their businesses; all these professionals are highly motivated to generate new potential leads. In turn, they can provide you with introductions to their clients who have just sold their businesses or are about to and who need professional help on how to invest the proceeds from their liquidity event. Through this process you should find at least one investment banker, business broker, and merger and acquisition attorney who would be interested in networking with you.

Once you have your team of professionals in place you can now expand what you offer prospective business owners and existing business owner clients, to include helping them increase the value of their businesses and develop potential transition strategies for their businesses through your network. This is of great interest to most successful business owners, and most financial advisors do not provide this kind of service. Your network of bankers, attorneys, and business brokers can provide expertise on exactly how to value their businesses and increase the value, and the mechanics of how a business is sold.

Once you have developed your professional network you can host periodic seminars for your network and potential business owner prospects who are interested in learning more about selling their businesses. The name of the seminar could be "Increasing the Value of Your Business and Transition Strategies." At the seminar, you should have each member of your network share with the audience his or her area of expertise. You would then discuss the importance of developing an investment strategy following a liquidity event and briefly describe the wealth-management process (see Chapter 9). Of all the investment seminars I have attended, this is one of the most popular and has among the highest invitation-to-attendance ratios.

I would also recommend that you join your local Association of Corporate Growth (ACG). The ACG is designed to facilitate networking between professionals who are engaged in the buying and selling of businesses. It provides an excellent opportunity to build and develop relationships with professionals that can become a resource to your business owner clients and prospects.

Business Owner Scripts

"Mr./Ms. Business Owner, my name is Jim Jones and I work with XYZ Financial. The reason for my call is that I have both experience and expertise in working with successful business owners like you. I position myself as a resource for my business owner clients in all aspects of their asset and liability needs to include increasing the value of their business and long-term transition strategies. I would like the opportunity to meet you, find out more about your business, and offer myself as resource to you."

"Mr./Ms. Business Owner, my name is Joe Advisor, and I'm with XYZ Financial. The reason for my call is to congratulate you on the success of your business, and also to discuss information that could have a positive impact on your bottom line. We compete very effectively with banks in the areas of lending and cash management and retirement plan management. I was hoping to visit with you next Thursday and provide you some of the details of how we can help you. Would you be available?"

"Mr./Ms. Business Owner, my name is Jane Advisor, and I'm a business financial services specialist with XYZ Financial. I want to congratulate you on the success of your business. If you are like most successful business owners I work with, you pay close attention to the bottom line. If I could have the opportunity to meet with you and find out more about your situation, I am confident I could save you money. Would you be available to meet next Thursday?"

"Mr./Ms. Prospect, this is Joe Advisor, a business specialist with XYZ Financial. XYZ Financial asked me to call you to tell you about the services we have available for successful companies such as yours that we believe can help you run your business more efficiently and more profitably. Since it's best to discuss this in person, I'd like to meet with you next Tuesday. Is morning or afternoon better for you?"

"Mr./Ms. Prospect, my name is Jane Advisor, and I'm a senior financial advisor with XYZ Financial. The reason for my call is, first, to compliment you on your success, and then to tell you that we are offering several new, innovative services for businesses, and I wonder if I could schedule a brief appointment with you to discuss them?"
If the prospect asks what type of services:
  "We have so many, I can best answer that question if I come out and meet with you to find out your specific needs and let you know about the services that are most applicable."

Investment Banker, Business Broker, M&A Attorney Scripts

Mr./Ms. Banker, Broker, Attorney, my name is Jim Smith and I'm with XYZ Financial and the reason for my call is that I work with a number of successful business owners who might have an interest in the future in selling their businesses. I work hard to assemble a team of experts to help my current and prospective business owner clients and wanted to invite you to a discovery meeting to determine if we could potentially add value to each other's business.

Script: If You Were in the Business Prior to Joining XYZ Financial

"Mr./Ms. Business Owner, my name is Joe Advisor, and I work for XYZ Financial. I'm calling you today because I was a business owner like you before I worked for XYZ Financial. Since coming to XYZ, I've been trained on what's available for business owners, and I wish I had known about some of this when I did what you do. I believe that my understanding of your business and of business services could help you. Would you be available for an appointment this week?"

Screener Scripts

What Is the Nature of Your Call?
"I am calling Mr./Ms. Business Owner to show him/her how to save money on his/her current banking relationship."

"I am Joe Advisor with XYZ Financial. The reason for my call is that I specialize in helping successful business owners bring more to their bottom line. I was hoping to schedule a brief appointment with Mr./Ms. Prospect to find out more about the details of his/her business. Can I do that through you, or should I talk to him/her directly?"

Realtors

REALTORS® CAN MAKE AN EXCELLENT TARGET MARKET if you approach them the right way. Many of the successful ones are affluent, it's easy to access information about them, they are easy to contact, they understand the sales process, and they have their own retirement planning needs. Most real estate firms do not provide retirement plans for their Realtors, so the retirement planning rests on the shoulders of the Realtors themselves. What's more, most successful Realtors have uneven cash flow. A significant home sale can result in a six-figure paycheck that might be the only cash flow the Realtor gets in months. The temptation to make a big purchase right after a big paycheck is high, and managing cash flow and developing a thoughtful retirement planning strategy can be challenging.

Most advisors overlook marketing to Realtors because so many Realtors are not successful that it's easy to disregard the successful ones. You can be assured that Realtors who have had consecutive years of success earn a high income and have plenty of money to invest. Realtors are also easy to access because they want potential clients to know about them, their successes, and how to contact them. There is no target market that is easier to access information about and contact than successful Realtors.

There is a pervasive myth in our industry that Realtors invest most of their money in real estate. In actuality, Realtor firms discourage their Realtors from investing in real estate because of the time it takes to maintain and oversee the real estate they own. A successful Realtor works many hours and doesn't have the time or interest to manage a real estate portfolio.

HOW TO ACCESS

Develop a list of the major Realtor firms in your market and visit their websites. You will find a list of all the Realtors who work for the particular firm. You can also find that in most cases, each of the Realtors has his or her own website and you can access that website by simply clicking on the Realtor's listing on the company website. At these websites you will find all the information you need about how successful the Realtor is, what his or her outside interests are, and other important information about the Realtor's level of affluence.

Any financial advisor who took the time to look at John's website could quickly determine that he was a highly affluent prospect worth pursuing. For example, a typical website might share that John Realtor has the following interests:

♦ Some $20 million in real estate sales in the past year (which signifies over $1 million in annual income)

♦ An extensive collection of single-malt scotch

♦ A vacation home on Cape Cod

♦ A passion for horses

♦ One of the most prestigious addresses in his city

♦ His cell phone number (unlike many affluent individuals, they want to make it easy for people to contact them and would never be on a "do not call" list)

HOW TO QUALIFY

There are so many Realtors who are unsuccessful and earn a modest income that prequalification is very important. Luckily, it is easy enough to qualify Realtors that it only makes sense to prequalify this target market. The easiest way to qualify Realtors is to find out how much in home sales they have generated in the past year, which you can determine simply by going to their websites. The gold standard for success among Realtors is an annual $10 million in home sales. This translates to between $400,000 and $500,000 in income and represents the top 1 percent of Realtors in a market. The next level of qualification would be a Realtor who generates at least $5 million in home sales; $5 million in home sales translates to between $200,000 and $250,000 in annual income, which represents roughly 5 percent of the

Realtors in most markets. I would encourage you to focus on Realtors who generate at least $5 million in annual home sales.

It is also worth noting that many successful Realtors are women whose household income could be even higher because of working spouses.

SCRIPTS FOR APPROACHING REALTORS

Because information about successful Realtors is so easy to access, taking the time to discover their outside interests is an excellent way to connect with them. The following example shows how this conversation can take place:

> "John, this is Joe Advisor with XYZ Financial and I have made it a practice to get to know the top professionals in my market. I know you are one of the most successful Realtors in our area and I would like to have the opportunity to get to know you. I also looked at your website and saw that you have a collection of single-malt scotch. I thought it might be fun to get together at one of my favorite restaurants after work to get to know each other and enjoy a nice dinner. I know they have a good scotch selection at [restaurant]. Would you be open to joining me for dinner?"

REALTORS AS A NICHE MARKET

Another way to approach successful Realtors is to make clear that you specialize in their niche market and have experience working with Realtors. In making your specialization clear it's important that you share your knowledge by pinpointing their specific needs, which typically include retirement planning. Making it clear to the successful Realtor that you understand and have expertise helping them with their specific challenges will make your offering attractive to them.

It also makes sense for advisors to consider joining local Realtor associations as an affiliate member. This provides exposure, sponsorship opportunities, and speaking and networking opportunities.

An example of how you can position yourself with a successful realtor might be:

> "John, this is Dave Davis with XYZ Financial. I am calling you because I have developed both experience and expertise in working with suc-

cessful Realtors like yourself. I have found that some of the biggest challenges they have is managing their cash flow and developing comprehensive retirement planning strategies. I wanted to provide you with a complimentary discovery meeting where I can introduce myself and find out more about your specific situation and provide you with some ideas on how I could add value to your current investment and retirement planning strategy."

"Mr. /Ms. Successful Realtor, this is Jim Smith at XYZ Financial and the reason for my call is that I have worked with other successful Realtors like you. I just learned that you have achieved [mention sales level, $5 million roundtable, etc.]. I have made a commitment to developing a high level of expertise in identifying the investment issues and needs of successful, affluent Realtors like you. I believe we have a lot in common and I would appreciate the opportunity to meet you, find out more about your circumstances, and share with you how I could potentially help you. Could we meet a mutually convenient time and place next week?"

DEVELOPING A NETWORK GROUP

One of the most effective ways to develop a relationship and build a strong connection with a successful Realtor is to invite one to join your network group. Realtors also want to increase sales opportunities and not only will they reciprocate, you will also build a stronger connection and put yourself in a good position to compete for their investment business. Realtors are ideal referral sources because they are often aware of and involved in the relocation of successful individuals. Refer to Chapter 23 for more information on establishing a successful networking group with Realtors.

COMMERCIAL REALTORS

Most of the same principles that apply to successful residential Realtors apply to successful commercial Realtors. Including commercial Realtors as well as residential Realtors will double the opportunities in your market. As with residential Realtors, it is easy to get access to commercial realtors' background information, and they are underpenetrated as a group.

CHAPTER 28

Executives

EXECUTIVES OF PUBLIC COMPANIES REPRESENT one of the highest percentages of millionaires in the United States. Information about them is readily accessible, and the need for professional financial advice is very high. For all those reasons, financial advisors who make a commitment to this market will be rewarded for their efforts. To be successful with this market, however, you must be committed to developing the required expertise. Successful senior executives have very specific and often complex needs that you must understand and be able to help them solve. The advisors I know who have successfully penetrated this market have developed the necessary expertise and made a major time commitment to understand the unique needs of the this market and are aware of the resources their firms have that are specifically suited for the executive market.

Just because executives are affluent doesn't mean that this niche market is for all advisors. Some markets have many publicly traded companies and some simply do not.

As a rule, senior executives are more sophisticated and require higher-level planning needs, so if you target this market you must be willing to be challenged, to broaden your knowledge base on specific financial instruments, and to be prepared before every meeting. Because of the regulations governing the shares of publicly traded company stocks, the issues can be complex, and most senior executives are not aware of the different strategies they can follow regarding their stock and options. I have been surprised by the stories advisors have told me of how little senior executives know about rules and regulations that involve their equity holdings and the strategies available to them to hedge and provide liquidity to their concentrated positions. Those advisors who make the necessary commitment to acquire the expertise and knowledge can meet a very important need these affluent executives face, and they will find themselves with a receptive audience if they can educate and help these executives with their unique and complex investment needs.

If you are willing to make the commitment and work in a market that has an abundance of high-level executives, you will find that one of the advantages of this market is the wealth of public information that is available about individual executives of publicly traded companies. One of the most successful young financial advisors I have worked with shared his story about how he decided to focus on executives. "When I first started in the business I started to call business owners but soon became frustrated because it was hard to find information about them in order to prequalify them. I attended an office meeting where a corporate executive specialist mentioned how easy it was to get information about successful executives. He explained you can get on their company websites and read information from the proxy statements and see everything you need to know—where they are from, their background, their concentrated stock position, their option holdings, their deferred compensation, how many shares of their company they own, if they are borrowing against their stock, and where they went to college. It's all public information and it's filed once a year on the proxy. I decided that since profiling is such an important part of our business, this is an affluent market I can do that with and decided right then to pursue."

ACQUIRING THE RIGHT EXPERTISE

I asked an advisor who had a great deal of success with executives how he acquired the necessary expertise he needed to pursue this market. He contacted his firm's specialist on concentrated stock positions, hedging strategies on those positions, and liquidity strategies and asked him 300 questions to learn as much as he could on these strategies. Then he contacted the specialists on exchange funds and asked them hundreds of questions. He was determined that he was going to know more about concentrated stock positions and options strategies and tax treatment of those strategies than anyone else.

Another essential ingredient in pursuing the executive market is exuding confidence that you know what you are talking about and have the required expertise to serve this market. Most senior executives are bright and understand the importance of surrounding themselves with bright and knowledgeable people. When you convey your knowledge and confidence to them, your appeal to the executive market will be high.

LOCATING SENIOR EXECUTIVES

The next step is becoming familiar with the sources of public information that are available on executives of publicly traded companies. To get the proxy information go to FCC.gov and type in the company information. Another source of information is the company's S-1 filing report (the registration statement that a company is going public). The S-1 filing also shows what executives own what shares and what their compensation is.

Another excellent source is local business journals. These business journals include information on local companies that are being bought and sold as well as the names of the top executives of these companies. Additional sources of information can include *PR Newswire, Bloomberg, Dow Jones News Plus,* and the local newspaper.

Additional sources for executive can be found in the Appendix.

APPROACHING SENIOR EXECUTIVES

Once you have acquired the needed expertise and are familiar with the different information sources, you are ready to get started in pursuing the executive market. It's always more effective if you know or have an existing client who is an executive inside a publicly traded company who can provide you with an introduction to other senior executives. If, however, you don't have any potential referral sources, making a direct marketing contact to a targeted executive is required.

Most senior executives have secretaries, assistants, or other types of gatekeepers whose primary role is to keep people away from the executive. One strategy to get around them is to get the targeted executive's direct number and call her early in the morning or later in the afternoon (before 8 A.M. or after 5 P.M.). This information is often found on the company's website or by calling into the company directory outside normal hours when the direct extensions can be provided.

Sample Scripts

"Mr./Ms. Senior Executive, this is Joe Advisor, financial advisor with XYZ Financial here in [city]. I'll be brief. The reason for my call is that

I/my team works with a select few corporate executives of public and private companies, helping them to navigate concentrated stock and option positions. What I would like to do is to sit down with you and tell you about some strategies that we've implemented for many of our executive clients to protect and grow their concentrated stock positions. Would you have some time next Thursday?"

"Mr./Ms. Senior Executive, this is Jane Advisor calling from the Private Client Group at XYZ Financial in [city]. My team and I provide financial planning and investment advisory services to successful executives like you who lack the time and resources to effectively manage their own financial affairs. I have other clients who work at your company and I am familiar with many of the benefits your company provides. After we meet, I can also provide you with references from other executives who work at your firm if you are interested.

"Mr./Ms. Senior Executive, this is Jane Advisor at XYZ Financial in [city] and I work with successful executives like yourself. I have found executives in your situation lack the time and resources to effectively manage their own financial affairs, and I wanted to see if you have had any experience in working with an advisor like myself who specializes in working with senior executives and would be interested in learning more about how I help successful executives like yourself."

"Mr./Ms. Senior Executive, this is Jim Smith calling from XYZ Financial, and we specialize in working with corporate executives of public and private companies, working with them on planning strategies that are specific to their situation. As you know you are going to be in a section–16 situation, you are going to have restrictions. Our job is to help you navigate through those restrictions with your concentrated and restricted stock and options."

"Mr./Ms. Prospect, my name is Jane Advisor, with XYZ Financial's Wealth-Management Group. We specialize in helping successful executives of public companies handle their restricted stock and options. If we could show you a way to manage your equity exposure effectively, would you be interested in a brief meeting?"

"Mr./Ms. Executive, my name is Joe Advisor and I'm a financial advisor at XYZ Financial. I'm calling you because I specialize in working with successful executives who have restricted shares and stock options. The timing, liquidity opportunities, and tax implications of options and restricted shares can have a meaningful impact on your net worth, and I believe I can offer you insights into your situation that can make a difference. I would be glad to work around your schedule and stop by your office. Your time will be well spent. What time would be convenient for you?"

One technique that is effective with successful executives is to contact them when you have something of value to offer. If through the discovery process after reviewing the proxy or S-1 reports you determine that an executive owns 350,000 shares of a $40 stock, you will know that he is going to be interested in his stock position. Knowing any information you can provide about his company, research opinions, and earnings estimates, earnings, or research updates will be a high priority for him. Having this information available and knowing he has a vested interest is an effective way to make an initial contact, get through the gatekeeper, or use as a follow-up connection. For example:

Advisor: This is Joe Advisor, with XYZ Financial. May I speak with Mr./Ms. Senior Executive?"

Ms. Gatekeeper: He is not available right now. May I help you?

Advisor: Sure, our firm just released a favorable report on your firm that I'm sure he would be interested in seeing. Before I send it to him I would like to make a brief introduction. Could you connect me to him or schedule a time I could call to introduce myself and offer to send him this research report on his firm?

Advisor: This is Jane Advisor at XYZ Financial. Is Dr. Jones available?

Mr. Gatekeeper: No, he is busy.

Advisor: Our firm just released a great research piece on your company and I'm sure he'd like to see it. It may update his earnings expectations and I'd like to send it over to him for his review. If you provide me with his e-mail address I would be happy to send it to him.

Once you get the e-mail address, send the research report to the executive and in the e-mail write: "Here is some research I thought you would be interested in about our firm's view of your company. I'd love a chance to sit down and talk about this with you."

Prospect Follow-up

"Mr./Ms. Executive, this is Jane Advisor, and our firm just released a very interesting research report on your company. As I mentioned to you during our last meeting I am committed to being a resource for you and providing you with information I think you would be interested in. I would like to e-mail the report to you and continue to stay in touch."

THE LAW OF LARGE NUMBERS

Penetrating the executive niche market involves making a lot of contacts. Many advisors I have interviewed who are successful in this market have shared with me that their victories rest within the law of large numbers. As a guideline, you should expect to make one hundred calls to get ten contacts and with experience you should expect to get one appointment. This means there is a contact-to-appointment ratio of between ten and twenty to one.

The following case studies show how persistence pays off.

Case Study 1

A team of two advisors who specialize in working with senior executives targeted a company and made many calls trying to reach the senior executives. They finally got the CFO to take their call. The team convinced the CFO to meet with them and after the meeting the CFO said, "I can tell you guys know what you are doing and I'd like to work with you guys. Unfortunately I have no money, just restricted stock." The team got his e-mail address and every time they received a research report or update on this particular company they sent it to the CFO. As they continued to communicate, mostly through e-mail, they started to build a stronger relationship. A year later they went out to see him again and he said, "All of my money is still in restricted stock, but I would love to work with you guys at some point." The team kept up the correspondence and within sixty days the company was acquired for $2.3 billion. The team didn't call the CFO; he called them.

Case Study 2

An advisor who specializes in working with senior executives called into a Fortune 500 company in her market and reached one of the senior vice presidents. After the initial call the executive said, "I understand you can explain concentrated stocks but our company pays for a planning company to work with us." The advisor responded by saying, "With respect to concentrated stock, are they doing prepaid forwards for you? Are you doing any exchange funds?" The executive was vague about the answer to the questions posed by the advisor and finally responded by saying, "You should call our CEO. He has a very large concentrated position."

The advisor contacted the CEO and referenced the senior vice president's suggestion. The CEO said, "My best friend works at ABC Financial, but you should call our corporate counsel; he probably needs to hear what you have to say about concentrated stock position strategies. I'll tell him I told you to call him." The advisor called the corporate counsel mentioned by the CEO and got the appointment and eventually opened an account with the corporate counsel for $20 million.

THE PROCESS

Once you get the initial appointment you want to focus on the discovery process. Begin the process by going through the fact-finding exercises, including previous investment experience and personal information. As a side note, it's easy to find the personal information because most people have pictures, awards, diplomas, etc., related to what's important to them all around their offices.

At some point in the first meeting, give her a taste of what you could do for her and the level of experience you have. You want the prospect, however, to do 80 percent of the talking—you want to learn about her. The goal is to ask questions about things she hasn't given a lot of thought to or doesn't know the answers to; position yourself as an expert through your questions. Examples of some potential questions could include:

+ "Do you have a strategy for your concentrated stock position?"
+ "Have you developed a long-term financial plan?"
+ "What are your future cash flow needs after you retire?"
+ "Have you made retirement plans? What is your potential time frame?"

+ "Have you developed any estate planning strategies?"
+ "Do you have incentive stock options or nonqualified options?"
+ "Do you have an irrevocable insurance trust?"
+ "Who is the trustee for your trust?"

End the meeting by positioning the value of the comprehensive planning process. At the end of the appointment you might say, "Why don't you let us analyze what you've got, and we'll come back to you with some recommendations on areas of inefficiencies that we can address." Or, "Thank you for taking the time to share with me all of this information [repeat highest priorities]. The next step is to go back and thoughtfully think through your situation and see how we might best be able to help you in the following areas [repeat highest priorities]. How does that sound?" Then get out your calendar and schedule an appointment with the executive, then send a meeting reminder when you get back to the office.

THE SECOND MEETING

The goal for the second meeting is to deliver on what you promised, give the executive an overview of your strategy, and suggest some recommendations she should consider to accomplish her long-term goals. The goal is to have the executive commit to a more in-depth planning process. The most important topic is goal-based planning and specifically developing a strategy around the executive's cash flow needs after retirement. Estate planning and the strategies surrounding it are high priorities for most senior executives. They want to know how they can keep their wealth for many generations and how to effectively pass down their wealth. Another potential topic is setting up charitable remainder trusts for their concentrated stocks, understanding gifting strategies and the lifetime gift exemptions.

The objective is to position yourself as the CFO of their family. Position yourself as taking care of their financial lives so they can concentrate on their jobs and be comfortable that all their investment needs are being handled. By discussing all these different issues you are making the case to go through the comprehensive planning process, and to get them to engage in the planning process and to include the spouse in this process, you have greatly increased your odds of getting the senior executive as a client.

SUMMARY

+ Senior executives are busy people who are difficult to reach. Persistence is necessary to attract their attention.

+ Senior executives often have gatekeepers whose job is to keep you away from them. E-mail is an effective tool to circumvent the gatekeeper.

+ It is easy to gather information about executives through several reports available to the public.

+ Using recent research reports on the company of a senior executive is an excellent way to start a relationship with the target executive.

+ Don't make the assumption that senior executives fully understand their options and restricted stock benefits, the tax implications, and what investment strategies are best suited for them.

+ Financial advisors looking to make this their niche market will need to be well-versed in the unique needs of senior executives.

CHAPTER 29

Influencers

BUILDING A NETWORK OF INFLUENCERS IS THE OBJECTIVE of this market action plan. Influencers are CPAs and attorneys, both of whom are powerful referral sources; these professionals have significant influence with their clients, and when they recommend a financial advisor to their clients, their clients often take heed.

The key to this strategy is quality, not quantity. If you can build a network of six CPAs and estate planning attorneys who consistently give you referrals, you will have built an excellent network.

The objective is to share your approach with these influencers and to demonstrate that this approach is better than the one their clients' current financial advisors use. But be aware that referring clients to you will reflect on the influencer and she will therefore be cautious in doing so. Explain to these influencers that you will do everything you can to help them (such as providing ongoing education and cost-basis research on anything they need) and to facilitate a professional relationship with them.

The key with this group is to educate them in areas of interest to them and in areas that will make them look smart in the eyes of their clients. Education on the capital markets and current events as they apply to the markets will be of high interest to them. Not only will you be providing value, but the influencers will appreciate your expertise; their confidence in you as someone they can refer their clients to will grow.

HOW TO BUILD YOUR INFLUENCER NETWORK

In Chapter 12, "Leveraging Clients to Get New Ones," a section was devoted to building relationships with your current clients' CPAs and attorneys. I would recommend that you review that section and use it together with the ideas presented in this chapter.

There are three suggestions for starting your network.

RETIREE SEMINARS

When you are presenting seminars to retirees (or to anyone, for that matter), invite one of your CPA or estate planning attorney prospects to join the program. This will add to the depth of the seminar and will create a partnership; it will allow the influencer to see you in action. This is an excellent first step in developing a relationship with an influencer who could be part of your network.

QUARTERLY EDUCATIONAL SEMINARS

This is an effective way to both start an influencer network and leverage it after you have built it. Identify all the CPAs in your market area. Personally contact each one and invite them to a relevant seminar on tax-related issues that would benefit them. Invite the CPAs a month in advance, and follow up several times before the seminar. I recommend that you present different seminars quarterly to the same group of CPAs.

Make sure you have expert speakers. Provide lunch, and be sensitive to the timing as it relates to their busy tax season. Take part in the presentation so that the CPAs can see your expertise and professionalism firsthand. Provide continuing education credits. Ideal attendance is twenty to twenty-five CPAs.

The objective of these seminars is to provide a valuable resource for CPAs so they have a reason to reciprocate—rarely will you be able to provide them with as many referrals as they provide you. Follow up with the CPAs in attendance every month; share with them your expertise, educate them, and familiarize them with your wealth-management process.

The topics of these seminars should not be product-related. Here are some ideas for topics:

- Changes in the tax law that will affect their clients
- How options and master limited partnerships are affected by the tax law and how to interpret the reporting received by their clients
- Defined-benefit plans
- Estate planning tax issues

- Medicare and Medicaid tax reporting
- Retirement issues and plan design
- Business valuations as it relates to tax law

How to Get Continuing Education Accreditation

To get continuing education accreditation for your presentations to CPAs, contact your state board of accounting and apply for CPA continuing education credits; for presentations to attorneys, submit your presentation agenda to your state supreme court.

Seminar Introduction

"Thanks for coming to our seminar. I want to reiterate our commitment to providing high-quality information on timely topics and to providing whatever service we can to the CPA community as a thank-you for the business we get from you. Please take the time to fill out the feedback questionnaire so that we can continue to improve our seminars. We are willing to provide all the resources we have available. We want to be on the list of advisors you refer your clients to when the occasion arises."

FACE-TO-FACE MEETINGS

Identify the CPAs and estate planning attorneys in your market territory. Do this by compiling a list of your clients' CPAs and attorneys and by calling CPAs and attorneys from the Yellow Pages. The objective is to get a face-to-face appointment with these influencers.

Introduction

"Mr. /Ms. CPA/Attorney, my name is Jane Advisor and I am with XYZ Financial. I am in the process of getting to know the best CPAs in my market with whom to develop a professional relationship. As I continue to build my practice, it is among my highest priorities to build a network with the right professionals. I also believe there is a possibility that in the future we could share mutual clients. I would like the opportunity to meet with you and find out more about your practice. When would be a convenient time for us to get together for an introductory meeting?"

"Mr./Ms. Influencer, this is Joe Advisor, and I am an advisor from XYZ Financial. I am building my wealth-management practice in this town/location. If we don't have any mutual clients now, I am sure we will in the future. I know you are a successful professional, and I would like to meet you, find out more about your practice, and tell you about mine. Would you be receptive to a meeting next Thursday?"

Introduction (Mutual Client)

"Mr./Ms. Influencer, my name is Jane Advisor with XYZ Financial and we have a mutual client, [give name]. I am in the process of building a network of successful professionals like you. I would like to meet you face to face to find out more about your practice and share what we do for our clients. Would you be available to meet?"

In the first meeting, spend the majority of the time understanding the CPA's or attorney's practice and what type of clients she is looking for. Also give a brief description of your practice and wealth-management process. Suggest a second meeting where you can share in more depth how you work with your clients and some ways that you could add value to them and their clients.

In the second meeting, focus on sharing your wealth-management process and your value proposition (See "Wealth Management," Chapter 10) and how you are different. The purpose of this meeting is to separate you from what the CPA or attorney perceives as the typical "stockbroker." Invest as much time as you need to understand the CPA's or attorney's practice so you can add value to her practice by giving her a good understanding of how your wealth-management process is unique. The most common reason for lack of referrals is that the influencer does not know what an advisor really does and a relationship of trust hasn't been formed.

After the first meeting, concentrate on providing valuable information to the influencer so that she looks at you as a true resource. Educate the CPA or attorney with information that can help her and that she is interested in. Some examples of this type of information are your firm's insight into tax laws and changes, market outlooks, wealth-management tools, current issues and how they affect markets, how the capital markets work, and innovative liability products. Provide this information on a regular basis. Once a month, have either a scheduled appointment or an informal drop-by.

This process should generate at least several new referral sources per year. If each referral source provides two new referrals a year and you can convert 90 percent of these referrals to clients, then this process should add at least four new affluent clients per year. This is in addition to the existing CPA/attorney network referrals you already have.

HOW TO LEVERAGE YOUR INFLUENCER NETWORK ONCE YOU HAVE STARTED IT

Referrals

Once you have started your network of influencers, one of the most effective ways to build it is to refer your clients to your network of CPAs and attorneys. Nothing gets more referrals from influencers than giving referrals. The best time to do this with a client is after a planning session, when you are discussing the client's current tax and estate planning situation and if she is not satisfied with her current CPA or attorney.

Seminars

Use your CPA network as a source of names for seminars. Suggest to the CPAs you work with that you would like to hold a relevant seminar for their clients, such as "Planning for Retirement: The Wealth-Management Process." Offer to mail and call the CPA's clients and invite them to the seminar. Provide lunch. Offer to follow up with each of the attendees the next day to discuss their individual situations. CPAs don't always know how to give referrals, and this is an excellent way to stimulate them.

Annual Update

Arrange an individual annual update meeting with each CPA and attorney in your network. Buy the person lunch, exchange ideas, share referrals, and solidify the relationship.

CPA Personal Account

Manage the CPA's account, even if it is below your minimum.

> "Mr./Ms. CPA, typically I accept only accounts with a minimum qualification of $250,000, but I would like to offer my services to you with no minimum so that you can experience firsthand the quality of our clients' experience."

Buy Lunch During Tax Season

Buy brown-bag lunches for CPA and staff members during the week before tax deadline. Have the lunches delivered with a card that says, "My compliments." This creates enormous goodwill.

Office Visits

Invite the members of your CPA network to your office and give them a presentation to explain what a client experiences with you. Share your wealth-management process and the tools you have, and introduce your team and the specialists you use, if any.

Quarterly Parties

Once a quarter, organize a nice dinner and cocktail party for your best clients. Have the dinner at a high-end, well-known restaurant to provide a good draw. Start cocktails at 6:00 P.M. After dinner, present a thirty-minute talk on a topic of interest to your clients given by an influencer who has given you referrals or is likely to be a good referral source. You should also spend 15 minutes giving a short presentation on an investment-related topic. If you have a sponsor for the party, have her share a relevant topic as well.

The purpose of this event is to give one of your best influencers the opportunity to speak to your best clients. The influencer will appreciate the opportunity and will be likely to reciprocate by giving you more referrals. The clients will appreciate being invited to a nice dinner with an interesting and relevant topic. This is also a great opportunity to encourage your best clients to invite an affluent friend.

CHAPTER 30

Alumni Marketing

MARKETING TO ALUMNI OF YOUR COLLEGE IS A GOOD STRATEGY for a number of different reasons. Successful people are typically loyal and grateful to their alma mater. In many cases their college years evoke strong, powerful memories and emotions. As a result, many affluent individuals are willing to give their college both their time and money. Becoming involved in your college alumni programs gives you the opportunity to meet and develop relationships with many affluent fellow alumni. What's more, marketing through your alumni organization gives you more than access to affluent individuals you may already know; it also provides you with priceless information.

There are four reasons why investing time in alumni marketing makes so much sense.

1. Access to affluent individuals
2. Important information
3. Common interests
4. Ease of involvement

ACCESS TO AFFLUENT INDIVIDUALS

Alumni organizations are set up to facilitate alumni interaction. The intent is for individuals of all ages, economic levels, and occupations to share their common college experience and connect behind a common goal: their commitment to their alma mater. If you are involved in your alumni organization, you will have access to some of the most affluent and committed alumni in your market and you will have a natural common interest to begin the relationship development required to do business.

IMPORTANT INFORMATION

One of the objectives of alumni organizations is to share information that helps connect fellow alumni. The amount of valuable information available to advisors whose intent is to market to fellow alumni's is considerable. Examples of information sources include alumni magazines, websites, and annual reports. From these sources of information you can determine where there is money in motion, significant events in fellow alumni's lives, amount of their contributions to the college, and networking opportunities. There are few marketing opportunities that provide more information about your target market than alumni organizations.

COMMON INTERESTS

Whether your common interests are in your alumni sports programs, your past major, past activities, common professors, or just love of your college, there is a strong tie between fellow committed alumni. One of the most effective ways to market in the financial services industry is to establish common interests with affluent individuals and build a relationship of trust. There are few better opportunities for financial advisors to establish and build stronger relationships with affluent individuals than their alumni organizations because of the strong and powerful shared college experience.

EASE OF INVOLVEMENT

Universities and colleges want to facilitate alumni connections because their alumni organizations help tie alumni back to the university/college and facilitate contributions. If you have any interest in getting involved with your alma mater and assuming a leadership position, nothing could be easier. Most schools have an entire alumni development department that is dedicated to getting interested alumni more involved; all you have to do is ask.

There are three primary ways the motivated advisor can organize her marketing efforts to build relationships with affluent alumni:

1. Becoming involved in established alumni organizations
2. Developing an alumni organization
3. Reading alumni publications and contacting featured alumni

BECOMING INVOLVED IN ESTABLISHED ALUMNI ORGANIZATIONS

In most major markets there are already established alumni organizations designed to facilitate strong relationships among fellow alumni. Regardless of whether you are in a market that is close to your alma mater or not, it is likely that there are alumni organizations to join. If you are in a market close to your college there are often many opportunities to become involved in local alumni groups. These opportunities can range from sports watching, networking, and luncheons to opportunities to be on boards of your college and travel opportunities. If you are a longer distance away there may be fewer alumni and alumni activities, but the alumni connection is often stronger. The goal is to become involved and put yourself in a position of leadership.

The closer your market is to your college or university the larger the numbers of your fellow alumni. The more time you have committed to this effort the more opportunities you will have. It also makes sense to narrow your focus to your individual college major (business school, arts and sciences, education, journalism, etc.). The value of the smaller groups within the alumni organization is that the shared experiences are more closely connected and the number of people in common is likely to be much higher. You may recall past classmates, a special professor, or a graduate assistant who made an important difference in your life, and those same factors can connect you to other alumni who had the same experiences.

As your involvement increases, so will your ability to access information. The website of your university and more specifically the individual college (major) can provide a wealth of information about successful alumni as well as access to e-mail lists of other alumni who are committed to your individual college (major).

Oftentimes when you are in close proximity to your alma mater there can be so many alumni in a concentrated area the alumni organizations are organized by county. This gives you the ability to access information and connect with affluent alumni who are in close proximity to where you live and work. You will also then share one more point of connection: where you now call home.

The best way to get connected with your local alumni organization is to simply go to your alma mater's website and look for the alumni relations department. Contact the department and let it know that you would like to get more involved. Ask about the scope of opportunities and alumni organizations you can get involved with. The same suggestion would apply to your individual major and department.

I can recall an example of a fraternity brother of mine who from the year he graduated became actively involved in our university's alumni program. He lived close to the university and generously gave both his time and money. He formed a young alumni organization that he remained committed to for many years and helped grow into one of the strongest alumni organizations at our university. Over the next thirty years his position and influence within our university continued to grow. He was recently appointed president of the national alumni association and in that role interacts with the president of the university, is the partner to the head of the internal alumni president, and interacts with the most powerful, affluent, and influential alumni. This gentleman made a long-term commitment but has been rewarded by having access to the all right people in a powerful and influential leadership role. For a financial advisor it doesn't get any better than that.

As the distance from your alma mater increases, you lose the larger numbers of alumni and the variety of networking venues, but the marketing opportunities are just as great for different reasons. The further the distance, in many cases, the closer the connection because you and your fellow alumni are so far from home that the rarity of alumni makes the connection more valuable and meaningful. The college experience for many people is so powerful that being a long distance away makes the need to stay connected even stronger.

Most major markets will have an established alumni chapter of the largest or most prestigious universities. All those out-of-town alumni chapters will be delighted to have you become involved in a leadership position. The objective is to become a chapter president, and while that might not happen overnight, it is certainly an obtainable position. It starts with a willingness to become involved in a leadership position and to make known your aspiration to lead the alumni chapter (become president of your alumni chapter).

For example, I live in Colorado, where there are two thousand of my fellow alumni, even though we are more than 1,400 miles away from my university. At first I was surprised to learn that there were so many of my fellow alumni in Colorado: I had met only one before I got involved in the local alumni organization. When I contacted the development office I learned that approximately 10 percent, or two hundred, of these alumni have either given to the university or have been targeted by the university as being capable of providing a gift of $100,000 or more. My estimation is that an individual would have to have investable assets of well over $1 million to be capable of a $100,000 gift—therefore these two hundred individuals would be exactly the kind of affluent individuals a financial advisor would like to make a connection with.

As chapter president you may not know exactly who those two hundred people are, but you would know who all the alumni are in your state and how to reach them. By having their names you can do some research to determine their positions and prequalify those fellow alumni you would like to build relationships with. Also, as the chapter president you will have many occasions to interact with your target list as you reach out to them on behalf of the alumni chapter that you head. In short, becoming an alumni chapter president is one of the easiest ways for you to increase prospects who have shared interests with you.

DEVELOPING AN ALUMNI ORGANIZATION

If you are in a market that is a long way from your alma mater, you may not have an existing local alumni organization, or it may be very small or weak. This is a perfect opportunity to become a leader in establishing or strengthening a long-distance alumni organization. If you are motivated, you could contact the alumni relations department from your university and offer to start a chapter or work toward upgrading an existing club to a chapter. After a screening and orientation process your university would provide you with the support, including a list of alumni in your market and all the resources you need to either start or elevate an existing club into a chapter.

READING ALUMNI PUBLICATIONS

Commit to gaining access to all the available publications and information that your alma mater provides. This is often as simple as making a small contribution and requesting all alumni publications. The first step is to visit your school website and the individual department you graduated from.

There are a number of different types of alumni magazines available at most universities and colleges, and I recommend requesting a copy of every single one of them because the value of the information is so high. Here's a dissection of an actual monthly alumni publication to show how much valuable information is available to connect you with potential prospects:

- Front-page feature on alumni who have made outstanding contributions to their fields
- Recognition of groups of individuals—Top 10 businesses and access to all nominations
- Feature on professors and university employees and the national recognition that they have achieved
- Human interest story about a professor who recently retired after thirty-eight years
- Featured alumni stories
- Class notes—alumni updates by class from 1940 through 2012 as well as alumni profiles of ten successful and influential alumni
- Calendar of alumni events, both national and local
- A listing of new books published by alumni
- 2012 alumni association awards luncheon invitation
- Nominations for the school's most outstanding "40 under forty" alumni

> Alumni magazines do a good job of identifying successful alumni and finding ways to recognize them. The strategy is to go beyond the magazine articles and look at the websites where all the nominees are listed. It's good to know who the owners of the top ten businesses are, but it is even better to know who the top one hundred are that were nominated, all of whom are proud of their accomplishments.

Outside of physical publications, many universities provide their alumni access to powerful search engines that allow you to search for alumni by job title. One financial advisor who graduated from a very prestigious university has the ability to identify all the CEOs in the nation who graduated from his university just by entering "CEO" in the alumni search engine.

Each department or college within a university can have its own website, alumni development officers, and fund-raising initiatives. As mentioned earlier, often focusing on your individual college gives you an even stronger connection with your fellow alumni. Look to these websites for detailed information about their activities, featured alumni, boards of directors, and opportunities to get involved.

Additionally these colleges have annual reports that among other things include alumni who have given gifts to a particular college, and while the exact amounts of gifts are not provided, the levels of giving are. It's not hard to determine by the level of gifts how successful these alumni are.

LinkedIn is another powerful tool to help you connect with alumni nationwide. That is discussed in detail in Chapter 22.

RECOGNIZING SUCCESS

In most alumni publications there is a section called "class notes," which is a listing of alumni by class year and specific accomplishments, achievements, and awards that they have received. That alumni take the time to submit these achievements means they are obviously very proud of them. For a financial advisor this provides a wonderful opportunity to both prequalify and recognize successful fellow alumni.

The following are some excerpts of class notes in my most recent alumni magazine, which is published monthly (the names have been changed):

♦ Jim Smith (BS 1954): inducted into the Tennessee Hall of Fame.

♦ Lee Jones (BBA 1959): named the 2011 Jewish humanitarian of the year.

♦ Rick Smith (BBA 1972): elected to XYZ board of directors.

♦ Steve Smith (BS 1979): elected by governor of the state to be the state treasurer.

♦ Greg Jones (BBA 1976): named Southeast innovator of the year.

♦ Tom Rogers (BBA 1980): appointed to position of senior vice president and CEO for a major hospital.

♦ Mike Miller (AB 1987): named senior vice president and general counsel for a major corporation.

One of the ways to make a connection with these successful alumni is to highlight their names in the class notes section and laminate the page and mail it to them with an attached note: "Congratulations on your accomplishments and being featured in our alumni magazine. I thought you might like an extra copy. I enjoy meeting and working with successful individuals, particularly from our college. I would like to call you next week and introduce myself. Again, congratulations on your accomplishments and I look forward to making a connection with you."

I would recommend that you follow up the mailing with a call one week later:

"Mr./Ms. Alumni, this is Jane Advisor with XYZ Financial and an alumni of ABC University. I noticed that you were recognized in our alumni magazine for your recent [promotion, recognition, publication] and I wanted to congratulate you on your success. I sent you a laminated copy of the page where you were featured. I hope you got it. I specialize in working with successful individuals like you and I wanted to invite you to [a meeting, lunch, coffee] to get acquainted and to share with you our wealth-management process and how I might potentially add value to your current investment situation. Would you be open to getting together at a mutually convenient time?"

Another version of the call might sound like the following:

"This is Joe Advisor with XYZ Financial and I hope you got the article I sent you from our alumni magazine—congratulations again on your success. In my practice at XYZ Financial I enjoy working with successful people like you. I would like to have the opportunity to meet you over coffee to make a connection and share with you how I could potentially add value to your current investment situation and at the very least provide you with a second opinion. Would you be open to meeting at a mutually convenient time?"

Your chances of getting an appointment with a successful alumnus have increased considerably by taking the time to notice her recognition and sending her a copy of it before you made the first call. Alumni are proud of their accomplishments and you are putting your best foot forward by taking the time to recognize them.

This same technique works for all the alumni information you have access to, whether it is being recognized in class notes, alumni profiles, top businesses, top forty under forty, or books published. People appreciate and like to be recognized, and as an active alumnus you have all the information you need to provide that recognition to a steady stream of successful alumni from your alma mater.

SUMMARY

♦ Alumni organizations are fertile ground for providing new prospects.
♦ Alumni groups located close to your university have the greatest con-

centration of members and provide the most opportunities to connect.

♦ Alumni groups located far from your university have a small concentration of members, but those members might feel a deeper connection to the university.

♦ Alumni publications of all sorts provide a wealth of information on potential prospects.

♦ The goal should be to become president of your local alumni chapter, a position in which you will have greatest access to alumni information in terms of charitable giving.

CHAPTER 31

Retirement Plans

IN TARGETING RETIREMENT PLANS, I recommend the following three steps:

1. **Specialize.** To be successful with qualified retirement plans, you should focus on retirement plans between $1 million and $50 million in size. This is the most advantageous segment.

2. **Gain expertise.** Before you begin prospecting, you must be willing to commit to developing a high level of expertise. This is a market in which knowledge is truly essential. Your firm's retirement group can give you much of the training and information you need, as can a mutual fund's partner education program (your wholesaler can guide you to these), and you can read books on retirement plans. Your efforts to continually increase your competencies will give you a definite competitive advantage in securing retirement plan business. Many retirement plans have problems with plan design or fiduciary responsibility, so introducing yourself as an expert in these areas is a great way to open the door to getting an appointment. There have also been increased regulations, requirements, and responsibilities for fiduciaries of retirement plans.

3. **Make contact.** Call the person who signed the 5500 form, identify yourself as a specialist in retirement plans, and ask if she will be putting the retirement plan out for bid, either now or in the future. Another tactic is offering a complimentary retirement review to evaluate her retirement expense ratio and fund performance as compared with other plans of her size. If she is open to a change, that is an excellent time to make an appointment. Remember, your goal is simply to gain an audience with the decision maker.

An excellent lead source for retirement plans is *Pension Planet*, which is featured in the Appendix of the book.

Retirement Plan Script

"Mr./Ms. Business Owner, this is Jim Smith. I'm a vice president with XYZ Financial and the reason for my call is I realize the importance of getting the most out of your business's retirement plan assets. I have found that many retirement plans pay too much for below-average returns. As a fiduciary I know you would be interested in getting the most from your retirement plan for yourself and your employees and I would like to offer you a complimentary review of your plan. My objective would be to show you how you could get a better return for potentially less cost. Could we schedule a mutually convenient time when I could come to your business location, introduce myself, and find out more about your retirement plan?"

"This is Jane Advisor, and I'm a financial advisor at XYZ Financial. I specialize in working with retirement plans, and I want to ask if you are going to put your retirement plan out for bid now or in the near future. [Or, when was the last time you made a change in your retirement plan?] I would like to have an opportunity to share with you the benefits of considering XYZ to handle your plan. I will be in the area on Thursday and would like the opportunity to introduce myself and show you how we could make a positive difference."

"This is Joe Advisor, and I'm a financial advisor at XYZ Financial. I specialize in working with retirement plans, and I wanted to find out if you have been at all concerned with the performance of your plan. If you are open to a second opinion, we offer an open platform with a wide range of investments and managers, and I would like to share with you some alternatives you might consider. Would you be available on Thursday for a brief meeting?"

RED ZONE MARKETING: PRE-RETIREES

The demographics have never been more in favor of the financial services industry than right now. There are approximately 80 million individuals who are approaching retirement age, the baby boomers. The need for retirement planning and developing a postretirement cash-flow strategy is critically important after an individual is over 50 and within ten years of retirement. I believe that the ten years before an individual retires are the most important in his investment life, and I call this period of time the Red Zone.

The first step in this market action plan is to find out who the biggest employers in your market are and develop a Red Zone strategy and a prospect list of these local companies. It is also worthwhile to determine whether their retirement plans permit in-service withdrawals. The best way to do this is to ask people you know who work for these companies; if you don't know anyone there, then simply call the company and ask for someone in HR.

Once you've targeted the company, the next step is to find individuals in the company who are 50 or older and who may be close to retiring. To find out who these people are, you must establish a contact within the company. If you already know someone who is at the company, the best method is to simply ask her about people she knows who are 50 or older or who may be close to retirement.

If you don't know anyone in the company, then you need to get a company directory. Here are some ways to go about that:

◆ Ask the receptionist who are some people you can talk to about sales (easy to get), purchasing, service, company information, or something similar. Start calling these people or departments. As you develop prospects and build relationships within the company, ask if they would be comfortable sharing a directory with you.

◆ It may be possible to get a lead on a directory by checking the company's website.

◆ Many companies post the names of their top employees in the building directory, and you can get names that way.

◆ Check the local newspaper (especially the online version, which is searchable) for promotions and other announcements.

◆ You can purchase directories from leads brokers (see Appendix).

LinkedIn is another excellent source for determining potential Red Zone prospects. Enter the name of the targeted company in the Advanced Search field of your LinkedIn home page. All the contacts and second-level contacts in that particular company will be shown. You can check their profiles to see how old they are (see college graduation date) and if they have changed companies to determine if they would be candidates for IRA rollovers.

If you have had past experience in the targeted industry or target a company where you have worked in the past, you have a real advantage in identifying qualified Red Zone prospects. You would know the particulars of the retirement plan and qualified individuals over 50 who work at your targeted company as well as having access to the corporate directory.

The next step is to identify and establish a relationship with centers of influence within the company; each center of influence can introduce you to prospects inside the company. Start this process by establishing contact with an insider who can identify five or six coworkers who are five years from retirement, or who can help you identify the centers of influence. This means that you must be willing to educate employees who are retiring in five years; this may not result in much business initially, but it is an excellent way to build a base within the company and to build a strong foundation for future business. Employees five or more years from retirement are not heavily marketed to and are appreciative of someone willing to invest time to educate them on their future retirement options.

Once you have identified five or six employees, have lunch with each one and discuss 401(k) allocation and your wealth-management process. In many cases, these employees may not have a lot of assets outside of their retirement plans and will appreciate your free advice on how to allocate their retirement assets. The key is to build relationships with these employees and ask them to refer you to other people who may need your help. Your objective over time is to be considered an insider by the retiring employees of the company.

Another excellent way to reach new prospects within the company is to invite your initial contacts to a pre-retirement seminar and give each of those prospects five or six seminar invitations to pass out to other pre-retirees in the company. This will greatly expand your contacts within the company. At each seminar, hand out response cards to set up the follow-up process. You will get people's e-mail addresses and will be able to e-mail them with relevant market research, reports, and research on their company, and to set up initial meetings.

Once you have a number of prospects within the company, organizing fun events that are tied to their interests is an excellent way to build relationships and enhance your reputation.

EMPLOYEES BEING "DOWNSIZED"

Individuals who have recently been laid off have money in motion, and they need help and guidance immediately. Their highest priority is dealing with their current retirement plan, and they need to know the intricacies of IRA rollovers and their tax implications.

To be successful in this market, you should develop an expertise in helping laid-off employees with financial issues as well as other critical issues such as how they can find another job and whether they can afford to retire. If you do this, you can position yourself as the one resource who can help them with their entire situation, either directly or by referring them to other resources (which is also an excellent networking opportunity).

You can generally find people who are being downsized in several ways:

♦ Establish a contact at a company that is downsizing. See if you can discover whether this company's plan allows lump-sum distributions.

♦ Get information from your existing clients and prospects. Ask your clients and prospects regularly for the names of associates or friends who were recently laid off.

♦ Monitor your local papers for news of companies that are downsizing, and ask existing clients who work at those companies if there is anyone they know who might be affected.

♦ Work with counselors and services that assist employees who have been laid off. You can find these services in the Yellow Pages or get referrals from your HR contacts.

BECOMING AN OUTSIDE EXPERT

Preparation is required to execute a retirement-oriented market action plan effectively. You must develop an expertise in retirement distribution strategies, including NUA (Net Unrealized Appreciation) and IRA rollovers. You also need to target at least one large company in your area and become an expert in its particular retirement plan. The turnover among HR professionals is fairly high, so if you can establish yourself as the expert on a particular company's retirement plan, you will have great perceived value among the employees of that company and will have a natural "calling card."

Red Zone Scripts

"Mr./Ms. Prospect, this is David Jones, financial advisor with XYZ Financial here in [city], and the reason for my call is that I have developed both experience and expertise in helping individuals prepare for the most critical phase of their investment lives: retirement planning. The decisions you will make in the ten years leading up to your retirement are the most important in terms of your long-term financial well-being, and I have developed a retirement planning process that I know could make a positive difference for you. I've found I am most effective with individuals who have accumulated at least $250,000 toward their retirement, would that apply to you?"

If yes:

"I would like to offer you a complimentary discovery meeting where I could introduce myself, find out more about your circumstances, and outline my retirement planning process, which I'm confident could add value to your investment circumstances. When would be a convenient time for me to introduce myself to you?"

If no, I'm not interested:

"Is there anyone you know in your company who is retiring in the next five years whom you believe I could potentially help?"

"Mr./Ms. Executive, my name is Joe Smith at XYZ Financial. The reason I am calling you is that I have developed a level of expertise in working with successful executives like you. In addition to my experience working with executives, I am a [state professional designation] and I focus on helping executives effectively plan for their most critical years: the ten years before and after retirement. The decisions made during these years have a profound impact on an individual's ability to retire comfortably. I call this period of time the investment Red Zone. I am going to be in your area next Thursday and I would like the opportunity to introduce myself and offer you a complimentary retirement plan review to see if I could potentially add value to your Red Zone planning. Would you be available on Thursday?"

"Mr./Ms. Prospect, my name is Joe Advisor, and I'm a financial advisor with XYZ Financial. I specialize in working with individuals who are 50 or older who are interested in knowing more about their retirement options. I would like to get together with you and share what we have at XYZ and how we can benefit you and your family. I will be in the area on Thursday and could work around your schedule. What time would be good for you? Is there anyone else you know who is close to retirement whom you think I should talk to?"

Or offering a seminar:

"I would like to invite you to a seminar our team is providing to individuals like yourself who are in need of Red Zone planning. The seminar is [provide details] and will address head-on the issues you need to address to ensure a successful retirement. Would you be interested in attending our seminar?"

"Mr./Ms. Prospect, my name is Jane Advisor, and I'm a financial advisor with XYZ Financial. I specialize in working with individuals at ABC Company who are 50 or older and are interested in knowing more about their retirement options. I am presenting a seminar on retirement planning issues and challenges next Thursday night at [time and place], and I wanted to invite you and your spouse to attend. Would you be interested? Can you think of anyone else whom I should invite who would benefit from knowing more about what their retirement options are?"

"Mr./Ms. HR Director, my name is Joe Advisor, and I'm a financial advisor at XYZ Financial. The purpose of my call is to offer your company a pre-retirement seminar that addresses the concerns and issues that employees who will be retiring in the next five years might have. There is no cost to your company, and we have had very good feedback on our past seminars. I would like to have the opportunity to review the outline with you. Would you be interested?"

CHAPTER 32

Retirees

QUALIFIED RETIREES HAVE BOTH TIME AND MONEY and are often reluctant to accept an offer for an appointment with you if they don't know you. Because of these dynamics, educational seminars and events are among the most effective way to meet qualified retirees.

SEMINARS

A key to attracting retirees is to recognize that they have the time and may be interested in working with you, but they are reluctant to agree to an appointment without knowing you first. A seminar is an ideal way to position yourself as an expert and give the retiree an easy way to get to know you, making a follow-up appointment much easier. The seminar market action plan provides the techniques necessary to accomplish this.

The place to start is by gathering names. I recommend that you use a list broker to generate a list of prescreened names (see the Appendix). For example, you might ask for retirees who have annual incomes over $100,000 or investable assets over $500,000. Make sure that you screen out names that are on the do-not-call list.

Contact retirees personally and invite them to a seminar that is tailored to them, with a free meal included. Raise their interest in attending by telling them how the seminar will benefit them. Follow up the contact with a written invitation, and then a reminder the day before the seminar.

The ideal time for a seminar is from 9:30 A.M. to 10:30 A.M., and you should hold it at a well-known location. Serve coffee and light refreshments before the seminar and consider offering brunch afterward so you will have a chance to socialize with the attendees.

There are many seminar topics that will be of interest to retirees, such as "The Big Three Factors That Affect Retirees: Taxes, Fees, and Inflation" or "How to Maintain Your Cash Flow During Your Retirement Years." Break the seminar into two parts. In the first part, present the facts, and in the second part, give the audience three or four ideas or strategies to use. Each part should last between fifteen and twenty minutes.

End the seminar by stating that you would like to meet with each of them to discuss their individual situations, and state that the only price of admission is to accept your follow-up call. If you follow up and have qualified retirees attending, you should expect at least one $250,000 client per event.

OTHER PROVEN STRATEGIES

- Contact the recreational directors of retirement communities and assisted-living facilities (not nursing homes) and offer to provide a seminar or a series of classes on investment topics that would be of interest to their residents.
- Referrals are another good way to get in front of retirees. Ask existing clients, prospects, and CPAs for introductions to other retirees.
- Host events for your retired existing clients centered on activities like golf, wine tasting, or cooking classes; ask your retired clients to bring along a retired friend.
- Look for specific clubs and organizations for retirees and offer to speak to them. Many companies have well-organized groups of retirees; an example is the "pioneers" of the Bell companies. Identify these retiree groups and provide investment information through seminars with good follow-up. You can also organize a retirees' group yourself. I've seen this done with excellent results.
- Build a network of influencers, then invite the members of your network to a golf outing and ask them to invite their best retired clients, or present joint seminars to retirees with the CPAs and attorneys in your network. This is a great way to help CPAs and attorneys get comfortable referring their retired clients to you.
- Retired military officers often have two retirement plans (military and their second career). There are two approaches to this group: You can advertise as a retirement specialist in one of the veterans' association newsletters, or you can host a seminar on "How to Make

the Most of Your Retirement Plan." See the Appendix for information on veterans.

Invitation Scripts

"Mr./Ms. Prospect, this is Joe Advisor with XYZ Financial. The reason for my call is that I want to invite you to a free seminar and brunch on the tax law changes and how they will affect your retirement plan. Do you currently have any retirement accounts?"

If the answer is yes, then:

"We have noticed that with many of our retired clients, there is some confusion as to how the tax law has affected mandatory distributions and beneficiary designations, which are topics we will be going over in our seminar. Would you be interested in attending?"

"Mr./Ms. Retiree, my name is Jane Advisor, and I'm a financial advisor at XYZ Financial. I am calling you because I am conducting a free seminar on investment issues that affect retirees. The seminar will be held at [give name of hotel] next Thursday, and breakfast will be included. Would you be interested in attending?"

"Mr./Ms. Recreational Director, my name is Joe Advisor, and I'm a financial advisor at XYZ Financial. The purpose of my call is to offer your community a special talk that is tailored to the retired investor. Our talks are timely and informative, and we have had excellent feedback on our past programs. I want to ask if you would like the opportunity to review the talk with me to see if there would be an interest on your part."

"Mr./Ms. Retiree, my name is Jane Advisor, and I'm with XYZ Financial. I wanted to personally invite you to a seminar that addresses three issues that retirees are concerned about: inflation, taxes, and fees. The seminar is [give date, time, and location]. Would you be interested in attending?"

CHAPTER **33**

Money in Motion

MONEY IN MOTION REFERS TO LARGER SUMS OF MONEY flowing into an affluent individual's life because of a change in her personal or professional circumstances. Examples of this are flows resulting from mergers and acquisitions, a high-level executive leaving a company, receiving an inheritance, a divorce from an affluent spouse, and the death of an affluent spouse. Each of these changes of circumstances generates money in motion, and this market action plan is designed to position you to compete for this money.

If you decide you want to pursue this market action plan, be prepared to spend the time necessary to develop your expertise. This market is highly competitive. Your knowledge must be specialized, particularly in the areas of mergers and acquisitions, senior executive changes, and Rule 144 transactions. If you don't have the right level of expertise, it will be obvious, and you will be wasting your time.

AN EXAMPLE OF THE GENERAL APPROACH

Each change of circumstance requires a specific approach, but the overall method is similar in most cases. To illustrate, let's say there is a business owner whose business is being bought or merged with.

When the news of the merger or acquisition becomes public and you become aware of it, you must move very quickly—if you know about it, chances are your competition does too. Your chances of getting through to the decision maker are much higher if you are among the first to make contact (by phone or overnight package) than if you are the twenty-fifth to do so. The day you become aware of the transaction, ship a package overnight.

The same day, make a call to the prospect. If the prospect does not return your first phone call but sees your name and then gets an overnight package from you, when you make a follow-up phone call two days later, your name will stand out, and he might talk to you.

Keep up your efforts because your competitors can be easily discouraged by the prospect's lack of response, and they will stop their marketing efforts. Eventually some of these prospects will take your call if you are persistent, if only to tell you that they are not interested. If you have enough of these opportunities outstanding, you will eventually have the opportunity to present to your targeted prospects. Your goal is to get a face-to-face meeting where you can gather information and where you can impress the prospect with your expertise and your ability to positively affect his situation.

You can use this same process with senior executives who are leaving or retiring from their company, and people involved in Rule 144 transactions.

Prepare and Customize

Preparation is essential. You must prepare and organize your different letters and packages in advance of the event. The first and last paragraphs should be customized to the particular situation, but the body of the letter can be the same, depending on the type of money-in-motion event. Also determine the sequence of the packages in advance and customize it as needed.

Here are my specific recommendations for the different types of money-in-motion situations.

MERGERS AND ACQUISITIONS

Bloomberg is a good source of information on merger and acquisition transactions. You can filter by geography, and you can get all the information about the transaction and the individuals involved. The main advantage of *Bloomberg* is the timeliness of the information; it is available the day the transaction occurs. Also useful are industry-specific trade publications; you can find these in the library or on the Internet. The advantage of both of these sources is that they are not as frequently used and often give you the information before your competition gets it, particularly for smaller transactions.

It's important that you focus on a couple of industries and really specialize in them so that you can stay on top of money-in-motion opportunities. As an example, one advisor who committed to this market action plan was able to uncover as many as twenty-five money-in-motion opportunities every day.

EXECUTIVE DEPARTURES

A senior executive leaving a public company is another excellent money-in-motion opportunity and one that is not as heavily prospected as merger and acquisition transactions. Executives who change jobs face IRA rollover and stock option consequences. Executives have less loyalty to their former companies after they leave and are more willing to diversify out of their concentrated positions.

If an executive is retiring, she has more time to evaluate different options and can be receptive to diversification. The role of the advisor also becomes more important, because the advisor becomes a retiree's connection to the business world and to the information she is interested in. Executives will appreciate you more after they retire than they did before.

The best sources of leads for executives who are leaving or retiring are the local newspaper, *Bloomberg*, and trade journals. This is where specialization in an industry is especially important because you can more easily be aware of the changes going on in that industry.

RULE 144 TRANSACTIONS

You can identify Rule 144 transactions through a number of sources, such as www.freeedgar.com. When an executive or past owner sells a block of stock, this triggers different opportunities for you to provide your expertise (tax liability, planning, diversification, and so on). The marketing process described in mergers and acquisitions can and should be followed in Rule 144 transactions.

INHERITANCES AND DIVORCE

You can find money involved in inheritance transactions by examining state records of probated wills with more than a predetermined amount of money over the past twelve months. Developing a network of estate and divorce attorneys is an excellent way to get in front of affluent prospects who are receiving inheritances or getting divorces.

DEATH

You need to handle the death of an affluent individual very carefully. The best source of information is your network of influencers (CPAs and estate attorneys). Alternatively, follow up with the surviving spouse six months after the death. It typically takes nine months for an estate to settle, and calling after six months takes much of the emotion out of the call and still leaves three months for tax arrangements.

HOME SALE

When someone buys or sells a home, large sums of money are in motion. These transactions are a matter of public record and can be easily identified (see the Appendix for sources). You can filter this list by dollar amount and date. You have opportunities on both the seller's and the buyer's side (buyers are also often new to the area). These real estate transactions are often listed in local newspapers.

EXECUTIVE RELOCATIONS

All executives who are transferring need a source of services in their new location, and this marketing technique will set you apart from your competition. Scan the local business journal and newspapers in your market for announcements of corporate executives who are relocating to the area. Overnight the most recent copy of the "Best of" (lists published by local papers giving the best services, restaurants, professionals, and other such providers in your area) to these relocating executives, along with a personalized note introducing yourself. Follow up with a phone call, preferably to where the executive works. Developing a network with successful Realtors will also help you identify relocating executives. Good Realtors are experts at identifying relocations.

Scripts

"Mr./Ms. Business Owner, my name is Joe Advisor, and I'm an advisor with XYZ Financial with experience in working with individuals like you who have had a significant change of circumstances. Hopefully you got the package I sent you that outlines our experience and approach. I would encourage you to give me the opportunity to meet with you and your advisors at your earliest convenience to share our approach and how we could help you."

"Mr./Ms. Executive, my name is Jane Advisor. I'm an advisor with XYZ Financial, and I have developed an expertise in working with senior executives like you. In changing firms, I'm sure you are considering different alternatives for dealing with the stock and options from your former company. I sent you a package that outlines our approach, expertise, and experience, and I would appreciate having the opportunity to schedule an appointment with you to share what we do and how that can benefit you. When would be the earliest we could get together?"

"Mr./Ms. Retiring Executive, my name is Joe Advisor. I am an advisor with XYZ Financial, and I have built both experience and expertise working with retired senior executives. I sent you a package that outlines our approach, expertise, and experience, and given your change of circumstances, I believe we could give you excellent investment guidance. I would appreciate the opportunity to meet with you at your earliest convenience to share our approach and how we could help you."

"Mr./Ms. Rule 144 Transaction, my name is Jane Advisor, and I'm an advisor at XYZ Financial. I have both experience and expertise working with executives involved in Rule 144 transactions. Our firm is highly ranked on the execution of large blocks of your company's stock, which reflects our ability to get you an excellent execution price on your stock. Additionally, we offer many products and services that could have a positive impact on your tax liability and investment performance. I would encourage you to give me the opportunity to meet with you at your earliest convenience to share our approach and how we could help you."

"Mr./Ms. Inheritor, my name is Joe Advisor, and I'm an advisor at XYZ Financial with experience working with individuals who have had a significant change of circumstances. I sent you a package that outlines our approach and expertise, and given your change of circumstances, I believe I could provide you with strong resources and excellent guidance. I would like to meet with you at your earliest convenience so that I can share our approach and provide you with specifics on how we could help you. Would you be available to meet next week?"

"Mr./Ms. Divorcee, my name is Jane Advisor, and I'm an advisor at XYZ Financial. I have spent a great deal of time working with people in your circumstances and have developed an expertise on the issues involved in your recent/current divorce. I understand that you might want a second opinion apart from that of your former spouse's advisor, and I want to offer that to you. If I could meet with you in the near future and find out the specifics of your circumstances, I'm sure I could provide you with valuable guidance. Would you be available for an appointment this week?"

"Mr./Ms. Widower/Widow, my name is Joe Advisor, and I'm an advisor at XYZ Financial. I understand that during the past six months, you have lost your spouse. First, I want to offer my condolences, and second, I want to make my advice and experience available to you. I understand the financial issues you are facing, and I know I could make a positive difference in your situation. Are you available for an appointment next week where I could learn the specifics of your circumstances and provide you guidance?"

CHAPTER 34

Nonprofits

DEVELOPING BUSINESS THROUGH PHILANTHROPIES is a natural approach to the high-net-worth market. Many high-net-worth clients are philanthropic; they may be philanthropic because they feel they can make a difference in society, or they may be philanthropic because the U.S. tax code rewards them with tax credits, or both.

Charitable contributions are tax deductible, and financial advisors can assist clients in a variety of ways in planning the best ways to give. Many high-net-worth clients employ strategies such as charitable remainder trusts, charitable lead trusts, private family foundations, donor-advised funds, and appreciated securities gifting. The beneficiaries of many of these strategies are public and private charities.

Financial advisors have two opportunities:

1. Affluent client relationships with board members and other community leaders
2. Management of a nonprofit's assets

These are not mutually exclusive, as you can do both at the same time and have individual clients who participate in both aspects of your business. You need to understand, however, that prospecting within nonprofits effectively can have a longer lead time than other market action plans..

BE PREPARED AND BE ORGANIZED

If you are to be successful in this area, you must understand how nonprofits create investment policy and how they manage their investments and monitor the performance of those investments. You must understand what nonprofits are looking for, who your competition is, and which products and services are offered in this market. If you target large-market nonprofits, you will also need a high level of expertise. The competition for the business of these organizations is high, and many of your competitors will have their Certified Investment Management Analyst (CIMA) accreditation. You can find out how to get the CIMA by visiting the Investment Management Consultants Association (IMCA) website (see the Appendix).

No matter how you choose to approach this market, you will be more successful if you are organized and gather the preliminary information that you will need:

1. Find out which nonprofit organizations are located in your area. The local chamber of commerce is an excellent place to start gathering this information. Some chambers of commerce even publish a "volunteer directory" that lists all the philanthropic organizations in the community.
2. Put together a binder of all the nonprofit organizations in your market. This will be your book for data and planning.
3. Gather as much information as you can about each of your targeted organizations. One way to do this is to enter the name of the organization into GuideStar.com, which will give you the organization's board members and largest contributors. Another way is to visit the website for each organization.

   You need to know:

   ♦ The mission of the organization
   ♦ Names, addresses, and phone numbers of board members, executive committee members, and officers
   ♦ Names, addresses, and phone numbers of fund-raising and finance committee members
   ♦ Names of significant donors (contributors who give $5,000 or more, which usually includes board members)
   ♦ Location of current assets
   ♦ Size of the endowment
   ♦ Major fund-raising events and calendar.
   ♦ Affiliations with other financial organizations (events sponsored by competitors)

♦   Brochures and newsletters

4. Categorize each of the nonprofits in your list by type:

   a. Large-market nonprofits, including large-market public charities, public colleges or universities, and large private colleges

   b. Small-market public charities, including community colleges and small private colleges

   c. Private charities

DEVELOPING AFFLUENT CLIENT RELATIONSHIPS WITH BOARD MEMBERS

In recent years, philanthropists have been taking a more active role in the organizations to which they give, and they may often be active members of the boards of directors. In many cases, the opportunity to manage an endowment account does not exist; instead, the business opportunity is strictly networking with board members and other community leaders who are involved with the organization. They are prospects for both your firm's wealth-management services and its expertise in charitable giving strategies.

Although you should have a minimum account level for individual accounts, a small endowment account could lead to affluent relationships.

GET ON THE BOARD OF A NONPROFIT

At the beginning of this market action plan, I recommended that you identify all the nonprofits in your market area, research them and make a list of names, and categorize the organizations by type. Take the list of people you developed and now do the following:

1. Cross-reference your list of people (top donors and board members) across all the organizations on your list to determine which individuals are on multiple boards and multiple donor lists. This overlap list becomes your target list (150 to 200 names is optimal).

2. Make a list of the nonprofit organizations that would give you the best exposure to the largest numbers of people on your target list and that you could afford to belong to (most nonprofits have minimum commitment levels that you must meet in order to serve on the board of directors).

3. Narrow your list to organizations that you have a true interest in; it would be difficult to spend sufficient time and energy on an organization otherwise.

4. Become a member of one organization in each category and take a leadership position. Leadership is essential to making this strategy work, because if you do not become a leader, your efforts may go unnoticed. (Being on the board is the ideal, but if you cannot meet the minimum level of financial commitment necessary to be on the board, there are other volunteer leadership roles you can take.)

5. Once you are on the board, take a leadership role. Show that you are smart and that you are a leader. The objective is to get on the finance or fund-raising committee, where your expertise will show. For female advisors, it is especially important that you aspire to board positions rather than organizing social events and galas. It is important to hold your own and emerge as a legitimate, contributing leader of the organization.

6. After establishing a strong reputation as a leader within the board, the next step is to use your firm's expertise to help your organization. Most financial service firms have expertise in philanthropic areas and can provide ideas on raising money through charitable remainder trusts, charitable lead trusts, appreciated stock, and other such strategies. Hold a luncheon for the directors of development on how to raise money. Bring in your firm's experts (or provide this information yourself if you have the expertise) on appreciated stock gifts, charitable remainder trusts, and charitable lead trusts, and show how these can save donors money. You can introduce the luncheon by saying, "I want to help you leverage the resources I have to help us raise money for this organization [the nonprofit]. My clients are wealthy individuals, and philanthropy is a high priority for them; they want to give money to charities they believe in and reap the benefits of charitable giving. If you know of individuals who need my expertise, let me know, and my firm and I can help them. I would like to introduce our expert, who will share with you some insights that can help us raise money for this organization."

7. Identify board members who could be potential clients and focus on building a relationship with them. Invite them and their spouses to dinner, identify their interests, and find activities you can do with them that are fun. Your objective is to build relationships with wealthy indi-

viduals with whom you have a common philanthropic interest. Over time, as you build the relationship, you will be invited into their social circles, and you will meet other affluent individuals. During the course of developing relationships with them, their investment situation will come up or they will ask questions about investments. Let them initiate the conversation; typically it may be, "I have an advisor I have worked with for a long time, and I feel good about our relationship," or, "I feel I am well taken care of." This is your opening to make the following statement: "I am serious about growing my business in the community, and if you are ever considering a change or want to know more about our practice, I would be happy to spend a few minutes with you to share what we do," or, "If you want a second opinion, I would be happy to share how we work with our clients," or, "If you know someone who might be interested in learning about our approach, please let me know."

NONPROFIT ASSET MANAGEMENT
Large-Market Nonprofits

The asset-management decisions of these organizations are almost always made by committee and are often turned over to an outside consultant. There are two paths you can take with these organizations (and you can do both and at the same time):

1. **Organizations seeking proposals.** Part of the fiduciary responsibility all nonprofits have is to check the marketplace periodically to ensure that they are aware of the available offerings and their pricing. Call your list of nonprofits, endowments, foundations, municipalities, Taft-Hartley plans, and police and firemen's retirement plans and ask if they are actively searching for a consultant now or will be in the near future. If they are currently searching, you should ask how to submit a proposal. Even if they are not currently searching, you should check back with them every six to nine months because change is constant in this market and you want the opportunity to compete whenever you can. If you submit ten proposals, you have a good chance of making the final cut four times and winning the bid once. As long as you offer a competitive product and have the expertise, you have a chance of winning.

2. **Any other nonprofit organizations you are interested in.** In most of these large organizations, an investment committee makes the deci-

sions and there is a CFO or business manager who handles the day-to-day operation of the endowment. The CFO or the business manager is the person you want to reach. In my experience, the easiest way to find this person is to call the main number of the nonprofit and ask to speak with whoever handles the endowment. These organizations get these calls daily, not just from solicitors, but also from people wishing to make grants or contributions.

Once you have the decision maker on the phone, try this script:

> "Mr./Ms. Decision Maker, this is Joe Advisor, and I am a financial advisor with XYZ Financial. We have found that in many cases we can help nonprofits get better returns and, in many cases, at a lower cost. I would like to have the opportunity to meet with you to find out more about your situation, so that I could potentially improve your returns at a lower cost. Could we schedule some time to meet?"

Remember, all you want is a meeting. At the meeting, you can move into a discussion of your firm's competitive advantages.

Small Municipality Funds and Police and Firemen's Defined-Benefit Retirement Funds

These are good leads to pursue. Generally, they fall into the $20 million to $100 million category, and they are often below the radar screen of institutional competitors. If you have the expertise and the product line, you can easily find yourself at the top of the competition with this group. Call the targeted municipality and ask for its annual report; they will send you the report, and that report will list how much the target has in its retirement funds (police and firemen included), and who the board members and investment committee members are. Contact the targeted municipality or retirement fund and use the same marketing process for large-market nonprofits.

Scripts for Finding Out If a Nonprofit Is Seeking Proposals

> "Mr./Ms. Prospect, my name is Joe Advisor, and I'm a financial advisor at XYZ Financial. I am a CIMA [assuming you are one], and I specialize in working with nonprofit/retirement funds like yours. I am calling to ask if you are in an active search for a consultant."

If the answer is no, then:

"May I ask who you are currently using to manage your endowment? When do you anticipate that you will be in an active search? I'd like the opportunity to keep XYZ Financial in front of you. When would be a good time for me to check back with you?"

If the answer is yes, then:

"I would like to have the opportunity to meet with you and find out more about your plan so that I can have the background information to provide a competitive proposal. I will be in your area on Thursday; could we meet sometime that day?"

SUCCESS COMES FROM PUTTING IT ALL TOGETHER

The purpose of this book is to enable you to learn exactly how many of the most successful advisors in our industry have created their own million- and multimillion-dollar practices. Many successful advisors have read the earlier edition of this book and have learned from it. Now it is your turn. I hope you've come to see that it is very possible for you to take your business to a significantly higher level.

Over the course of my thirty-two-year career as an advisor, manager, and now as a trainer to financial advisors, I have seen many successful professionals reach the million-dollar goal by following these practices. My training techniques have been validated by my interviews with top advisors, many of whom consistently brought in $25 million in new assets every year. This is why I believe that any advisor who has the desire and the motivation to succeed can master the lessons in this book and build a significant business.

Once you put all the lessons in this book together and begin to implement them, there is little standing in your way. Start by making the needed changes to the way you are currently working, implementing the lessons and tactics this book provides you. Don't try to do everything at once; prioritize first—implement those high-priority action steps and then move to the next priorities and corresponding action steps. Reaching a million-dollar practice is not easy, but it's within your reach if you combine a high level of motivation, a commitment to action, and the right blueprint, which I have provided you in this book.

Appendix

RESOURCES

Here are some of the better sources of names for your market action plans. These are grouped into categories so you can more readily see how each source is applicable to your needs, and the market action plans in which they can be useful are also listed. You may want to take some time to look through the entire list of sources and note the ones you want to explore further.

GENERAL AND MIXED SOURCES

These sources provide both commercial and consumer information or both general and specialized information.

Bank Directors

A list of directors can often be found on specific bank websites.

Corporate, Association, and Country Club Directory

www.elusiveleads.com

This is a phone directory for corporate employees, association members, country club members, university alumni, and other such groups. It often includes direct dial numbers and e-mail addresses.

Free Erisa

www.freeerisa.com

This website provides information from 5500 filings and includes the value of the assets in the plan, annual contributions, the office manager and his or her phone number, and the names of partners. You can then visit the websites of the individual practices for the names of the individual plan members and their phone numbers.

Go Leads

www.goleads.com

This fee-based site offers low-cost leads for businesses and consumers: names, addresses, phone numbers, number of employees, value of house, and other such information. Filters let you customize a list.

InfoUSA

www.infousa.com

This fee-based site is an excellent source of names of business owners, names of executives, number of employees, revenues, lines of business, and other such information, and of consumers by name, address, and so on. The site has comprehensive filters. You can search by location, industry code, revenues, employees, key individuals, address, phone number, or other field. Some databases are available in public libraries.

Internet White Pages

1. www.whitepages.com
2. www.switchboard.com
3. www.superpages.com

You can use these sources to find residential addresses and phone numbers for names. You can also get reverse information: Looking up a phone number will retrieve the person's name and address, and looking up the address will retrieve the person's name and phone number.

Internet Yellow Pages

1. www.switchboard.com
2. www.yellowpages.com
3. www.superpages.com

Use these sources to find businesses in your area by category, including business names, addresses, and phone numbers. In some cases, the business owner's name is included. The following categories are available:

- ♦ Attorneys
- ♦ Bankers
- ♦ Churches and synagogues
- ♦ CPAs
- ♦ Home builders
- ♦ Medical professionals
- ♦ Mortgage brokers
- ♦ Nonprofit organizations
- ♦ Real estate professionals, Realtors
- ♦ Retirement or retiree communities and associations
- ♦ YMCAs or YWCAs

Larkspur Data

www.larkspurdata.com

This site offers databases (for a fee) on high-net-worth individuals and company retirement plans. You can search by all the usual fields you would expect, but also by many unique fields, such as yacht ownership or purchase.

Local Newspapers
http://www.naa.org
Choose your newspaper at this site, which is a listing (searchable by state) of media sources and news sources.

Use this source to find:

♦ Businessmen and women who have been recognized or promoted or who have relocated
♦ Networking clubs and speaking opportunities
♦ News on local companies, individuals, and events
♦ Real estate transactions and listings, and advertisements from brokers and agents

Marquis Who's Who
www.marquiswhoswho.com
This source contains a list of influential men and women, including extensive biographies and home and work addresses. Entries are listed both alphabetically and by geography. Separate databases include only women, attorneys, medical professionals, or business professionals. This source is also available in public libraries. Use it to find:

♦ Executives
♦ Successful attorneys
♦ Successful medical professionals

Pension Planet
www.pensionplanet.com
This source maintains the largest and most timely database of qualified retirement plans and qualified health and welfare plans available anywhere. It is provided by individuals who are experienced in the design, administration, and investment management of qualified retirement plans.

Search Engines
♦ http://news.google.com
♦ www.google.com
♦ www.metacrawler.com
♦ www.yahoo.com

Use these sources to search for groups such as:

+ Associations and association news
+ Attorneys
+ Churches and synagogues
+ Company news (promotions, layoffs, and other such information)
+ CPAs
+ Hispanic newspapers
+ Home builders
+ Local newspapers
+ Medical professionals and professors
+ Names of and news on executives and business owners
+ Realtors
+ Retirees
+ Teaching hospitals and hospital staff
+ YMCAs/YWCAs

Search Systems: Public Records Online

www.searchsystems.net
This fee-based site offers business information, corporate filings, property records, deeds, mortgages, criminal and civil court filings, births, deaths, marriages, unclaimed property, professional licenses, money in motion, and other such information. It has all the public records you could ask for, but you will need to dig and be a little creative.

Sourcebook to Public Record Information

This book explains how to find the information you want from municipal, county, state, and federal records. It is available in many libraries.

State Licensure Boards

Use a search engine to search for the terms "[your state] state licensure board" (example: Nebraska state licensure board). This will return a list of websites for various professions that are licensed in your state. Many sites list individual license holders, retired status, continuing education credit status, and other such information.
Use this source to find:

+ Attorneys
+ CPAs
+ Medical professionals
+ Retirees

U.S. Census Bureau

www.census.gov

Use this source to find census data, including neighborhood ethnic makeup, income, and ages; business types and revenue estimates; and much more.

BUSINESSES, COMPANIES, INDUSTRIES, AND EXECUTIVES

American Society of Appraisers

www.appraisers.org

This site provides business valuation reports.

BenefitsLink

http://benefitslink.com/index.html

Use this site to find:

♦ Information and articles on retirement and benefit plans
♦ Information on specific plans

Business Sales Leads

1. www.salesgenie.com/Business_Leads
2. www.eloqua.com/Leads
3. www.onesource.com
4. www.goleads.com
5. Zapdata.com
6. salesleadsplus.com
7. www.database101.com
8. www.businesssalesleads.net

These fee-based sites provide low-cost leads of businesses and include contact name, address, number of employees, and other such information. Filters let you customize a list.

Business Schools

Use a search engine, and use the following terms: "[your state] association business schools officials" (example: Ohio association business schools officials). Business schools host conferences for professional development where it would be appropriate for you to speak. These sites also usually have a list of officers and directors.

Central Contractor Registration

www.ccr.gov

Businesses have to register with this site before becoming government vendors. Government vendors have guaranteed income and make a good product. You can customize your search to match your niche market: minority-owned, nonprofit, and veteran-owned businesses, for example. Use this source to find successful businesses in your area, including contact information.

Chambers of Commerce

www.2chambers.com

Most of the smaller towns have chamber of commerce websites. These sites typically include a business directory that includes business name, address, and phone number. Sites also usually have a link to the local town newspaper. Use this source to find your local chamber of commerce, which can provide:

♦ Lists of member businesses in your area, which often include owners' names
♦ Nonprofit organizations

Company Financial and Executive Records of Public Companies

www.freeedgar.com

This site provides access to insider filings, company annual reports, and other financial filings.

www.investor.reuters.com

This site gives the names of senior executives and directors and copies of the company's annual report (online as well as hard copy).

www.prars.com

This site provides free company annual reports that are public records (hard copy), as long as the report is in the site's inventory.

www.sec.gov

Provides access to insider filings.

Corporate Events

www.bloomberg.com

Bloomberg offers many news services that focus on corporate executives, companies, and industries, for a fee. You can find information on executives, such as news on insider buying and selling, information on filers, filing dates, shares filed, price, and the broker used to sell securities. You must subscribe in order to use Bloomberg's more specialized tools.

Dun & Bradstreet

www.dnb.com

This company provides online and hard-copy directories of businesses, for a fee. Available information includes names of business owners and executives, credit reports, business history, financial analysis, and other such information. Both private and public companies are covered. Information is available in many formats, such as in-depth company information and mailing lists filtered by many possible filters. You can search for leads by revenues, number of employees, name, and other categories. Some databases are available in public libraries.

Gale

www.gale.cengage.com

This company has a number of fee-based databases covering trade groups and associations (areas covered, contact information, convention information), public and private companies (lines of business, revenues, number of employees, business history, articles about them, competitor information, industry analyses), articles (general interest, academic, specialized and technical, newspaper articles), and health, among others. Many of these databases are available in public libraries.

Google News

http://news.google.com

You can search for terms relating to corporate executives changing companies, executive compensation stories, and mergers and acquisitions.

Hoover's

www.hoovers.com

For a fee, this site offers comprehensive information on companies and executives, including credit history, lines of business, lists of executives, former positions, and other such information. It is also available in many public libraries.

Layoff Reports

Google News at http://news.google.com. Search using the keyword "layoffs" or "downsizing."

Local Business Journals

1. http://newslink.org/biznews.html
2. www.bizjournals.com

At these sites, you will find a list of business journals published in your area. These journals are a good source of information on local businesses and executives. Every week the local business journal in most markets will have stories on individuals and companies that often focus on changes of circumstances. Become a diligent reader of your local business journal and read it to find prospects. Use this source to find:

+ Businesses being recognized
+ Executive relocations and promotions
+ Information on specific businesses
+ Lists of the top real estate brokers or contractors
+ New businesses in the area
+ Successful businesses and their owners

National Human Resources Association

www.humanresources.org

Provides information from the Association of Human Resources Professionals.

Society for Human Resource Management

www.shrm.org

See also the sites for state chapters, where you can give financial seminars and network.

Standard Industrial Classification (SIC) Codes

www.ehso.com/SICcodes.htm

This site provides a full list of SIC codes.

State Websites of Business Registration Information

www.state.co.us

If you enter your two-letter state abbreviation instead of "co" in this URL, it will take you to the state's official website. Most of these websites will display public records for every business registered in the state. Each state website puts this information in a different place. Look for links such as "Secretary of State," "Corporate Records," or "Bureau of Corporations." You can generally search by business name, SIC code, location, and other such fields. Public records usually list business owners' names, contact information, tax status, and other such information.

Trade Publications

www.tradepub.com

This site lists many trade publications that you can subscribe to free of charge.

Use this source to find information that will help you to become an expert on an industry.

Venture Capitalists
www.vfinance.com
Venture Capital Resource Library lists more than 1,400 venture capital firms.

ATTORNEYS AND CPAS

Attorneys
1. American Academy of Estate-Planning Attorneys at www.aaepa.com
2. Divorce Headquarters at www.divorcehq.com
3. DivorceNet at www.divorcenet.com/money
4. FindLaw at http://lawyers.findlaw.com
5. Lawyers.com at www.lawyers.com
6. National Network of Estate Planning Attorneys at www.nnepa.com /public

Law offices specializing in land and house sales, estate planning, real estate, and divorce are great places to find influencers or clients. Attorneys are also a good source of information. Use these sources to find:

♦ Attorneys
♦ Attorney conventions and meetings
♦ Divorce attorneys
♦ Estate planning attorneys

CPAs
1. www.aicpa.org/yellow/ypascpa.htm; click on the name of the state you're interested in.
2. www.aicpa.org/yellow/ypsboa.htm; then choose your state.

CPAs are good sources of information on mergers and acquisitions, divorces, company relocations, and other such events. Use the above sources to find:

♦ CPAs
♦ CPA associations
♦ CPA conventions and meetings
♦ State licensure boards

Use a search engine to search for the terms "[your state] state licensure board" (example: Nebraska state licensure board). This will return a list of websites for various professions that are licensed in your state. Many sites list individual license holders, retired status, continuing education credit status, and other such information. Use this source to find attorneys and CPAs.

MORTGAGES, REALTORS, AND HOME BUILDERS

1. www.monster.com
2. Local classified ads

Look for top real estate agents by searching classified ads. Look for a Realtor who is looking for a first or even second assistant. If he needs an assistant, then he is more than likely successful and is looking for ways to concentrate his business. Many real estate companies allow brokers to have an assistant only after they hit a certain sales volume. A great online site for looking for these is Monster.com; you can search for classifieds just for real estate assistants.

County Clerk and Recorder's Office

Mortgage records are public. You can track specific mortgage information, such as addresses of properties, lien information, and property owners' names, through the county clerk and recorder's office. This information is available to anyone.

Home Builders

www.home-builders.com
You can find builders in any state through this website.

National Association of Home Builders

www.nahb.org
This site has links to builders' conventions and conferences. Also look for "NAHB Community," which has a link for "Find Your Local Builders' Association."

National Association of Realtors

www.realtor.org
Look in the directories for names and contact information for Realtors. For the Realtor magazine, look for a link to *Realtor Magazine*, which is published by this association. It has a listing of the nation's top Realtors and Realtor teams by sales volume.

Real Estate Brokers

1. National Association of Real Estate Brokers at www.nareb.com; you can

search for broker listings by state for any state and then click on "Find a Realtor."

2. Council of Real Estate Broker Managers at www.crb.com; click on "Find a CRB" (commercial real estate broker) and choose "accept," then choose a state to get an alphabetical listing of commercial brokers.

Real Estate Guides

Check real estate guides in your Sunday paper and in free literature distributions. Some search engine phrase or keyword suggestions are (try these both with and without the quotation marks):

+ "Top commercial real estate brokers"
+ "Top home builders"
+ "Top mortgage brokers"
+ "Top Realtors"

CHARTERED INSTITUTE OF MANAGEMENT ACCOUNTANTS (CIMA)

www.cimaglobal.com
This is a membership organization that offers an internationally recognized professional qualification in management accountancy.

INVESTMENT MANAGEMENT CONSULTANTS ASSOCIATION (IMCA)

www.imca.org
This is a professional organization devoted to financial management and cost accounting.

LARGE COLLEGES, UNIVERSITIES, PRIVATE COLLEGES, SMALL COMMUNITY COLLEGES, AND SMALL PRIVATE COLLEGES

Simply call the college and ask for the CFO or manager of endowments. If you have access to *Bloomberg* (see that listing previously), you can find this information there.

RETIREMENT COMMUNITIES

www.retirementhomes.com
This site gives you the ability to pick any state and includes pictures, phone numbers, descriptions, and links to these communities' websites as well as care levels and home pricing. This allows you to prequalify prospects' net worth before calling or visiting.

National Retirement Living Information Center

www.retirementliving.com

This site has a directory listing under "Retirement Communities and Senior Housing." You can search by state. It arranges these listings by level of care offered, from independent living to nursing homes; you can use it to build your list of properties where residents still handle their own financial decisions (independent living or assisted living facilities). This site also has a listing of local papers or newsletters from senior housing complexes, which lists decision makers and boards and committees within the complexes. The site also has tax information for seniors by state.

Senioresidences.com

www.senioresidences.com

This site provides a list of retirement communities.

The Senior Times

www.theseniortimes.com

This site offers lots of information that is of interest to retirees, with which you may be able to develop leads or sharpen your market action plan.

Veterans

1. American Legion at www.legion.org; you can search for Legion posts in any location and find addresses and contact information.
2. Veterans of Foreign Wars at www.vfw.org; find contact information for the locations you want to focus on.
3. FindLaw at http://lawyers.findlaw.com; you can find attorneys who work with veterans by searching for legal issues of "veterans" or "military law" and limiting the search to your city.

Volunteers of America (VOA)

www.voa.org

One of the best groups to join is Volunteers of America. This group is very large nationally. Many high-net-worth individuals are on the VOA Guild.

NETWORKING

www.bni.com

Although your business networking group will be unique to your needs, you may want to take a look at the frequently asked questions on the BNI website to gain a basic idea of how its meetings operate.

www.konnects.com

This is a networking group; its website also provides networking tips.

LEADS Groups

Contact your local chamber of commerce for information.

LeTip

www.letip.com

This is a professional organization with the primary purpose of giving and receiving qualified business tips or leads. Each business category is represented by one member, and conflicts of interest are not allowed. No outside speakers are allowed at LeTip meetings, and you need to be a member of this networking group.

National Professional Associations

Many special interests have national professional associations that have e-networking or local networking options. Use a search engine to see if your outside interest has a national professional association.

Networking Books

1. Allen, Scott, and David Teten. *The Virtual Handshake: Opening Doors and Closing Deals Online.* New York: AMACOM Books, 1995.
2. Stanley, Thomas J. *Networking with the Affluent and Their Advisors.* Chicago: Irwin Professional Publishing, 1993.

Networking for Professionals

www.networkingforprofessionals.com

This works like a networking "matchmaking" service. You join, you search for professionals you want to speak with, then you contact them and meet.

Online Business Networking Articles and Resources

http://entrepreneurs.about.com/od/onlinenetworking

This site offers excellent articles about networking, including links and other resources.

Ryze Business Networking

www.ryze.com

This is a networking tool used in the entire United States.

State Offices of Economic Development and International Trade

www.state.co.us

Enter your two-letter state abbreviation instead of "co" in this URL, and it will take you to the state's official website. Look for links to the state office of economic development. Websites for offices of economic development offer connections to Internet business resources, guides to small businesses, and offices for minority businesses in the state.

CERTIFICATIONS

Certified Divorce Specialist, Financial Divorce Association

www.fdadivorce.com

You can take classes (four days) to become certified, or you can study at home. This association also has newsletters and member listings by state.

Chartered Institute of Management Accountants (CIMA)

www.cimaglobal.com

This is a membership organization that offers an internationally recognized professional qualification in management accountancy.

Divorce Financial Planner, a Division of Certified Financial Planner

1. www.cfp.net
2. www.divorceandfinance.com

Anyone who is registered with the federal Certified Financial Planner Board of Standards, Inc., can be part of the Association of Divorce Financial Planners. This is a great networking opportunity for client referrals, resource listings, and membership events.

PHYSICIANS

American Medical Association

www.ama-assn.org

You can search by state, city, or zip code for doctors by specialty. The site gives name, biography, education, specialty, and phone number.

University Medical School Websites

On some sites, you can search by faculty, alumni, and associations, and you can also access faculty research papers and other such information. In most cases, however, you must go to the library in person if you are not an affiliate of the medical school. Also, you can call the university medical library and ask it where to access research reports. Use this source to find names of affluent medical professionals.

SALES PROFESSIONALS

www.salesprofessionalsusa.com

Here are some search engine phrase or keyword suggestions:

- Supplier awards (then the name or abbreviation of your state)
- "Manufacturers representatives" (try this both with and without the quotation marks)
- "Business brokers" (try this both with and without the quotation marks)
- "Licensed sales professionals" (try this both with and without the quotation marks)

AFFLUENT INDIVIDUALS

www.mergernetwork.com

Business owners who are in the process of selling their businesses have huge capital potential. You can search by state, city, region, or even internationally. Lists provide the business owner's contact information and sale price. The basic membership is free of charge.

Cole Directory

www.coleinformation.com

This is a cross-reference and reverse directory for residence names and phone numbers. It includes recent home sales, homeowner's insurance status, and related information. The price varies depending on the type of information you are requesting. This directory is also available in many public libraries.

CIS Marketing

www.cismarketing.com

This fee-based site offers leads specifically tailored to the financial industries.

House Values and New Home Buyers

1. http://newslink.org/biznews.html
2. www.bizjournals.com

First, find the website for your local business journal using these websites. Then go to the individual site for each journal in your area. Many have links such as "Sales Leads" or "New Home Buyers."

Local Land and House Sales

Identify individuals with large blocks of land for sale in your community either through the Multiple Listing Service (MLS) directory or through contact with your local Realtors. Often these individuals are facing very-low-cost basis issues and have a need for professional advice and planning, not to mention someone to invest the proceeds of the land sale.

Your county tax assessor's office can provide a listing of all new deeds to homes or land. Give the parameters of what you are looking for (deeds in the last three months, over $400,000, for example), and it can e-mail or send you a list.

Polk City Directories
www.citydirectory.com
These are cross-reference and reverse directories, one for each city or for a larger area. You can search by name of individual, phone number, address, household income, or other such fields. These directories are also available in many public libraries.

Professors and Executive MBA Students
You can contact professors or admissions people of executive MBA programs, or offer to teach a quick seminar during a class. The average salary for an executive attending an executive MBA program is $93,000, but it can go up to $250,000. The professors are professionals themselves and are usually high-net-worth individuals because schools want successful people to teach their methods.

U.S. Search
www.ussearch.com
This fee-based site offers basic information (full name, address, and phone number) plus former addresses, basic financial and tax status, age, spouse's name, background check information, value of house, and other such information.

Index

Printed in the USA
CPSIA information can be obtained
at www.ICGtesting.com
JSHW030049110424
60979JS00010B/141